Many Worlds, One Life

Hermann Simon

Many Worlds, One Life

A Remarkable Journey
from Farmhouse to the Global Stage

Gregory Carpenter,
Companion on the
roads of marketing,
with best wishes
Bonn, June 17, 2024
Hermann Simon

C

Copernicus Books is a brand of Springer

Hermann Simon
Bonn, Germany

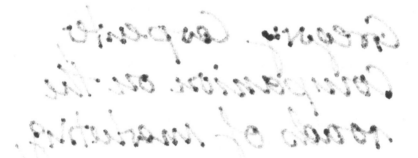

Adapted from Original German Language Edition Zwei Welten, ein Leben: Vom Eifelkind zum
Global Player by Hermann Simon Copyright © Campus Verlag GmbH 2018.
ISBN 978-3-030-60757-9   ISBN 978-3-030-60758-6   (eBook)
https://doi.org/10.1007/978-3-030-60758-6

This Copernicus imprint is published by the registered company Springer Nature Switzerland AG
The registered company address is: Gewerbestrasse 11, 6330 Cham, Switzerland

Preface

The perceived midpoint of one's life, according to a US publication, lies at age 18. Roughly speaking, that means that the first two decades of one's life subjectively seem to last as long as all the decades that follow. I can confirm that this hypothesis applies to me. My first world—where I lived until shortly before my 20th birthday—was a small village in the Eifel Mountains, a region sometimes called Germany's "Wild West," and in former times its "Siberia." Time passed very, very slowly during this phase of my life. In the ensuing 50 years, my life changed radically. Time seemed to rush by faster and faster, so that I really feel as if I have spent the same amount of time in each world.

I have indeed encountered many new worlds. Defined in regional terms, these worlds span Europe, North America, and Asia. Defined in professional terms, they include the military, science and research, consulting and entrepreneurship, and even some brushes with politics. My development from farmhouse to the global business stage was neither destiny nor predetermined. It did not follow any plan or prescription. In contrast, it came about step by step, with outcomes often driven by luck and coincidence. Time and again, forks in the road emerged, offering opportunities that I usually seized.

The encouragement of my wife Cecilia played a decisive role in many of those choices. Her standard advice was "of course you'll do it" and I followed it. My children Jeannine and Patrick played along, both when we "schlepped" them around the world and when their father was constantly on the road. I thank all three for their invaluable contribution to the person I was allowed to become.

In the early years of my professional career, my orientation pointed primarily toward the West, in particular the American and European business schools. But the time I spent in Japan in the 1980s left an indelible impression on me. Later in my career, the Asian countries—especially China, South Korea, and Japan—would become increasingly interesting and important. Asia turned into a late love for me.

Despite my role as a global player, I have preserved a close relationship with the small village I grew up in. I believe I can say that I have lost neither my roots nor the down-to-earth attitude those roots nurtured in me. Whenever I want to escape the industrialized world—which I often refer to as "Globalia"—I retreat to my old village. Staying at our old farmhouse transforms me into a child of the Eifel. The polarity between the boy from the village and the global player shone through on the occasion of my 70th birthday in February 2017. My family prepared two surprises that touched me deeply. The first was for the village child: an appearance by three local choirs with a total of 70 singers. The other surprise was directed at the global player. They showed 25 video greetings from friends and colleagues from 12 countries.

Global stage and farmhouse are not incompatible, but rather the two inseparable sides of my life.

Bonn, Germany   Hermann Simon
                                                             Spring 2021

Praise for Hermann Simon's *Many Worlds, One Life*

"Hermann Simon is one of the very few people who combine a truly global mindset with strong local roots. This rare combination makes him a superb bridge-builder at a time of increasing friction in our global trading system. World-renowned management scholar, successful entrepreneur, engaged citizen—this book tells his life's amazing story in a compelling way."
— U. Mark Schneider, CEO, Nestlé

"From the moment I met Hermann Simon, through each successive encounter, I have enjoyed increasing returns which are rare in most relationships. Hermann, please continue to open further fields of inquiry in business theory and practice, always with an eye to aligning profit, high purpose, and passion."
— Philip Kotler, Professor Emeritus of Marketing, Kellogg School of Management, Northwestern University

"This book describes the life of a truly global citizen who supports companies in globalization and thus promotes understanding between countries and peoples. Personally, I learned a lot from Hermann Simon for my own Hidden Champion strategy. I have also noticed that more and more small- and medium-sized enterprises in China are beginning to implement the Hidden Champion strategy and benefit from the theories he proposed. I recommend the book to each entrepreneur with global ambitions."
— Yang Shuren, Owner and CEO, Shandong Moris Technologies, Inc.

"Hermann's description of the handling of the nuclear bombs in the fighter bomber squadron is very impressive and illuminating. Most people today are not even aware of how lucky we were that nuclear weapons were not used during the Cold War. We must not under any circumstances return to such a situation."

— Helmut Ganser, General, German Army

"Since our first encounter in 1983, our paths have crossed many times. His books led me to the world of pricing. Each encounter with Hermann Simon was intellectually enriching. This book tells the exciting story of a wanderer between many worlds, enticing and relevant for both practitioners and academics."

— Takaho Ueda, Professor, Gakushuin University Tokyo

"This book shows what can become of a boy growing up on an almost medieval farm in the age of globalization. A great encouragement for all those who come from modest backgrounds."

— Martin Richenhagen, Chairman, President, and CEO,
AGCO Corporation

"Hermann, surely you sometimes look back on your life and think 'this can't be true.' You have truly experienced a spectacular life and are still incredibly active."

— Gert Assmus, Professor Emeritus, Tuck School,
Dartmouth University

"This book tells the fascinating journey of a global citizen, brand builder, and networker. Hermann Simon, the inventor of the Hidden Champion concept, is himself a hidden champion from a farm in the middle of nowhere. He mastered the omnipresent but neglected topic of price management and successfully bridged the gap between theory as university professor and hands-on management practice. The perfect role model in challenging times."

— Bernhard Steinruecke, Director General,
Indo-German Chamber of Commerce, Mumbai

"Among the politicians, officials, scholars, and entrepreneurs that Hermann Simon has close acquaintance with, it is a great honor that I am writing a letter of recommendation for this book and Dr. Simon.

As a worldly renowned business manager and scholar, his wise words have always inspired and awakened business leaders (and engineers) like me. I bought the book and finished it on the spot before I left the bookstore.

This book is about his life rather than his studies. This book also proves that he is a good essayist as much as he is a scholar. As you navigate into his youth in a German farmhouse, you will notice that he has always captured the details of daily life and social surroundings. It is the encounter of such details and awakening of his senses that have led him to become the pride of modern Europe's business management studies.

My favorite part in his book is the chapter, 'The School of Life'. He has listed the things he has learned throughout his life and said they are 'subjective and incomplete.' As I read through his book, it felt as if I were having a cup of tea with him over family, future, health, management, leadership, time management, and other lifetime subjects. His value and love for humanity is truly special.

In this book, he acknowledges that his life is divided into two: one from his Eifel village and one from the globalized word. The division of the old and the present, or the division of time and space, which usually starts from village and ends in a city, was unavoidable to anyone our age who has gone through rapid urbanization and industrialization. Such sense of separation, however, does not always lead to enlightenment. The enlightenment that he is sharing with us is the fruit of his lifetime effort.

When you read his stories from his childhood to recent research and studies, you will learn the never-changing truth that 'Great discernment is cultivated rather than is born.' I also think this book will be a milestone for the younger generations who still have more road to travel."

— Dr. Chang Gyu Hwang, former CEO,
Samsung Electronics and KT Korea Telecom

"Rarely have I been so fascinated by the times you describe. Memories came back, like the short phase we served in the same squadron."

— Andris Freutel, Starfighter Pilot and General, German Air Force

"There are thousands of books on globalization, but only this one offers a personal story by one of the most inspiring business thinkers of our times. He writes about the unlimited opportunities offered by the globalized world."

— Dr. Marek Dietl, CEO, Warsaw Stock Exchange

"Hermann, though this is a down-to-earth book about your life, it brought the poetry of Goethe and Erlkönig to my mind. I was reminded of the beginning *'Wer reitet so spät durch Nacht und Wind...'* ('Who rides so late through night and wind?') Is that not what we do in our careers and lives, travel through night and wind?"

— Evert Gummesson, Professor, Stockholm School of Economics

"Hermann, in your ingenious, inimitable way, you have connected your own career with the current events of the day and their philosophical considerations.

I didn't put the book down. Your development process from the 'agrarian Middle Ages' to the internet age is probably unique. Your research on price management and Hidden Champions have become global benchmarks."

— Dr. Michael Thiel, Investor, Munich

"What particularly intrigues me is how Hermann has felt at places I myself have visited. The book also proudly reminds me that we have shared lots of common experiences in the past three decades."

— Pil Hwa Yoo, Professor, SKK Business School, Seoul, Korea

"Your book has given me great joy and enriched me with many insights."

— Klaus Brockhoff, Professor of Innovation Management,
WHU Beisheim School of Management, Koblenz, Germany

"The exciting chapter about his time in the Air Force is very good. The personal experiences and feelings are wonderfully integrated into the overall security policy context. Compliments!"

— Joachim Rodenkirch, Mayor of Wittlich, Germany

"This work is really very impressive. It's a lifetime achievement that hardly any-one else could boast of."

— Eckart Zwicker, Professor, Technical University of Berlin

Excerpts from Published Reviews of the German Edition

"It's a book about a career and the growing up of the Federal Republic of Germany. And about the contradictions of the modern world. Rooted in humility, it counters the vanities of the elites."

— Hans-Jürgen Jakobs, Former Chief Editor, *Handelsblatt*

"In his autobiography, Hermann Simon describes his fantastic journey from the Eifel village to the great world of management. He writes about adventures, encounters with great personalities of world history, his time in America, Japan, China, and many other countries, and gives advice for readers of all ages."

— Peter Doeppes, Chief Editor, *Eifelzeitung*

"It's not in Tokyo, London, or Stanford, but in the Eifel where Hermann Simon, feels most at home. When the 71-year-old management consultant, who is counted among the world's most influential management thinkers, wants to leave the global business world through which he continues to jet for his lecture tours, he is drawn back to his tranquil village."

— *Volksfreund*

"This autobiography is a story of globalization. Hermann Simon describes his path from his parents' farm to becoming an internationally successful management consultant known for his analysis of medium-sized world market leaders."

— *VDI-Nachrichten*

"This entertaining book is the ideal companion for a long reading evening by the fireplace or in a hotel room. Whoever is interested in business stories and biographies can dive straight into it."

— *Managementbuch.de*

"Simon not only writes about his life story. He also delivers lessons for brand and market success in the global competition of the twenty-first century."

— *Absatzwirtschaft*

"In his memoir, Hermann Simon always searches for the universal, the interesting, the things that take a reader further. The question of 'why?' and the search for the pattern behind the individual runs through the accessibly written book like a red thread. Anyone who has read it will understand Hermann Simon's pattern for success."

— *General-Anzeiger,* Bonn

"Hermann Simon fans get their money's worth: from elementary school to his academic stints in the United States and elsewhere to his consultancy work, Simon describes his career in every detail. The personal merges with the professional."

— *Harvard Business Manager*

"Open and honest, the 74-year-old describes his very rich life between his home village and the big, wide world. It is also a book about the German post-war period in which Hermann Simon grew up. It is a book about globalization and how Simon became its role model."

— *Manager Magazin*

Contents

1

Roots

Time and Space

"Where am I from?"

At some point, most people will inevitably ask themselves that question and search for deeper answers.

The former German finance minister Theo Waigel—who gave the Euro its name—was asked how former German chancellor Helmut Kohl succeeded in winning over guests at state visits. Weigel answered by saying "That was an art. He would ask them where they were from, what their parents did, and what they have done with their lives."[1]

The *"Where are you from?"* question interests me because I myself am rooted to a particular place. If I want to withdraw from my current global business world for a few days or even a few hours, I return to the place of my childhood. When I meet people for the first time, I often ask where they are from and where they grew up. The answers always have "time" and "space" dimensions.

I am no exception. The farmhouse where I was born stood in the "Prussian Siberia," in the Eifel Mountains, far away from bustling city centers.[2] The rugged volcanic landscape has molded me and left its marks on me. To this day, one can hear my Eifel roots in my accent.

---

[1] *Frankfurter Allgemeine Zeitung*, August 7, 2017, p. 4.

[2] The exact coordinates are 50 degrees, 3 minutes, and 10.03 seconds north and 6 degrees, 54 minutes, and 37.01 seconds east.

But do I also come from a time? I entered the world at 2 a.m. on Monday, February 10, 1947.[3] So I missed earning "Sunday child" status by only two hours. Like every living being, I was the latest link in an endless chain of ancestors. Each of them exists only because this chain never broke. This thought, of course, is not new. As the Roman philosopher Seneca said, no one comes from nothing. Our ancestors extend from the origins of time to the present day.[4] The German-Jewish historian Michael Wolffson dedicated a book about the history of his family by saying "Ancestors—they have shaped us more than we know" (Wolffsohn 2017). Another observer wrote "Where we come from is more than a historical or genealogical question. It is something philosophical. And one feels frustrated, because one in the end does not quite know how to answer that question. Something vague and mysterious has been poured into the foundation of our existence" (Kleinschmidt 2017). We have all emerged from the depths of time. The development and the experiences of our endless line of ancestors have coalesced in our genes and been transferred to us. How and where we are raised leaves marks on this foundation and accompanies us our whole lives.

Deeper Connections to the Past

One evening years ago, I arrived at Alpine University in Kitzbühel, Austria, which is McKinsey's European training center. I had not eaten supper yet, so I went to the restaurant. Only one guest was there, who had likewise arrived late. Because I had met him before, I asked if I could join him. He welcomed me, and we struck up a conversation as we ate together.

After about an hour, perhaps shortly after 9 p.m., another guest entered the lounge and joined us. He was American, so we switched to English. My two companions at the table quickly discovered things they had in common. We became immersed in a discussion that lasted past midnight. I was more an observer than an active participant, asking a question only every now and then.

The guest I had joined was Reinhold Messner, the first person to make a solo climb of Mount Everest. The American who joined us was Robert Thurman, who edited *The Tibetan Book of the Dead*, a classic text about afterlife and reincarnation (Thurman 1993). I had read Thurman's book after it had caught my eye in the library of my long-time friend, Professor Pil Hwa Yoo in Seoul.

---

[3] Between February 10, 1947 and the day I first wrote these lines (March 15, 2017) a total of 25,601 days have elapsed.

[4] Seneca, *Aus den moralischen Briefen an Lucilius* (English: *Letters on Ethics: to Lucilius*) Position 6406 in the Kindle Version.

After Thurman had suffered an accident that cost him an eye, he settled in Tibet and became the first Buddhist monk with western roots. During this time, he studied with the Dalai Lama, with whom he remains close friends to this day. When he returned to the United States, he gave up his monkhood and became professor for Buddhist studies at Columbia University. He also founded the Tibet House in New York City together with actor Richard Gere. The Academy-Award-nominated actress Uma Thurman is his daughter.

The meeting between Thurman and Messner—whose own connections to Tibet and the Himalayas run deep—was a meeting of two kindred spirits. I was privileged to eavesdrop on their discussions about reincarnation and about Buddhist teachings. People in other cultures believe in more comprehensive connections to the past. Thurman's version of the *Tibetan Book of the Dead* provides detailed conceptions about the transition from the previous life to the new life.

Do I also come from the depths of time? Right now, I know as little about the answer to that question as I did 20 years ago. But that does not change how some things seem strangely interconnected.

On a trip to India, I read in a book about reincarnation that souls of the dead enter a state of waiting between two lives. The souls prefer to remain within their own families and return in the next-born children. The teachings of reincarnation explain that one's fears in the current life stem from experiences in prior lives. Someone who has a fear of water drowned in a previous life. Personally, I have a fear of water, especially deep water. I do not swim very well. But is the number of people who have drowned not much less than the number of people who have a fear of deep water?[5]

The theory of the return of souls within one's own family made me think about my own life. The last person in our family who passed away prior to my birth had drowned in the depths of the Black Sea. After he had endured and survived life-threatening dangers in Russia in World War II, he finally appeared to have been rescued. In Sevastopol, he boarded a ship that was supposed to bring German soldiers to safety. But the ship was shelled and sunk by the Russians. That happened in May 1944. We only learned about this tragedy eight years after the fact. In 1952, we received a message from the Red Cross that a comrade of my uncle, Jakob Simon, had seen him board that ill-fated ship. He was declared dead and was honored with a funeral service in our home village.

---

[5] In the year 2016, 537 people in Germany died from accidental drowning. But that number seems high to me, relative to the number of people killed in traffic accidents (3214 people), an historic low. See also "Wieder mehr Badetote," *Frankfurter Allgemeine Zeitung*, March 17, 2017, p. 6.

Why am I afraid of water? I cannot recall any direct experiences around water that would have instilled that fear. And why has my uncle Jakob, whom I never met, appeared to me in a dream with unusual clarity?[6] But then another tragedy of an ancestor emerged. My wife Cecilia, with whom I had shared my thoughts on reincarnation and my fear of water, recalled a story about an event that happened almost 150 years earlier.

"Your uncle Jakob isn't the only person in your family who drowned," she said. "Have you forgotten what happened to your great-grandfather in Paris?"

My great-grandfather Andreas Nilles came from Lorraine. He took a job as postman in Paris and moved there with his wife. Shortly after the birth of his first son Johannes on November 18, 1875 he was assaulted and thrown into the Seine, where he drowned. His widow moved back to her family in Lorraine, which had since become part of Germany after the war of 1870–71.[7]

Two family members drowned. Their direct descendant has a fear of deep water. Is that a coincidence? I do not know. I cannot say that I believe in reincarnation. But I know many people from Asia who are convinced that it is real. And what reasons should there be to consider that teaching any less plausible than the Christian belief in life after death?

Across Centuries

"What is time?" wondered Augustine of Hippo.

His answer was merely: "I know what time is if nobody asks me; if somebody asks me then I don't know."[8]

Albert Einstein was more pragmatic with his simple definition: "Time is what the clock says."[9] In the mid-1800s Heinrich Heine warned that the "elements of space and time have become shaky. Space is killed by the railways and we are left with time alone" (Kortlaender 2014).[10] According to Henri Bergson, we have a grasp only of space, but not time.

It seems clear, then, that our notion of time is less concrete than our notion of space. We use words such as short, long, far, and high to describe space. Yet

---

[6] See Chap. 13 of this book.

[7] After World War I, Lorraine once again became part of France.

[8] https://www.osho.com/osho-online-library/osho-talks/einstein-mystery-saint-augustine-4452b948-65c?p=356d142ff374e5e1e80cbae079cfe69e.

[9] https://www.philosophie-raum.de/index.php/Thread/24555-Gehirn-Bewusstsein-Nichtlokalit%C3%A4t/?postID=544600; the original quote is in German "Zeit ist, was die Uhr zeigt."

[10] The original quote is German "die Elementarbegriffe von Zeit und Raum sind schwankend geworden. Durch die Eisenbahnen wird der Raum getödtet, und es bleibt uns nur noch die Zeit übrig."

we also use the exact same adjectives to describe time. We say that life is short, but we also speak of long periods of time and of things far in the past. If something must be done urgently, we will say that it is "high time." The mathematician Kurt Gödel has said "the world is a space, not a time" (Yourgau 2005). The American philosopher Ralph Waldo Emerson understood space and time to be a unit, as he said "the sense of being … is not diverse from things, from space, from light, from time, from man, but one with them and proceeds obviously from the same source whence their life and being also proceed."[11] But perhaps the German comedian Karl Valentin expressed the most succinct way to reduce space and time a common denominator: "I don't know anymore whether it happened yesterday or on the fourth floor." In any event, it is no wonder that the place I came from seems much more concrete to me than the era I grew up in.

Having said that I have made my way through life in equal measure along the dimensions of time and space. In previous centuries, a person might have traveled a grand total of 10,000 miles in his or her life. Farmers went into the fields and occasionally ventured into town to buy or sell goods in the marketplace. Once a year, they would make a pilgrimage. The distances they traveled were always short, unless they were going off to war or making a pilgrimage to a distant location. Thus, the accumulated distance during one's life came to a few thousand miles. Even the soldier Johann Peter Forens, who came from my hometown and fought in wars all across Europe with Napoleon, is said to have traveled "only" a little over 10,000 miles in his lifetime. The 72nd *Wehrmacht* (German army) division, originally stationed in our regional capital city Trier, fought on all fronts in World War II and covered about 4000 miles on foot.[12]

Nowadays, we cover a distance anywhere from 20 to 190 times faster than our ancestors, depending on the mode of transportation. A person can walk three miles per hour, but a car can travel at 60 miles per hour and a high-speed train runs at speeds of 180 mph and higher. A passenger jet reaches speeds of 570 mph. The distance between Seattle and the famous shrine at San Luis Capistrano in southern California is approximately 1200 miles. If a pilgrim walked 20 miles per day on average without a day off, the journey would take 60 days. A flight would take less than three hours. In other words, the journey by air takes 1/524 the time of walking. People today travel as much in a few days as people centuries ago did in their entire lives.

---

[11] Ralph Waldo Emerson, *Self Reliance (Illustrated)* Kindle Edition, p. 14.
[12] See also *Die 72. Infanterie-Division 1939-1945*, Eggolsheim: Nebel-Verlag/Dörfler Utting 1982.

Today when I fly to Beijing to give a speech, I can return to the Frankfurt airport two days later and will have traveled a total of roughly 10,000 miles. A one-way trip from Frankfurt to Sydney takes 20 hours and covers 10,250 miles. I completed my fastest around-the-world journey in seven days, flying from Frankfurt to New York, then to San Francisco, then Seoul, and finally back to Frankfurt. That distance was 17,340 miles. In my 70-plus years, I have traveled several million miles, a distance that in times past would have required several generations, if not centuries to cover. Measured in miles, my journeys have taken me—metaphorically speaking—through many centuries. Andrzej Stasiuk, the most highly acclaimed contemporary Polish writer, expressed a similar thought: "Those who travel live several lives."[13]

Moving now from time to space: when I was born in that small village in the Eifel Mountains in 1947, life there was not much different than it was in the Middle Ages. When I compare living conditions then with today, I can observe that more has changed in those few decades than over the many preceding centuries. My feeling is that the extent of change between my Eifel village of 1947 and what I call the Globalia of the twenty-first century is much greater in extent than the change in the period from 1650 and 1850, and probably also more than in the century from 1850 to 1950. But perhaps every generation that has lived since the Middle Ages feels that its own era has been the time of greatest change.

In Chap. 2, I will go into greater detail about that transformation and will attempt to make a more objective measurement. But the statement that I have "traveled" centuries through time and space does seem accurate. Many people of my generation have traversed even greater metaphorical distances. One example is Mohed Altrad, who was born to Bedouins in the Syrian Desert. He does not know his exact birthdate. In France, he became a billionaire and a member of the French Legion of Honor. He said: "I grew up similar to Abraham, who was a Bedouin and only knew the desert. When people ask me how old I am, I answer '3000 years.'" He is expressing that he has experienced a development in his life that in the course of history took millennia to unfold.[14]

---

[13] "Im Gespräch: Der polnische Schriftsteller Andrzej Stasiuk," *Frankfurter Allgemeine Zeitung*, March 9, 2017, p. 40.

[14] *The Wall Street Journal*, June 17, 016.

The West, Warsaw, and Back

Answering questions of ancestry begins with one's parents. My mother Therese Nilles was born in 1911 in the village of Hemmersdorf, which is located in the Saarland close to the border with Lorraine.[15] My father Adolf Simon came into the world in 1913 in Hasborn, a small village in the Eifel Mountains. Both of my parents are thus children of the far western part of Germany.

How did they meet? Given the distance of about 100 miles between the two towns, it would have been unlikely for the two to have met under normal circumstances. In that day and age, almost all people married within their own neighboring towns. That a spouse would come to the Eifel from such as "great" distance would have been extraordinarily rare. The roll of the dice that brought my parents together—and altered the course of many millions of other lives—was World War II.

My mother trained with the Red Cross as an auxiliary nurse. She was drafted at the start of the war and stationed first at the Hotel Schulz, a beautiful classic lodge on the shores of the Rhine in the town of Unkel am Rhein, near the famous Bridge of Remagen. The well-known hotel and the nearby church-run convalescence home had already been converted into military hospitals in 1939, in preparation for Germany's invasion of France. As that campaign progressed westward, she was stationed in Metz (today part of France) and then later Wiesbaden, before the transfer came that would change the course of her life. In 1941, she was relocated to Warsaw, where she worked for the next three years. That is where she got to know Adolf Simon, a lance corporal in the medical corps. They worked in the same hospital the Red Cross had set up. These two children of far western Germany first met far in the east, more than 700 miles from home. Something must have sparked between the two of them, or otherwise I would not be here to tell this story.

They married in May 1944 in my mother's hometown. One day after the wedding, my father had to travel to the Atlantic coast, where his next assignment awaited him. Only a few weeks later, on June 6, 1944, the Allies landed on the beaches of Normandy and the Germans began their retreat from the western front. My mother, who had taken the family name Simon, did not return to Warsaw. The Soviet troops had already reached the outskirts of Warsaw by July 1944. They stopped their forward march there because Stalin had no interest in supporting the Warsaw Uprising, launched by the Polish underground resistance. He allowed the Germans to brutally crush the uprising (Borodzie 2004).

---

[15] Lorraine belonged to Germany at that time, but is currently part of France.

I have never visited the place where my parents were stationed in Warsaw. To this day, German–Polish relations remain under the shadow of history. I have Polish friends and know many Poles. But my oldest Polish friend suffered greatly under the Nazis, as did his family. I know that he speaks and understands German, and occasionally I have sent him German newspaper clippings, which he read. But even though we have known each other for 40 years, we have never once conversed in German. Many people from that time still carry the scars of what they suffered from Germans.

Germany's unconditional surrender on May 8, 1945 brought World War II to end in the European theater. My father was held as a prisoner by the French, while my mother returned to her hometown. Because public transportation had broken down completely, my mother rode by bike from there to the Eifel. That was a precarious adventure because of the chaos all around. The war had reduced streets, bridges, and entire cities to rubble. On her journey, she had to pass through French and American checkpoints. Nonetheless, she arrived safely in the Eifel. That was also the first time she encountered the small village and the farmhouse where she would spend the rest of her life. Had she imagined her future in that way when she fell in love with the farmer's son Adolf Simon in Warsaw? The contrast between the agricultural and "backward" Eifel and the comparatively modern, industrialized Saarland must have been striking to her.

My mother's family had its own turbulent history. Shortly before the outbreak of World War II and several months before the invasion of France, the region around her hometown was declared a Red Zone. That meant that the entire population from Basel in the south to Aachen in the north had to evacuate with whatever they could take with them. My mother's family—together with their livestock and all their household goods—was resettled in Thuringia in central Germany. They left behind a small farm, a grocery store, and a wagoner's shop. The war officially began on September 1, 1939 when German warships attacked Danzig (now Gdansk) in what is now Poland.

In May 1940, the German army attacked its western neighbors France, the Netherlands, Belgium, and Luxembourg. After the German troops had passed through the Red Zone and reached Paris, the residents of the Saarland were allowed to return, but what greeted them was a shocking surprise. My in-law's house was gone. Confronted by a curve too narrow for their tanks to pass, the German army had leveled the house completely. The family was left with nothing.

Exactly 50 years later, I accompanied my mother and her sister (my godmother) on a visit to Unkel, where my mother was stationed as a nurse when the war began in 1939. The Rheinhotel Schulz was still in operation, and we entered it through a stone archway. A sense of calm and comfort permeated the courtyard. Because the hotel is right on the shores of the Rhine, the terrace offers an unobstructed panorama that includes the ruins of the famous Drachenfels Castle. It is exactly the perspective that many artists in the nineteenth century used to paint their romantic pictures of the Drachenfels and Nonnenwerth Island in its foreground.

We told the young lady at the reception about the events of September 1939. She was interested and for her age she knew a lot about that period. The waitress who served us coffee knew even more. She was older and had grown up in Unkel. She also told us that the hotel owner was still alive at age 88. My mother remembered him.

As we looked out onto the Rhine, we were moved by the sight of an unusual ship traveling downstream. On the ship's deck, which had been transformed into a stage, a band played music and songs from around the time the war began. Individual soldiers in military dress from different eras stood aboard ship as if they were keeping watch. Chills ran down my spine as the remembrance of that time came to life before our eyes.

The ship served as the setting for a theater production of Bertolt Brecht's *Ballad of the Dead Soldier*, which was being performed in the cities of Verdun and Bitburg, on a ship on the Rhine, and in the city of Bonn. Brecht originally wrote his ballad with World War I in mind, but the contemporary producers shifted that focus forward by one World War. In Brecht's World War I setting for the ballad, a German soldier dies at the Battle of Verdun, one of the longest and deadliest battles in human history. He is buried in his imperial military uniform. He is then dug up from his grave and sent back to war, this time World War II. He dies in battle again and is buried in his *Wehrmacht* uniform at the military cemetery in Bitburg. That is the same cemetery that attracted headlines worldwide after the controversial visit by US President Ronald Reagan and German Chancellor Helmut Kohl on May 8, 1985, the 40th anniversary of Germany's unconditional surrender.

In this updated version of Brecht's ballad, the soldier does not rest in peace after his burial at Bitburg. He is removed from his grave again, dressed in the uniform of today's Germany army (*Bundeswehr*) and sent off to war once again. The soldier in this controversial ballad travels his last stretch on the ship I was referring to and finds his ultimate resting place high above the Rhine in the old customs tower in Bonn, which was still the capital of West Germany at that time.

I consider this interpretation of Brecht's ballad as a remarkable artistic device to bring space and time together. An interesting side note to the performance is that the mayors of Bonn and Bitburg at the time openly tried to stop the project. But why? Both mayors were taken to court and quickly lost. The producers' victory in court allowed me to sit on September 1, 1989— exactly 50 years after the beginning of World War II—together with my mother and godmother on the terrace of the Hotel Schulz and experience such a moving performance. It is hard to imagine two worlds more different along the Rhine than the one in September 1939 and the one in September 1989. The thought occurred to me once more that the true elapsed time in that intervening period was centuries and not merely 50 years.

Exactly 30 years later in 2019, I stood at the same place again, reflecting on my life. What luck I have had to live for over 70 years in peace! No other German generation before me was so fortunate.

Europe: Fate and *Patria Nostra*

The fates of my family reflect the turmoil of Europe in the nineteenth and twentieth centuries. My great-grandfather worked and died in Paris, where my grandfather was born. My family in the Saarland lived alternately under the rule of the French, the Germans, and for a time under the League of Nations.[16]

In World War I, my paternal grandfather caught malaria while deployed in Bessarabia, a region which now lies mostly within the country of Moldova in Eastern Europe.[17] In St. Gabriel near Vienna, my uncle Johannes Nilles studied theology and was ordained as a priest in 1935. He then spent the ensuing 53 years as a missionary in Papua New Guinea. My parents ended up in Poland during World War II and met in the military hospital where they both worked. Two of my uncles fought in Russia and one of them did not survive the war. My father was dispatched to St. Nazaire on the Atlantic Coast in 1944. One of my mother's brothers and an uncle by marriage served under Field Marshall Erwin Rommel in North Africa. They came across each other later in an American prisoner-of-war camp on a farm in Kentucky.

The fact that my family's history has been so closely intertwined with the continent's and the neighboring countries' fates has definitely played a role in my being a staunch European. I do not share the rather skeptical viewpoint of the French philosopher Bruno Latour, who said "Europe, that is what I

---

[16] Between 1920 and 1935, the Saar Region was under the League of Nations (Geneva) and governed by an international commission.

[17] Most of Bessarabia now lies in the Eastern European country Moldova. The name has nothing to do with Arabia. It is derived from the name of the House of Basarab, a royal family from Walachia (Romania) that ruled the region in the thirteenth and fourteenth centuries.

hesitate to call the European fatherland" (Latour 2017). Either Europe is our *Patria Nostra*, or we do not have one.

The numerous strokes of fate experienced by my ancestors exemplify the difficult times in Europe. Four of the eight children of my paternal great-grandfather died either at birth or at a young age, as did my father's twin brother. One uncle died in a train crash in 1940. Four years later, his brother drowned in the Black Sea. My grandfather from the Eifel fell from a barn loft when he was 75 years old and did not survive. Fate also hit my mother's side of the family hard and often. Not only did my great-grandfather drown in the Seine, but three siblings of my mother did not live beyond early childhood. Such chains of catastrophes occurred in many families. Child mortality, war, and accidents claimed many lives. Is it coincidence or providence that the chain of ancestors that led to me never broke?

Eifel

After my father returned from Allied captivity in September 1945, my mother went to the Eifel Mountains for good. She moved into the farmhouse where three older people lived: my grandparents Johann and Margarete Simon and an unmarried great aunt. All three were around 70 years old at the time. My grandparents had seven children, five of whom were still alive after the war. All of them had left home and were therefore not available to keep the farm going.

Although the matter was never discussed in my presence, my grandparents must have been very concerned both about their advanced age and the future of their farm. That left my father—who had worked as a milk inspector prior to the war—with no choice but to return to his parents' house and become a farmer. In the 1930s, he had studied for two semesters at an agricultural school, but he was never passionate about farming. After the war, his generation had few options. Roots, family tradition, and economic realities conspired to prevent him, like many others, from striking out on his own path. The sense of duty to take care of his parents in their old age and not leave them alone precluded alternative plans for his life.

In nothing else, the fact that my father, who was already 32 years old, left the war as a married man must have offered my grandparents a glimmer of hope. But to the family and the village, his wife was a very unusual person. She came from far away, she spoke a different dialect, and thanks to her years in Warsaw and other places she had a certain worldliness. The women from the neighborhood, in contrast, only knew their own village. Some had worked as maids in other towns or for wealthier families in nearby cities. But my mother never regretted moving to Hasborn. Although she could have easily done so, she did not speak High German with the villagers. She spoke in her Saarland dialect, and gradually learned the idiom of the Eifel. People from the Eifel, Luxembourg, and Saarland can communicate in their dialects, which belong to the so-called Mosel-Franconian language group. Mosel-Franconian was once the official idiom of the powerful archdiocese of Trier, which also existed as a city-state until 1789.

I bring this up because speaking these dialects can bring some important advantages, as the following story shows. Alois Mertes, who would later become an undersecretary in the German foreign ministry, came from a town in the Eifel and had perfect command of the Eifel dialect. At the height of the Cold War, he served as a diplomat in Moscow. Every diplomat knew that the KGB would listen in on conversations. So he and the ambassador from Luxembourg would use the Mosel-Franconian dialect. That apparently frustrated the KGB to no end because they did not have any agents fluent in this dialect. Sometimes it can be a big advantage to speak a strange or rare language.

The Bonds of Language

I essentially grew up bilingual. And I thought that a household with two languages was the most normal thing in the world. My mother spoke in her Saarland dialect. My father and his village spoke in the Eifel dialect. That was the language I actively used, even when talking with my mother. As a child, it did not dawn on me that my mother used a different dialect than my father. Growing up bilingual in that sense was perfectly natural for me. Perhaps children whose parents communicate with them in two truly distinct languages have a similar feeling.

I have retained my mastery of the Eifel dialect and use it regularly when I am in my hometown. It contributes significantly to the level of comfort I feel there. But the number of people fluent in the dialect continues to decline. Only a small number of young people still learn it from their parents, who prefer to speak to the kids in High German in order to prepare them better for the outside world. Because a dialect can only be passed along orally, the survival prospects for the language of my childhood do not look rosy. But I have not forgotten it and will use it for the rest of my life. It is part of me.

The dialect has many words that do not exist in High German or have disappeared over time. One example is the word for chaff. In High German, the word is "Spreu," but in my home dialect the word is "Koff," which is a distant relative of the English word chaff. Such words apparently share a Germanic origin and spread into Low German as well as English.

A shared dialect forms an important part of the identity of a village or a regional community. If you speak the dialect, you belong. A closeness arises spontaneously when two people speak a common dialect. It makes people feel less distant. As the most famous German poet, Johann-Wolfgang von Goethe said: "Every province loves its own dialect: for it is, properly speaking, the element in which the soul draws its breath."[18] An essay on homesickness uses the phrase "Language is home" (Kals 2017).

Common languages engender feelings of trust and security. At international management seminars and similar events, participants from different countries or regions are intentionally mixed together. They work in multinational groups, discuss issues, and make presentations. The common working language is generally English, which is a foreign language for most participants. But I have observed a particular tendency hundreds of times at these events. People of the same language spontaneously form their own groups during the breaks and the meals. The French, the Japanese, and the Italians (and of course, many other nationalities with a common language) sit together. This retreat into the cocoon of one's own language hinders and sometimes even undermines one important goal of these events, which is to familiarize people across national and linguistic boundaries.

Several hundred colleagues from the firm I co-founded gathered one evening at a brewery in Cologne's Old City. I went from table to table to greet them. At one large table sat only colleagues from Paris. When I suggested that this arrangement was not in the spirit of our firm's World Meeting—designed to bring together colleagues from different countries and offices—they had an immediate on-point answer: "In Paris we never have to time to get together. We find it great to be able to finally sit together at one table." And even though all of our Paris colleagues speak English well, they apparently feel more comfortable using their native language. At the same time, they appreciate it when someone communicates with them *en français*.

Personally, I have frequently experienced that my language gives away my origins and also creates enduring bonds. That starts with the recognition of a common hometown or home region. Time and again, I meet people who come from the Eifel or the nearby Moselle Valley, famous for its wines. In the course of a speech, discussion, or consulting project, people often homed in on my accent and recognized my roots. I also do the same with others. Michael

---

[18] Johann Wolfgang von Goethe, *The Auto-biography of Goethe: Truth and Poetry: from My Own Life*. H.G. Bohn. Kindle Edition.

Naumann, a former federal minister of culture, said "dialects can have the same effect as personal ID documents that some people carry with them their entire lives, whether they want to or not"(Naumann 2017).[19]

In this sense, I am reminded of a visit to the firm Bosch Rexroth. The CEO invited me to join him and his team for lunch. In the midst of our conversation, one of the other executives suddenly interjected: "Mr. Simon, you talk exactly like our Dr. Hieronimus."

"Who is Dr. Hieronimus?" I asked, following quickly with the question "and where is he from?"

Dr. Albert Hieronimus was a board member at Rexroth who would later become CEO of Bosch in India and conclude his career as CEO of Bosch Rexroth AG, the global market leader in hydraulics. He answered for himself: "From a small village in the Eifel that you have definitely never heard of." But I insisted on knowing, and he said "Immerath, in the county Daun, in the 'volcanic' Eifel."

My great-grandfather came from Immerath. He was the one who brought the name Simon to my home village.

Over the years, I have had several similar encounters with children of the Eifel. Is it a coincidence that my paths crossed those of so many Eifelians? These encounters gave me the idea to bring the successes, careers, and experiences of these personalities back to their roots. Nearly all of them had left their home villages and towns at a young age. Back home, only a few people knew what became of them and what unusual and impressive paths their lives had taken. So I initiated a series in a regional newspaper under the title "Children of the Eifel—Successful in the World." Each week there was a new story about someone with Eifel roots, and eventually I compiled the series into a book under the same name (Simon 2008).[20] Both the series and the book were well received. The Eifelians were proud of their children who had carved noteworthy paths in the outside world.

There was another situation in my life in which language played both a unifying and also a segregating role. Starting in 1958, I attended the Cusanus High School (*Gymnasium*) in the nearby city Wittlich. Many of the students came from local villages and were fluent only in their own dialects. High German was effectively a foreign language for them. On the other hand, the

---

[19] See also: "In den Rollen seines Lebens," *Frankfurter Allgemeine Zeitung*, April 22, 2017, p. 12.

[20] This series continues from time to time in the newspaper *Eifelzeitung*. Through 2018, around 140 profiles had been published. A second series, "Children of the Eifel—from other times" included some 400 profiles through 2018 and was also published in book form. Gregor Brand (Autor), Hermann Simon (Editor), *Kinder der Eifel—aus anderer Zeit*, Daun: Verlag der Eifelzeitung 2013; Gregor Brand (Autor), Hermann Simon (Editor), *Kinder der Eifel—aus anderer Zeit*, Band 2, Books on Demand 2018.

students who grew up in the city generally spoke High German, even if it was tinged with a regional accent. These were the children of civil servants, doctors, lawyers, and businesspeople. This separation due to language endured beyond school and remains more or less unchanged even today. The village kids spoke among themselves in their dialects, while the communication with the city kids took place in High German. If I meet someone with whom I previously spoke in dialect. I automatically fall back into our common idiom. I find it difficult to speak with them in High German, and others seem to have the same difficulty. One time at Oktoberfest in Munich, I was having a good time with several friends. One of the people was Dr. Michael Thiel, who grew up in my home village and is the son of my elementary school teacher. It was clear to both of us that we could only speak in our dialect. Anything else would have felt strange to us.

References

Wlodzimierz Borodzie, *Der Warschauer Aufstand 1944 (Die Zeit des Nationalsozialismus)*, Frankfurt: Fischer 2004.

Ursula Kals, "Wehe, wenn das Heimweh kommt," *Frankfurter Allgemeine Zeitung*, July 15, 2017, p. C3.

Sebastian Kleinschmidt, "Zeuge der Dunkelheit, Bote des Lichts, Rezension eines Gedichtes von Ulrich Schacht," *Frankfurter Allgemeine Zeitung*, February 11, 2017, p. 18.

Bernd Kortlaender (ed.), *was die Zeit fühlt und denkt und bedarf*, Bielefeld: Aisthesis Verlag 2014, p. 36.

Bruno Latour, "Das grüne Leuchten," *Frankfurter Allgemeine Zeitung*, October 7, 2017, Frankreich Spezial, p. L7.

Michael Naumann, *Glück gehabt. Ein Leben*. Hamburg: Hoffmann und Campe 2017

Hermann Simon, *Kinder der Eifel – erfolgreich in der Welt*, Daun: Verlag der Eifelzeitung 2008.

Robert Thurman, *The Tibetan Book of the Dead: The Great Book of Natural Liberation Through Understanding in the Between*, New York: Bantam Books 1993.

Michael Wolffsohn, *Deutschjüdische Glückskinder—Eine Weltgeschichte meiner Familie*, Munich: dtv 2017.

Palle Yourgau, *A World without Time: The Forgotten Legacy of Gödel and Einstein*, New York: Basic Books 2005, p. 115.

2

Leaving the Middle Ages

A slightly older contemporary of mine once wrote that his "childhood and youth would appear medieval by today's standards, but that was the reality barely half a century ago. And then seemingly overnight, a sudden change came that was more radical than anyone could have ever imagined." (Nosbüsch, 1993).

The person who wrote that passage, education professor Johannes Nosbüsch, came from my home region. His words also accurately describe my childhood. It is not an exaggeration to say that agriculture in my village after World War II was still medieval. Some progress had occurred since the nineteenth century, but handicraft, self-sufficiency, and traditional habits still predominated.

Hundreds of authors have written about what it was like to grow up on a farm, and the detailed descriptions in those biographies generally reflect my own childhood. So I will spare the reader yet another repeat of those typical experiences, and instead limit my stories and comments to a handful of situations that stand out to such an extent that I still recall them vividly today.

With a few exceptions such as the teacher, the postal clerk, and the policeman, all of the families in our village lived from subsistence farming. The largest farm covered 28 acres, and the average size was 20 acres. Almost all of the work was done by hand. In terms of farm equipment, the Eifel trailed more advanced, mechanized parts of Germany by a couple of decades. On our farm, the family had two devices that barely earned the name "machine": a mower and a seeder, both horse-drawn. My grandfather had purchased the mower on January 10, 1940 for 341.50 Reichsmark, which was about $136 at the time. Compared to mowing with a scythe, it represented an enormous step forward. But hay-making still took place by hand. The advantage of using the seeder vs. seeding by hand was a more uniform distribution of seed across the field. Other than that, though, the world of the Eifel farmer in 1950 was not much different from what a farmer did a century or two earlier.

The role of the Catholic Church still displayed some of its medieval power. The most powerful figure in village life was the Catholic pastor. This was reflected in how we addressed him. He was called "Lord," not "Lord Pastor."[1] When we encountered him, we would kneel and quietly say "Praise be to Jesus Christ." The Lord determined whether farmers could work the fields on Sundays during harvest. That was only permitted when he "proclaimed" it at Sunday mass, and of course everyone stuck to that rule.

The belief in supernatural powers was also common. The village had "sorcerers" that farmers would call to heal sick animals. But people also feared them because they could impose curses. During a thunderstorm, we lit candles and consecrated branches to keep lightning away from the house.

Our farm was designed for self-sufficiency. Except for salt, sugar, and spices, we grew almost everything ourselves. We gathered firewood in the forest. My father made our tools, such as rakes and baskets. And until just a few years before I was born, people made their own wool cloth and linens. We still have a lot of bed sheets and tablecloths with the monogram JS (for Johann Simon) that my grandmother weaved on our own loom.

In such an economy based on self-sufficiency, money does not play a big role. What little money we needed came from selling milk, hogs, or young pigs. Money was always tight, but we felt neither constrained nor poor. We always had enough to eat even though the variety was limited. An orange or a banana was a treat we only enjoyed at Christmas. Even sweets, chocolate, and soft drinks—all of which we craved—were rarities. My "spoiled" cousins from the city once visited on vacation and brought a case of soda pop with them. That was a party week for me!

Life was hard. As children we had to help out regularly with the farming and chores. My grandmother passed away when I was nine years old. From that point on, my parents ran the farm alone and needed all the help they could get. The small farms could not afford farmhands or maids. One type of work that I absolutely despised was pulling the shoots from beets in order to create proper separation. Originally, the beet seeds were sown in the garden and the smaller plants then replanted in the field. However, if there was a dry spell during planting, the replanted seedlings would not grow. When we switched to a new method and sowed the seed directly in the fields, we solved

---

[1] This is "dä Hee" in my native dialect.

one problem but created a new one: too many shoots that needed to be pulled. Beet plants require about one foot of separation in order to grow to their full potential. The development of mono-germ seeds made the pulling process simpler because each seed produced only one shoot. But these needed to be pulled as well because the spread of the seeds in the field was not uniform.

All of this pulling work—my most hated task of the entire year—consumed days that we spent bent over, crouched, or kneeling in the rows. It also demanded endless patience. Part of the problem was that there was neither a feeling of accomplishment nor visible proof of success. All I had done was simply pull some plants out of the ground.

Harvesting potatoes was a more social and therefore less monotonous activity. Digging up the potatoes left them strewn across the whole field, and we needed to pick them up by hand. Hands were always in short supply, so we hired a few women who did not have farms of their own, and we compensated them with potatoes. Most of the women would bring their children, who frolicked together in the fields. If the weather cooperated, there were few finer experiences than this for me when I was growing up. The kids needed to work too, but we always had time left for play. We drank homemade raspberry juice, and it was a pleasure to enjoy jam and bread with coffee out in the field. Late in the afternoon, we would start a fire and roast fresh potatoes. That was great fun, despite the occasional blackened potato or singed finger.

Toward evening, my father would come with the horse and wagon to load up the sacks. The sacks bore different markings, depending on the field and the potatoes' intended use: food, animal feed, and seed tubers. The nicest, largest *pommes de terre* were set aside for our own consumption. Smaller, withered, or damaged ones were sorted out for our hogs. The ones to be used for the next spring's planting—usually medium-sized, well-formed ones—were also separated out.

On good days, we would collect more than 30 sacks, so that the horse could barely pull the heavy wagon from the field. Every now and then, we needed to hitch on a horse from one of the neighbors. The horse had an easier time once it reached a paved surface. Because it was usually dark when we left the fields and we took public streets back to the village, each wagon carried an oil lantern for light. But these were another source of frustration. Either the oil was used up, the wick had rotted, or the lantern simply did not work. The trip home in the twilight or darkness thus often turned into an adventure. There were only a few cars and we never had any accidents, but we lived in constant fear that the policeman would show up and issue us a ticket, or worst of all, a fine for driving without a lantern. Once at home, we still had to tend to the livestock and unload the wagon. That happened with the help of a chute that we tipped the potatoes onto. They slid directly into the cellar through small holes. In good years, the potatoes would fill the cellar to the ceiling. The seed tubers would be stored in special areas in the cellar or in pits in the garden. Most of the feed potatoes ended up in a large pile behind the house.

My life as a child and a younger man followed the daily and annual rhythms of farm life. That changed little even after I entered high school (*Gymnasium*), which required a train trip to a nearby town. When I got home at around 2 p.m. during harvest, I would hop on my bike and head out to the fields. In the evenings, I would help feed the livestock and only then do my homework.

Under normal circumstances, I found this schedule neither unusual nor hard. I did not have any problems with school although I was not a stand-out student. The 1959 school year, however, was a tough one. My mother was hospitalized for several weeks during the harvest and then spent a month at a spa to recuperate. We had sent my younger sister to stay with an aunt, so my father was alone with me, a 12-year-old boy, during this work-intensive phase. In addition to my school work, I now needed to contribute an adult's workload.

In order to cope, my father purchased a milking machine so that I could milk the cows mornings and evenings. I was fascinated by the machine's vacuum technology. My father sometimes worked in the fields until midnight. We would occasionally sit exhausted at the dinner table, and my father would bring out two beers, a lager for him and a non-alcoholic malt beer for me. We toasted ourselves, and I felt like a man.

My grades in school dropped precipitously during this hard phase. That bothered me to such an extent that in the following year, when my mother was healthy again, I bore down and achieved the best grades of my entire school career.

The fear that something could happen to one of my parents—and make it extremely difficult to continue operating the farm—became my constant companion. Running a small farm with only two adults is a risky undertaking. There was no one in reserve if someone got sick. Although I have absolutely no reason to complain about my current situation in life, that feeling of economic insecurity has never left me. I trace the roots of that feeling back to the events of that time.

Another source of this insecurity is that agriculture is so sensitive to external factors such as weather and pests. For this reason, I make no effort to hide my reservations toward any business subject to such forces beyond one's control. Of course, I realize that external influences are an inseparable part of economic activity. No business operates in a vacuum. In the Great Recession of 2009, the revenue of Simon-Kucher—the firm I co-founded—fell by around 10%. That dredged up the experiences of my youth and the ever-present sense of economic insecurity.

Our village childhood was a strange contradiction of coercion and freedom. Many parts of my life were regulated by adults and subject to strict enforcement. That was especially true for anything related to church and prayer, but it also applied to school or to being at the table on time for meals. Our behavior with respect to authority figures such as pastors and teachers was tightly controlled. But at other times, we children were left to our own devices and enjoyed complete freedom. Our parents simply did not have the time to hold constant watch over us or provide for our "entertainment." We played outside almost all the time, wandering aimlessly through the village or through the nearby oak grove. We could do whatever we wanted without any adult supervision or intervention.

I was the oldest of a group of six boys in our neighborhood, so a natural leadership role fell to me. Serving as leader and instigator was the first and probably best leadership schooling of my entire life. It was my job to come up with ideas and then motivate, agitate, or divide up the group in order to keep everyone in line. These tasks were not fundamentally different from the leadership challenges I needed to cope with decades later. Was it luck or coincidence that I grew up with such a group of boys? Would I have turned out the same if there had only been girls in the neighborhood, or no children at all?

As kids, we were exposed to the full "circle of life," in contrast to modern children who experience only a tiny sliver of it. When someone in the neighborhood died, of course we children attended the wake and saw the body lying in state. We were also allowed to see newborn babies. We witnessed the cows having their calves and the hogs giving birth to their litters. We saw hogs getting slaughtered, and no one sent us away or covered our eyes when a chicken had its head chopped off and later ended up in the cooking pot. We saw dead animals of all kinds, before the workers from the rendering plants would pick them up. What does this direct exposure to the "circle of life" mean compared to the protected, sheltered way today's children grow up? I do not have an answer.

Another facet of our life was the profound sense of community within the village, something I came to appreciate only years later. This sense of community has two foundations. One was the relatively high degree of social equality. There were no families that were really rich, and on the other end of the wealth spectrum, none that were truly poor. The entire village participated in festivals and other community activities. Farming also contributed to the sense of community. Each family grew the same kinds of crops on the same stretch of fields. This meant that all the farmers and their families came together during the potato or grain harvest on the same land. For us children, this was a paradise because we could play in large groups in the fields. The world was not "all work and no play" for the adults either. They took time to chat with their neighbors across the field. In the evening, the fully loaded wagons made their way in one long procession back to the village.

It was comforting that everyone knew everyone else, but the downside is that everyone *knew* everyone else. Nothing remained secret or undiscovered for long, a fact which created a remarkable level of social control. Whoever violated the boundaries of social norms faced condemnation from the community. As young kids we were not really aware of these constraints, but the older we got, the more confining they became.

Between the Middle Ages and the mid-1950s, you could count the "breakthrough" changes in our region on the one hand. Basically, little had changed for centuries. In the year 1726, our village was allocated a stop on a newly established postal coach line. That represented the first connection with the "big" outside world. Around 150 years later, in 1879, the railroad reached our area. Starting in 1912, we got public water service, and electricity from 1918 onward. But by 1947, when I was born, no one in our village had an indoor bathroom or a television.

Little else changed until the mid-1950s, when the transformation of our remote area began to gather steam. The first automobile and the first tractor made their appearance. As the figure shows, groundbreaking innovations then seemed to come at a rate measured in years, not centuries.

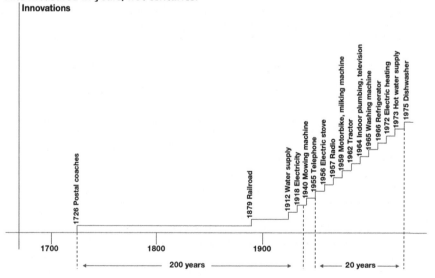

More technological innovation occurred between 1955 and 1975 than in the two preceding centuries. And within those two decades, the world of my childhood dissolved completely. Today, there is not one single farmer left in the village. The tradespeople and craftsmen, the businesses, the customs, and the role of the church all fell victim to this radical progress. What I miss the most, though, is the close sense of community of my childhood. I would give a lot to return once again to these "Middle Ages" and spend another day helping out on the harvest with the entire community.

Made of the Earth of My Homeland

One fundamental change, which few are aware of, affects our bodies and the molecules that constitute them. At the time of my childhood, the question "what am I made of?" had one clear answer: "From the earth of my homeland." From conception through the nursing stage, one's body receives its molecules from the mother in a natural way. After that, the cells of the body are built from the materials one takes in from food. And this food came exclusively from the earth of my homeland. With a few exceptions such as sugar, salt, and spices, everything we ate was self-produced. That was as true for the vegetables from the garden as well as the grains we used to bake our bread. Even the meat, milk, and eggs we consumed came from our own animals, who likewise lived on the yield of our fields and meadows. We were literally made from the earth, air, and water of our homeland.

And what we are made of today? We do not know. Or at least we cannot answer that question with any precision. "From the earth of the whole planet" comes close to the true answer. I once tried to count the countries of origin of what I found at a produce stand. Apples from Chile, kiwis from New Zealand, oranges from Spain, grapes from South Africa, mangoes from Egypt, figs from Morocco, mushrooms from Poland, and tomatoes from Holland, and so on. Where does margarine come from? It is probably manufactured from palm oil sourced from Malaysia or Indonesia. Where did the cattle graze and the fish swim before their meat ended up on our tables? In most cases, we do not know.

Being self-sufficient requires a wide range of skills that have disappeared from today's world. We are no longer required to raise a variety of plants and animals, and we have also lost the ability to prepare and preserve what they yield. We used to know how to smoke, salt, or can meats in order to preserve them. Preparing fruits and vegetables for conservation required specialized culinary skills. Fruit was dried, cabbage was made into sauerkraut, plums were pickled, and carrots were stored in sand. Surviving the long winters without purchasing anything seemed to require a thousand clever tricks and subtle techniques. But despite all these efforts, the diet was rather bland. Today, we no longer need those skills to survive the winters, and we have a much greater variety of foods available to us.

The fact that our constituent molecules currently come from all over the world—and not from a small village or local region—is one of the most significant yet barely noticed differences between the world of my childhood and the world of today. How relevant is this difference and what are its consequences? I do not know, but there is some concern.

Does the global nature of our food chains affect our immune systems? I do not know the answer to that either. But the mere fact that our molecular composition is fundamentally different today makes such questions worth pondering. This change describes my own route through time. In its material makeup, my body reflects my transition from a farm boy who only knew his local environs to a global player who feels at home anywhere and whose body comprises molecules drawn from the entire world.

Eight Grades ... in One Room

Today, it is hard for me to imagine that a teacher could handle eight school grades in one classroom. But that is the way it was in the elementary school I attended starting in April 1953. I have few specific recollections of my five years in that school, probably because of the constant noise and chaos in that one room. Despite all that, learning was not too difficult for me and I did not take school very seriously. The material that the teacher had prepared for the older students usually interested me more than the material intended for us, the younger students.

Our teacher got very sick and died a few years later. This forced a series of substitute teachers from neighboring villages to jump in. Consistency was not restored until a young teacher was transferred to our school. My motivation to learn increased after she arrived, but at the same time I enjoyed provoking her. Detention was a teacher's special punishment back then, and for me it became a regular weekly event. While my class was usually free after 11 a.m. on Saturdays, I needed to stay behind with the older students until 1 p.m. Because this happened every Saturday, my parents never noticed what was going on. And I never told them anything about my pranks or the resulting detentions. Had I done so, I probably would have drawn additional punishment. My goal was always to maintain a clear separation between home and school.

Detention, of course, was not the only form of punishment. "Spare the rod, spoil the child" seemed to be a motto of this era, and the teachers did not spare the rod. It was an essential part of their toolkit. Mild misdeeds would draw a whack on an outstretched hand. More serious wrongdoing earned whacks on the behind. Our pastor, a Catholic priest, meted out even worse punishment than our teacher. He was a competent and beloved priest, but he had a violent temper that serious misbehavior would bring to a boil. I can recall some rather hefty beatings. One such occasion happened when some friends and I disrupted the Stations of the Cross prayers that the older girls conducted with us during Lent. Another time the pastor heard that we had been caught smoking.

Sometimes, it was our more innocent misdeeds that drew severe punishments. My friends and I were fascinated by military vehicles, and tanks in particular. French and American units frequently conducted maneuvers in our town. During one recess, a column of tanks drove by the school and took up an offensive position in the nearby oak grove. We could not restrain ourselves any longer and forgot all about school. The tanks were far more interesting. After recess, the pastor stood before a classroom full of girls, with not a boy in sight. When we finally returned to the school, the pastor exploded and whipped us all.

Life was easier once the female teacher took over. I do not recall her ever striking us. In general, the girls did not suffer any corporal punishment.

From today's perspective, I really do not feel I learned very much in my five years of elementary school. The illness of my original teacher, the constant stream of substitutes, and the simultaneous instruction for eight different grades made it almost impossible for teaching to be effective. The situation did not improve until the final year, when a new teacher named Jakob Thiel was transferred to our school and a second classroom was established. Mr. Thiel was an engaged and energetic teacher from whom—unfortunately—I was only able to learn for a few months.

A monumental Morning Decision

Very few students were selected to attend the advanced high school (*Gymnasium*). My grades were only average in that one-room elementary school, so I was not a clear candidate for selection. I was also known as a punk, which did not exactly encourage the teachers to recommend me for such programs. Furthermore, the pastor played a decisive role in determining who got to attend *Gymnasium*. Unstated in the background of this process was his hope that the boys who advanced would eventually become priests.

The pastor recommended a neighbor of mine for *Gymnasium*, but not me. The recommended boy (his name is Heinz) was one grade below me, but stood out because of his good grades and exemplary behavior. We grew up side by side and played together every day, so I knew him very well. The fact that he was selected for *Gymnasium* while I was not set off a thought process inside me. That probably marked the first time I had ever thought about what education meant and what would become of me. I may have also felt somewhat humiliated. This prompted me to raise the issue with my parents. They applied no pressure; ultimately, what I did would be my decision and mine alone. I can recall exactly what my father asked me on the last day of school registration, as he stood next to my bed early that morning.

"Shall I sign you up for the advanced high school or not?" he asked.

After a brief moment of hesitation, I said "yes."

That one simple word—uttered early in the morning of January 15, 1958—marks what might be the most important decision of my life. But registration was only the first step. The next step was to pass an entry examination, which was not easy for kids from the villages to do. Everyone knew that we were not optimally prepared for such a test—due to our schooling situation—so Mr. Thiel offered tutoring in order to get us ready for the test. Because Heinz was registered early, he had already completed several weeks of test preparation. I joined him on January 15th when the test was only a few weeks away.

The tutoring sessions took place in the teacher's living room. My first visit there impressed me. He had an entire bookshelf filled with books. I had never seen anything like it in a private home. I had the opportunity to borrow books from the parish library and took full advantage of that.

The first session revealed just how far I was behind Heinz even though I had had one additional year of schooling. Either he was better than me, or the weeks of tutoring he had had were showing their positive effects. In any event, Mr. Thiel was satisfied neither with my effort nor with my progress. His temper would flare, and once when I failed to solve a division problem his patience finally wore out. He expressed his displeasure rather loudly and that led to a reaction that is unfortunately typical for me. Similar to my not returning the dentist for several years after one yelled at me for not opening my mouth, I stopped attending Mr. Thiel's tutoring sessions after this dressing down.

Gymnasium

The day of the entry exam for *Gymnasium* finally arrived. My mother took me by train to Wittlich and then returned home. I found myself among more than a hundred other candidates, and Heinz was the only other person I knew. This was a strange situation for me because in the village, we usually knew every person at any given time.

I undertook no other preparation on my own after breaking off the tutoring sessions with Mr. Thiel. Perhaps for that reason, I wasn't very nervous during the test. Decades later, my son Patrick complains that he finds himself under enormous pressure when it comes to education, while I suffered no such pressure at all. And he is right. During this potentially life-altering test, I felt neither pressure nor the burden of expectations. My parents, however, probably had mixed feelings about the prospect of my success. I was their only son and had only a younger sister, so I was the natural next-in-line for the farm. At that time, farmers in our community labored under the illusion that farming still had a viable future. So if my family's only son went to *Gymnasium*, it could doom the future of the family farm. Even though my mother had two brothers who had completed advanced studies, she did not apply any pressure on me to do the same. She seemed torn by the conflict between the life an academic course of study would offer and the life that would result if I took over the farm.

The written part of the test took place in the morning and included dictation, an essay, and math problems. In the dictation, a word came up which I did not know. It was a word related to the vineyards and meant draff or dregs. The word was obvious to the children who grew up in the nearby Moselle Valley because they had experienced the harvest and pressing of grapes first-hand every year. But it was a foreign word to children from the Eifel.

A lunch break followed the written part of the exam, and we were supposed to return to the room at 2 p.m. By that time, some students would be accepted based on the written exam, while others would need to sit for oral exams. When farmers would go into the city, they would take a modest sandwich with them and would go to a butcher shop for soup. So that is what Heinz and I did. It was the first time we were alone in town. We had some money with us and could eat at a butcher shop that also housed a restaurant. That was enough of an adventure for us that we quickly forgot about the morning tests.

At 2 p.m., we signed back in at the *Gymnasium*. To my surprise, I learned that I had passed the exam, which meant that unlike many others, I would not need to take the oral exams. Without much effort or enthusiasm, I had taken the first hurdle along an educational and academic path that would occupy me for the next 22 years and accompanies me to this day. It also made it more or less official that I would be the first in a long line of descendants on my father's side who would not become a farmer, but instead pursue a completely different path in life. As for my mother's side, one could indeed say that I was about to follow the footsteps of my academically trained uncles.

Leaving behind my local school to attend *Gymnasium* in the nearby town proved painful. I felt as if I was being torn away from the familiar environment I had known since birth and in which not only all the students, but also all the adults knew each other. Like everything else outside the village, I perceived this new environment as big and hard to figure out. At that time, the *Gymnasium* had around 600 students, with 38 students from the entire county together in one class, and roughly 30 teachers. Those numbers may seem small from today's perspective, but they were gigantic through the eyes of a young village boy whose only school experience had come in a one-room school. Although the town was less than six miles away and connected to our village by rail, I felt like a foreigner for a long time in these new environs and occasionally had strong bouts of homesickness.

In English class, we learned the Scottish song "My heart's in the highland, my heart is not here." That refrain became a kind of earworm because it accurately described my mood, especially during the afternoon trips home from Wittlich, located deep in a valley, to the Eifel highlands. The red rail car hummed on its way up the steep hill, and I was happy when I arrived at home, where my mother greeted me with supper. When I came back during the planting or harvest time and needed to go into the fields, she would keep my supper warm. She did this with the help of a tower cooking pot, a clever construction with a pot of boiling water at the bottom. Steam came up through double walls to warm three other pots stacked above it. This construction kept food fresh and warm. I enjoyed many meals that way when my parents worked the fields because they had no other help. I turned my attention to homework only after the work in the fields was completed for the day.

On rare occasions, I went back to my old elementary school for a few hours. This was possible because we had a free day, in part or in whole, when teachers were out at the *Gymnasium*. Mr. Thiel, with whom I maintained a good relationship despite my abrupt end to his tutoring, always welcomed me back. We became friends and would later go hiking together. I remain friends to this day with his son Michael, who works as an investor in Munich.

But these brief stays at my old school gave me the feeling that I did not fully belong there anymore. At that time, very few students from the villages attended the "higher school," as we colloquially referred to the *Gymnasium*. The ones who did quickly achieved a special status and more than a few of those students let this status go to their heads. Some spoke only High German, especially those who attended boarding school and only came back to the village during vacations. Because I was a commuting student, I had an easier time remaining part of the village community and participating in local club activities. But the "higher school" still conferred a special status that made me a bit of an outsider.

We students were accustomed to corporal punishment from our time in elementary school, and this violent form of punishment continued in *Gymnasium.* The most common form was a slap; spankings were much less frequent. Some teachers developed their own personal tactics. One teacher would pinch a student's cheek, hold on tight, and then deliver a hard slap to the other cheek. Another took a similar approach, except he pinched the neck instead of the cheek. At home, many students did not fare much better; they would experience slaps or beatings depending on the severity of what they did wrong. These habits varied by family. The most feared form of punishment came in the summer, when some kids would be hit with a switch on their exposed legs. I never experienced that in my house, but it seemed to be standard practice at some neighboring houses.

From today's perspective, corporal punishment by teachers, clergy, and parents seems like catastrophic misconduct. One might attribute some of the abnormal development of my generation to these practices. But we had a different view of what we went through at the time. Of course, the beatings and punishments were unpleasant. But the recipient often felt like a hero afterwards and was often seen in that light by others. It was a way of "scoring points" with the other boys, so to speak. The fact that I had to serve detention every Saturday likewise earned me a measure of respect from my fellow students. The corrective effects of these punishments on our behavior, however, were short lived. The more valuable lesson for us was to not get caught the next time (such as when we smoked.) We also intensified our threats against the people (mostly girls) who tattled on us.

In *Gymnasium,* we began in an all-boys class. The weeding-out process showed its effects quickly. Only five of the 38 from my county made it to high school graduation without repeating a grade. Three of those five came from villages, only two from the town. In the parallel track, which included the girls as well as the Protestant students, the percentage of students who made it to graduation without repeating a grade was significantly higher. The culture in the two tracks was completely different. Ours was a macho culture, while the other track was more balanced and lacked the in-your-face attitude we displayed. After six years, the two tracks were united, and looking back I see that as a lucky break. One cannot say that our macho attitude was fully eradicated by the time we graduated, but it was definitely toned down. Only five of the 22 graduates came from "our" side, a clear minority.

What teachers stood out and left an indelible impression on me? I can say which teachers, but I cannot precisely articulate what those impressions were or what differences they have made to me. Adalbert Puhl taught German, history, and geography. I feel he was quick to recognize which students had talent, and his hunches were usually spot on. I also had the feeling he thought I was very capable, and that motivated me. Puhl was a personality pre-destined for a political career, but his stubbornness was his downfall.

Locally, we did have a political role model, Matthias-Josef Mehs, who was mayor for many years. He had been shunted aside by the Nazis, and left behind a comprehensive diary for the years 1929–1946.[2] After the Federal Republic of Germany was established, he joined German Parliament as a member of the Christian Democratic Union (CDU). But at the start of the 1950s he voted against rearmament, which landed him in Chancellor Konrad Adenauer's doghouse. That essentially ended his political career at the federal level, so he focused thereafter on his mayoral post and devoted himself to research into the history of his home region. He is credited with starting the most beloved festival in the region, the so-called Wittlich *Säubrennerkirmes* or Sow Burner Festival. The annual festival kicks off on the first Sunday after August 16th, the day dedicated to the town's patron saint, Rochus. It welcomes over 100,000 visitors, and more than 100 pigs are roasted. The idea behind the festival traces its roots back to a medieval legend. One evening the city guard could not find the bolt for the gates, so he closed them with a carrot instead. Later that night a sow ate the carrot, leaving the doors unlocked and allowing an enemy force to enter the city. As punishment, the citizens of Wittlich rounded up and roasted all the pigs, hence the name "Sow Burner."

Puhl was cut from the same cloth as Mehs, with unbending and clear political stances derived from a Catholic worldview. He read a national weekly newspaper that in its heyday held a strong influence in Catholic circles. Puhl procured a steady stream of engrossing and captivating things for us to read. Each student received a copy of the biography of Lenin by David Shub. That was the first biography I ever read, and likely sparked my lifelong interest in biographies.

Perhaps because of his staunch positions or his stubbornness, Puhl switched to the other *Gymnasium* in town several years later. I would occasionally see him on walks in the large nearby forest. If I encountered him during a drive along the winding road through the forest, I would stop to talk. That was always an emotional experience. He asked about my progress and told me emphatically that a person with my talents should go into politics. Was he trying to make his own dreams come true vicariously through the success of one of his students? Several times in my life, I have come to a decision point that could have led me into politics, but ultimately I always stayed on the

---

[2] See Günter Wein and Franziska Wein (2011). In these very comprehensive diaries (1305 pages), one can get a first-hand understanding of how Nazi ideology was implemented at the local level.

sidelines, as I describe in Chap. 5, "Political Bystander." Today, I would say that I am estranged from politics. Perhaps I would have suffered the same fate as Mehs and Puhl because I have no shortage of stubbornness, at least according to my colleagues.

Puhl lived to the age of 97 and my encounters with him certainly left their mark on me. His primary form of communication was not what he said, but rather who he was. For me, the most decisive personality trait is the ability to live independently from the applause of the masses. That describes Puhl.

Another heavyweight among our teachers was Heinrich Deborré. For the first two years, we had a religion teacher who was good-natured and had mellowed with age. Then came this young priest, Deborré, a "man with a mission" who radiated energy and could be a polarizing presence. He was the first of our teachers to employ modern methods such as copied worksheets. His lessons, which often focused on hot topics, were outstanding, contemporary, and compelling. He did not confine himself to the Catholic catechism. We read the Quran, we discussed communism, and we studied Asian religions. Deborré also conducted trips during every summer vacation. They created some of the most unforgettable experiences of my youth and that I will elaborate on later in this chapter.

I am not exaggerating when I describe Deborré as fanatical. He wanted to be a missionary to the world, and time and again he motivated us to act. When a Jesuit preacher was traveling through Germany and attracting large crowds, Deborré thought that his actions were worth imitating. So we took part in a subscription drive for a monthly Catholic magazine. Within the two main villages of our parish—where maybe 600 people lived—I sold 40 subscriptions to the magazine. As a premium, I was proud to receive a leather briefcase. I doubt that many of those subscriptions lasted very long because the magazine was too sophisticated for the simple folks in our villages.

Another action was our effort to convince drivers to put an SOS ("Save Our Souls") sticker on their back windshields. The sticker signified that a Catholic priest should be called if there were ever an accident with life-threatening injuries. We would also hang posters at campsites to encourage tourists to attend Mass on Sunday.

Deborré died on July 30, 2014, shortly before his 90th birthday. We buried him a week later in Trier. Only a few familiar faces from those old times took part. Nevertheless, we will never forget what he did for us in our youth.

What did we learn from individual teachers? What lessons stuck with us? We did a more or less good job of learning English and French, along with Latin. What I retained from German classes is less clear. Many details from science and history have slipped my mind over the years. Yet I do not have the feeling that this knowledge has been lost. Rather, it has provided me a basis to understand things and hold my own at a certain level in conversations. What has clearly remained are a handful of statements and lessons that transcend basic facts and specifics. I will explore a few of them in Chap. 14, "School of Life."

For more than a few of our teachers, the era of National Socialism cast a long shadow over our school years. Granted, we had scant hard information, and mostly just rumors, about what any individual may have been involved in during the Nazi era. That also applies to the fate of the Jews who lived in Wittlich. They comprised around five percent of the population. Supposedly, only the city of Frankfurt had a higher share of Jewish citizens. The synagogue in Wittlich, erected in 1910, survived the Night of Broken Glass in 1938,[3] but later stood behind a wooden fence topped with barbed wire. Overgrown with elderberry bushes, it appeared as if it were in a very deep sleep. One would look away as one went by. The synagogue was later renovated and now serves as a cultural center.

In school, the fate of Wittlich's Jewish population was never mentioned. And we never asked what happened to them. No one had ever openly declared the topic taboo, but that is often the very nature of a taboo: one never speaks of the topic anyway, even without an explicit ban. It was not until the 1980s that young people started an initiative and invited former Jewish citizens to Wittlich. The encounter with them is one of the topics in Chap. 13, "Magic Moments."

From our teachers we heard the slogan that we should strive to be "tough as leather, hard as Krupp steel and fast like greyhounds." In one of my religion books, I found the sentence "if you want to do something great with your life, toughen your body." In a retrospective on this generation of teachers, someone wrote "our gym teacher was a typical slave driver" (Fasse, 2009). That statement reflected our own experience. Statements such as "we're supposed to win the next war with ones like you" were commonplace in school (Fasse, 2009). I heard a similar tone after joining the German Air Force, especially in boot camp. Quite a few of the non-commissioned officers (NCOs) had served in the German *Wehrmacht* in World War II and used training methods that bordered on oppression. The commissioned officers, who were younger, showed a more modern spirit and treated soldiers more as free-thinking citizens.

---

[3] The Night of Broken Glass, known as *Kristallnacht* in German, started on November 9, 1938, when Nazis attacked Jewish people and property. The name is derived from the glass shards from broken windows.

At *Gymnasium* I was an "active" student, but in some classes that led to destructive criticism. The German teachers bore the brunt of these attacks. I constantly badgered them about the relevance of texts to us and to our time, including many German literary classics. I was also a pest in other classes, particularly music. My over-the-top criticisms and my standoffish attitude robbed me of an opportunity to get a better education in the finer arts. In short, I could have used my nine years in *Gymnasium* more effectively. That was largely my fault, though I must say that motivation was not the strong suit of some teachers. Today, we know from neurological research that motivation is essential for successful learning.

When I graduated I had spent 13½ years in school, but it is hard for me to assess definitively how much I learned or how good that overall education was. In the first five years (elementary school), I do not believe I learned much. Perhaps this is incorrect, because I cannot rule out that in the one-room school I may have absorbed a lot of content meant for the older students. Judging the quality of my time at *Gymnasium* is difficult because I did not go to college right after high school. Instead, I joined the military. I asked a classmate who did start her studies right away at the University of Bonn, and she said that the students from our school could certainly compete at the same level as other graduates; they put their pants on one leg at a time just as we do, as the saying goes. My experience in my Air Force platoon, where I served with many other high school graduates, confirmed that. I was elected as spokesman for my platoon.

In his commencement address, the school director offered some visionary recommendations. He said: "The future will show that the competition among peoples will become tougher in all aspects. We must muster all of our abilities to ensure that this competition does not steamroll us. The key factor in achieving this is education. That is the only opportunity for people to advance."[4] That statement carries even more weight today than it did in October 1966.

Breaking Boundaries

One characteristic of village life back then was the lack of mobility. No one had a car or a motorbike, which made it remarkably difficult to get anywhere beyond the village. Our parents also had no time for travel or vacations. This

---

[4] "Die höhere Bildungsarbeit nicht lähmen, Oberstudiendirektor Quast sprach in Wittlich zu den Notständen an den Gymnasien," *Trierische Landeszeitung*, October 29, 1966, p. 5.

meant that as children we stayed in the village. Even a trip into the county seat was a big event. School trips to cities such as Trier or Cologne were among the highlights of the year. People were envious of me because my mother came from the Saarland and we would travel to visit relatives there once or twice a year. That was always exciting because we needed to pass through customs. (Saarland was still part of France until 1959). Our relatives in Saarland were much better off than we were. My godmother owned a grocery store. On every trip, my mother would load up on coffee and other products that we either could not get in our village or could buy at much cheaper prices in Saarland. There was always a risk as we returned through customs on the way home, but we were never caught.

My sense of confinement grew as I got older. How often my friends and I would sit together and dream of the great big world beyond us! Some of the tearjerker hit songs we heard on Radio Luxembourg fueled our wanderlust. A few older kids had succeeded in breaking away. One went to sea as a ship's cook, while others were stationed at distant posts when they joined the army. Among the men, there were a few who commuted for the week to Cologne or the Ruhr Valley for work. When they returned home, the "scent of the big wide world" wafted from them, in the spirit of a popular slogan for the Peter Stuyvesant cigarette brand in the 1960s.

Then all of sudden, someone opened up a portal for us to explore that big wide world. It was Heinrich Deborré, our religion teacher. He invited us to travel to Italy! That has been the dream destination of Germans since the time of Goethe. We began the planning and preparation a year before the trip took place. To raise the necessary money, we made and sold Advent wreaths and looked for sponsors. We learned Italian and studied up on our destinations. For us, this was more than a trip, it was an adventure that broke the boundaries that had defined and confined us. At the start of the school summer vacation in 1963, a hundred students in two buses set off on the 24-day odyssey.

It was like a fairy tale: Venice, Florence, Pisa, Assisi, and Rome as well as several days camping at Lake Garda. We spent the nights in cloisters and pilgrim guesthouses. The trip cost only 280 Deutschemarks (around $70 at the time.) Nonetheless, that was a lot of money for my parents. But that was not the reason for my guilty conscience; it was because I would be leaving my parents alone during the harvest. At age 16, I could contribute as an adult and I normally helped my parents several hours a day on the farm. It was hard for my parents to do without me during the summer break, and I have no idea how they managed all that work on their own. But they left no doubt that I should go on this trip. To this day, I am thankful to them for that.

One cannot underestimate how important it was that Deborré assumed the responsibility—during his own vacation time, no less—for traveling with a hundred young students to Italy. The trip was a purely private undertaking, unaffiliated with the school. And thank God that nothing bad ever happened. I have no idea what liability would have looked like if we had experienced an accident or other misfortune. But I did notice that Deborré was tense during the bus rides and moved his rosary between his fingers.

As a religion teacher, of course Deborré took us to visit churches and pilgrimage sites such as Assisi. We also attended mass frequently. At the same time, he granted us a considerable amount of freedom when we were in the cities. We were free to roam through Venice, Florence, and even Rome. On one evening, we sat on the steps of the Florence Cathedral and sang German folk songs until midnight. In Rome, we visited the gravesite of Nikolaus von Kues (1401–1467), better known to his fellow Germans as Cusanus. A Renaissance Man in the pure sense of the term, his ideas still intrigue scientists to this day. Some 200 years before Galileo, Cusanus claimed that the earth revolves around the sun. To this day, his most famous writings—"Learned Ignorance" and "Conjectures"inspire several dissertations every year. Cusanus is buried in the Church of St. Pietro in Vincoli, but his heart was taken back to his hometown of Bernkastel-Kues on the Moselle River.

This trip to Italy remains one of the most wonderful and emotional experiences of my life, for two reasons. First, it afforded me my first opportunity to break away from the confinement of my home village. Second, it exposed me to a world of unsurpassed beauty. In my view, Venice and Florence rank among the world's most beautiful cities. As a young man who had only know life in his small village, the impressions of Italy left their mark on me as if I were a roll of film that had never been exposed to light.

Heinrich Deborré was restless and driven. Two years later, he organized an even larger trip to Spain, Morocco, and Portugal. Around 50 students traveled in one bus for 35 days, almost the entire summer vacation period. Deborré once again offered this trip at the unimaginably low price of 420 DM (or a little over $100.) The guilty conscience from leaving my parents alone was even greater this time than it was on the Italian trip, but I have never regretted making this one either. It enriched me immensely and vastly expanded my horizons. As I write this, I immediately recall the cloister at Montserrat. I recall Barcelona, the palm groves of Elche, Granada with the Alhambra, and Cordoba. The ship "Virgen de Africa" took us from Spain to Africa and the Spanish enclave Ceuta. I will elaborate on this crossing of the Strait of Gibraltar, which I count among my "Magic Moments," in Chap. 13.

In the Portuguese pilgrimage site Fatima, named after the favorite daughter of Mohammed, we were impressed by how deeply devout the pilgrims were. The phenomena behind myths of this location were reality for Deborré and for us. Today, I still struggle to wrap my head around those emotional experiences.

Around 30 years later, in the mid-1990s, my wife and I toured Italy, Spain, and Morocco with our children. These trips were big events for our kids, but we and they had already seen so much of the world by that time, that the wonder and astonishment I experienced as a young man on these trips did not repeat itself for them. I sent Deborré a postcard from Rome as a momento of our unforgettable trip there in 1963. He called me, and we spoke for the first time in 20 years. He was still his old self. He told me enthusiastically about his missionary work in the state of Thuringia in central Germany. Communism in East Germany had turned many people into atheists. His goal was to bring them back into the fold of the church, but he did not appear to have had success on the scale he had hoped. When I saw him again at a baptism, he was in his 80s and weaker physically, but his voice still had the same unquenchable fire. The sermon he held that day would have been right at home with his preachings during my school years in the 1960s.

When one reads my descriptions of these journeys, one might think I had grown sick and tired of life in the small village I grew up in. Nothing could be further from the truth. I had a case of wanderlust when I was young, but on these trips, homesickness caught up with me and lured me back. This unusual and apparently contradictory feeling accompanies me to this day. Wanderlust and homesickness are not a contradiction to me, but rather represent the two sides of me as a person. Leaving home and returning home are two of the most exciting parts of any journey.

References

Markus Fasse, "Hart wie Krupp-Stahl," *Handelsblatt,* July 11, 2009, p. 9.

Johannes Nosbüsch, *Als ich bei meinen Kühen wacht'.... Geschichte einer Kindheit und Jugend in den dreißiger und vierziger Jahren,* Landau/Pfalz: Pfälzische Verlagsanstalt 1993, p. 15.

Günter Wein und Franziska Wein (Hrsg.), Matthias Joseph Mehs (Autor), *Tagebücher November 1929 bis September 1946,* Trier: Kliomedia-Verlag 2011

3

Years of Thunder

The Shattered Dream

A famous song from German songwriter Reinhard Mey includes the lines:
"Above the clouds/Freedom must be boundless/All fears, all worries they say/
Are hidden below the sky." Mey wrote and sang those words almost 50 years
ago, but they are an accurate description of how I felt when I was young.

Another saying—and one that Thank God did not apply to Germany in
my lifetime—is that "after the war is before the war." My birth in 1947 makes
me a member of a fortunate generation, the first in German history that has
lived its entire life in peace. Germany has not experienced a "hot" war since
World War II ended in 1945, but the first lines for what became the Cold War
emerged about a month after I was born.

The Cold War actually began on March 12, 1947, when US President
Harry Truman announced the doctrine that would eventually bear his name.
According to the Truman Doctrine, the United States was prepared to offer
military and economic support to any and all countries threatened by
Communism (Peter Ochs 2016). Many tense flashpoints highlighted the confrontation between East and West in the decades thereafter. They include the
Berlin blockade and airlift (1948), the Korean conflict (early 1950s), the
uprising in communist East Germany on June 17, 1953, the suppression of
the Hungarian revolt in 1956, the Cuban missile crisis (1962), and the march
of Soviet troops into Czechoslovakia in 1968. These events left their lasting
marks on my homeland by turning it into "Fortress Eifel." Because a military
strike from the Warsaw Pact could only come from the east, important Allied
military bases were shifted to West Germany's westernmost region, the Eifel.

H. Simon, *Many Worlds, One Life*, https://doi.org/10.1007/978-3-030-60758-6_3

This included the establishment of US air bases at Bitburg, Spangdahlem, and Hahn, as well as a German air base at Büchel.

During my childhood and teenage years, the roar of fighter jets filled our skies. I remember the first jets that thundered overhead, the Americans' Lockheed T33, which were primarily used for training. More modern jets followed, including the F-86 Sabre, the F-4 Phantom, and Germany's own F-104G Starfighter. The flight maneuvers showed little regard to the civilian population below. On countless occasions, the fighter jets broke the sound barrier and shocked both people and animals with an ear-splitting bang. It was indeed Years of Thunder.

I was fascinated by these super-modern planes. One of my first encounters with them came at an air show at Spangdahlem in the mid-1950s. The local interest was so high that I got to experience my first-ever traffic jam on the way there. Imagine what a line of cars over a half-mile long would look like to a young child who was growing up in a village where no one had a car.

Time and again I would look to the skies, follow the jets along their trajectories, and try to imagine what it would feel like to sit at the controls in the cockpit. I became a fan of flight and knew all of the aircraft types, even those from World War II. I managed to scrounge up a copy of a book distributed to citizens during the war to help them identify German and enemy aircraft. The walls of my bedroom were covered with posters and models of every conceivable aircraft type. My favorite, though, was the elegantly designed Starfighter, the Lockheed F-104. The first magazine I ever subscribed to was called "Flugrevue," or *Flight Revue* in English.

The Americans in our area caught my attention. On occasional visits to Spangdahlem, I was able to catch a glimpse of their world. I eagerly devoured any information I could get my hands on. To this day, I can still recite from memory this fluffy passage from a US Air Force brochure:

> In space so vast
> It ends where no one knows
> Our giant birds seem gnats
> As distance grows
> We measure flight
> In miles and speed and men
> And quality of craft
> But mostly men

It should come as no surprise that this youthful obsession with flight gave rise to a dream: to become Starfighter pilot. And I was not the only one from our region with that dream. The allure of the jets screaming overhead in the Eifel was irresistible for many of us kids. Several students from my *Gymnasium* and a disproportionately large number of young men from my region would become military pilots, flying either fighters or transports.[1] One of them, Erhard Gödert from Wittlich, holds a most unusual and unofficial record (Portrait 2008). He is likely to be the only German pilot who broke the sound barrier *below* sea level. How did he pull that off?

In 1961, Gödert was trained as a test pilot for the German version of the Starfighter, the F-104G. One test flight led him into Death Valley, whose deepest point lies 282 feet below sea level, the lowest point in North America. At about 100 feet above ground—but almost 200 feet below sea level—Gödert roared over the valley and broke the sound barrier. He told me that the only thing he could see behind himself was a gigantic dust cloud. He made a quick getaway and can be happy that no one noticed his adventurous joyride.

One graduate of our *Gymnasium*, Andris Freutel, rose to the rank of general in the German Air Force. Another who became a pilot was Jürgen Bücker, who grew up near Spangdahlem and wore US military clothes so often that we nicknamed him "Joe." Later, he established himself as a "global milkman" by setting up dairies in 42 countries. Along with Dr. Gerhard Neumann— alias "Herman the German," whom you will read about in Chap. 12—"Joe" was one of the few true adventurers I have met in my life (Portrait 2009).

When the 33rd Fighter-Bomber Wing in nearby Büchel was equipped with Starfighters in the 1960s, my dream became even more tantalizing. Theoretically, I could now realize it without leaving home. I drove to Munich for a screening test, but failed in the first round due to slight color blindness. At the time, I was devastated. But looking back, I consider that rejection to be a lucky break. Who knows if I would still be alive if I had my dream of being a Starfighter pilot had come true? Nonetheless, I did join the Air Force.

In the Air Force

How often we sat in our village bar and dreamt of the big wide world! Wanderlust simmered inside us. Our village and the Eifel were too confining.

---

[1] Erhard Gödert and Andris Freutel from Wittlich, Bruno Barzen from Flussbach, Peter Bayer from Greimerath, Mike Koske from Ulmen, Frank Bischof from Kerpen/Eifel, Kurt Leyendecker from Deudesfeld, Reiner Heck from Hillesheim, Guido Dedisch from Bitburg, Alexander Matzner from Kaisersesch, Axel Pütz from Thür, Albert Weber from Nachtsheim, and Olli Kootz from Kehrig were fighter pilots or flight systems officers. Andris Freutel became a brigadier general. Peter Becker from Binsfeld and Jürgen Bücker from Großlittgen flew transports.

We dreamt of long trips to faraway lands. When a local butcher told us of his adventures as a sea cook, it poured even more fuel on our fantasies.

High school graduation gave me an opportunity to escape those confinements. On January 2, 1967, a troop transport took me and 600 other recruits from the Rhineland to the city of Ulm on the Danube in southern Germany. My service time with the Air Force had begun. Military service was compulsory at that time, but even without the draft, there was never any doubt that we would "serve." The growing waves of anti-war protests in major cities had yet to reach rural Germany. One of my classmates was very disappointed that the army had found him physically unfit to serve. Another classmate who was declared unfit actually appealed the decision successfully and joined the army.

What explains this attitude among young people at that time, an attitude that would change radically in the ensuing years? The constant tension of the Cold War certainly played a role. We all believed in the impending threat of the Soviet Union and the Warsaw Pact. The fear that "the Russians could be coming" was very real and present to me. Also, one could not describe our teachers as pacifists, even though almost all of them had lived through the terrors of the Nazi era and World War II.

I completed my basic training in the 4th Air Force training regiment, 16th company. As with all other young people who leave their parents' home for the first time and need to get their bearings in foreign surroundings, I anxiously anticipated what would come my way. Our company comprised mostly high school graduates drawn from throughout the entire country. How would I prove myself in this new environment? How would I—an inexperienced, naive village kid from the countryside—hold my own against the streetwise recruits from the big cities? And how would I hold up physically during basic training?

This anxiety started to ebb away after just a few days. I discovered that I could handle this perceived adversity with relative ease. The marching and the training exercises were not so stressful because laboring on the farm had made me physically fit and accustomed to hard work. I even gained 20 pounds during basic training, probably due to the starch-heavy diet. But I was not picky and was satisfied with the food. The barracks were heated and I had everything I needed. After six weeks, the recruits had gotten to know each other and the time had come to select a spokesperson. The fact that they chose me certainly did not dent my self-confidence. By then I knew that I could "man up" in this new situation.

Nonetheless, I had some problems with the instructors. First, I did not like their tone. Second, obedience was (and still is) not one of my strengths, especially when I do not think an order makes sense or when it simply does not suit me. The higher ranking officers and the older non-commissioned officers had served in the *Wehrmacht*, a situation that Retired General Christian Trull confirmed in an interview in 2017: "When I joined the army in 1966, all of the commanding officers I came across—from the battalion commanders to the generals—were former *Wehrmacht* officers, as were the older non-commissioned officers."[2] These formative experiences influenced how they led troops, but two decades after the end of the war, they and their tone were anachronisms, especially in light of the new guiding principle of the citizen soldier.

After basic training, I stayed in Ulm as an instructor and participated in an officer candidate training in the summer of 1967. The tone there was markedly different. The instructors understood that their task was to prepare us for leadership roles. That was even more pronounced at the officers' school in Munich, which I attended one year later. We were treated similarly to university students. The German military, in fact, later established its own university at that location.

At the officers' school, I was impressed by an old colonel, a World War veteran who had only one eye. He held the lectures on strategy, and I will never forget how he defined that word: "Strategy is the art and science of developing and deploying all of a nation's forces in such a way that an opponent is deterred, or in the event of conflict, weakened to the greatest possible extent." In a slightly modified form, I have applied this definition to business: "Strategy is the art and science of developing and deploying a company's strengths in such a way to ensure its profitable survival over the long term" (Simon 2003). I prefer this concise definition to the more widely known definition from Harvard Professor Alfred Chandler: "Strategy is determination of the long-term goals and objectives of an enterprise, and the adoption of courses of action and the allocation of resources necessary for carrying out these goals" (Chandler 1969). This is one example of how I can directly connect my officer training to my later activities as an economist and a consultant, more than 20 years before I met Chandler at Harvard.

I completed officer's training ranked first in my class. This led to an altercation between me and the colonel who led the officers' school that one could classify as a refusal to follow an order, if not outright mutiny.

"Simon, you're staying here at the officers' school," the colonel said after summoning me. "I need you as an instructor."

---

[2] "Eigentlich kann sie so nicht weiter führen. Ein Gespräch mit Generalmajor a. D. Christian Trull über die Bundeswehr und über das Wesen des Soldaten," *Frankfurter Allgemeine Zeitung*, June 27, 2017, p. 9.

Well, that rubbed me the wrong way. I was under the reasonable assumption that I had been sent to the officers' school for one training course, after which I would return to the 33rd Bomber Wing, where I had been assigned since the start of the year. So I blew a fuse.

I do not know why I was wearing a steel helmet at that meeting, but I took it off, slammed it to the ground, and screamed: "There's no way I'm staying here! I'm going back to my squadron."

Such behavior is completely unacceptable for a soldier. Today, I wonder whether I would have been better off staying at the officers' school after all. But that incident showed that a latent tendency to insubordination and refusal to follow orders would have probably doomed my military career.

My wife Cecilia and I once discussed why both of us gave up the lifelong security of civil servant positions and started our own businesses. We came to the conclusion that neither of us wants to have a boss. I later apologized to the colonel for the argument, which did not have any consequences. And I did return to my squadron.

Deadly Grenade

In my brief military career, I did not escape the touch of tragedy.

One recruit completed his boot camp with the 4th Air Force training regiment. For the maneuver that concluded boot camp, the recruits needed to build foxholes covered with boards and branches. A smoke grenade, thrown by a lieutenant who was simulating an enemy attack, exploded in the hole where the recruit was sleeping. It took a few minutes for him to free himself from the hole with the help of his comrades. But these few minutes were too many. He succumbed 11 days later to the effects of smoke inhalation.

He was buried in his hometown of Zell, along the Moselle River. Because our Bomber Wing was the closest Air Force unit to Zell, a group of us was sent to his funeral, where I served as a pallbearer along with five other comrades. Our Wing had nothing to do with the accident, but at the cemetery one had the feeling that the sentiments of recruit's relatives and the residents of Zell were directed against us. We were representatives of the German armed forces, in whose service their relative and fellow citizen had made the ultimate sacrifice. A report on these events appeared in the national news magazine *Stern*.[3]

---

[3] The incident happened on March 6, 1968. The report in the news magazine *Stern*, "Giftgas vom Leutnant" appeared after Norbert Theisen's death on March 17, 1968, pp. 240–241.

Beisetzung des toten Rekruten Norbert Theisen
»Das Teufelszeug hat ihm die Lungen zerfressen«

Funeral and burial of recruit Norbert Theisen. Source: *Stern*, March 1968, Hermann Simon (right rear), Wolfgang Wawrzyniak (front left)

This incident later took on another personal dimension. When I was studying in Bonn after leaving the military, one of my classmates was Richard Engel, who remains a friend of mine to this day. He came from a village on the Moselle called Kaimt. His wife Ursula grew up in Zell. Decades later, I just happened to mention that I was a pallbearer at a funeral there. It turns out that the recruit was her cousin.

The Banality of Bombs

Within the context of "nuclear sharing," the 33rd Fighter-Bomber Wing had a sensitive mission. Should the Cold War ever become hot, our Bomber Wing would drop nuclear bombs on predefined targets behind the Iron Curtain.[4] Each pilot was assigned two targets and he knew the respective route in detail. In some cases, the targets were so far away that the Starfighter's range would not permit the pilot to return to base. In such situations, the pilot would drop his bombs, continue by flying back as far as possible, and then eject. This is one reason why survival training was an essential part of all Starfighter pilots' basic training.

---

[4] The 33rd Fighter-Bomber Wing was renamed the 33rd tactical Air Force Wing on October 1, 2013.

At that time, very few people knew that German fighter jets, flown by German pilots, would be carrying US atomic bombs. These special weapons were under the control of a US Air Force unit stationed in barracks right next to ours on the air base. Former Starfighter pilot Hannsdieter Loy provides a detailed description of this mission in his book *Years of Thunder*, which inspired the title of this chapter (Hannsdieter Loy 2012).

To handle this special situation, we had two security units. ULS was for non-commissioned officers' training and security, and S was for guarding the "special weapons" (hence the "S".)[5] I belonged to the ULS. Our duties included conducting officer training as well as general base security. If NATO sounded an alarm, we needed to guard the transport of the nuclear weapons from their depot outside the base to their positions by the aircraft. Back then, these transports traveled on a major public roadway. Only later did the military build a dedicated access road with a bridge over the public road.

The teams in both security units represented a full cross-section of society, in contrast to the people I had met in the units in officer training. Some soldiers had even served time in prison, while others showed up drunk to their posts. So one can imagine the tone and the language. Leading such soldiers was a big challenge for me. I was just 21 years old at the time.

During this period, I was also confronted with the massive bureaucracy of the German military. My promotion to cadet did not occur as expected. All other comrades who started with me had long since been promoted. I had not been, even though I had placed first in my class at the officer school.

The good news is that within the German military, you can file an official complaint for just about anything. The bad news is that there is one clear and notable exception: you cannot appeal a promotion decision because no one is entitled to a promotion at a particular time.

So what could I do? Instead of challenging the lack of a promotion, I filed a complaint alleging discrimination, which is legitimate grounds. My first filing on March 7, 1968, made its way from my fighter squadron to the central personnel department of the German armed forces. Following "completion of the documentation," the complaint ended up on the desk of the German minister of defense, who rejected it, citing the fact that I had been promoted in the meantime.

I objected, claiming that I had filed a complaint about discrimination and not a delayed promotion. The minister delegated the matter to the federal office of military administration in Bonn, which in turn said it did not have jurisdiction. The authority instead rested with the regional Area IV

---

[5] The security unit S in Büchel had the top personnel and was charged with a special task: guarding the "special weapons." This required the constant presence of a large number of specially trained soldiers, 24 hours a day, seven days a week, no exceptions. They worked in cooperation with US soldiers. Source: http://www.sondereinheiten.de/forum/viewtopic.php?t=4199.

administration in Wiesbaden. After an exchange of maybe a dozen additional letters, this office acknowledged my complaint on December 4, 1968.[6]

This Kafkaesque process was a huge lesson for me. I learned about dealing with a large bureaucracy with its tightly controlled procedures and file numbering systems. The experience also heightened my distrust of my direct superiors, who were convinced that my complaint had no chance of success. In the end, I won. My promotion was backdated and I received full retroactive compensation for the difference in pay.

The machinery of a bureaucracy can be very efficient if one uses it astutely. Decades later, I suspected a dentist of criminal activity. Falling back on my experience from the military, I filed complaints against him with numerous authorities all across the judicial system, and this led to his downfall. He eventually ended up in prison.

One of the greatest crises of the post World War II period occurred during my service in the 33rd Bomber Wing. In August 1968, Soviet troops marched into Czechoslovakia. This triggered several NATO alarms for us, and I was the officer in charge during one of them, a "quick train alarm." Six Starfighters in the alarm zone already carried atomic weapons with pilots ready at the controls. When the sirens went off at 11:30 p.m., it meant that we needed to equip all the remaining Starfighters with atomic weapons.[7] Under a NATO alarm, the security details manned their posts armed with live ammunition.

Under normal circumstances, this is a standard drill. But on that particular night, half of the company was drunk. I quickly needed to figure out how to get this unruly bunch under some semblance of control. As I mustered the troops, I heard one of them threaten me within earshot of everyone else.

"Simon, if you don't leave me alone, you'll be the first one that I blow away," he shouted.

Remember, everyone had live ammunition that night.

The source of the threat was a private who was not only drunk, but had a well-established reputation as a bully. A corporal who was one of my best pals heard the threat and put some of his previous civilian training to good use. He was middleweight boxer who boasted a hefty punch with both fists and who remains a legend to this day in his local fight scene.

I will not elaborate on how this awkward situation was resolved. Let us just say that I ordered my pal to restore discipline within the ranks, and shortly thereafter the drunken private was no longer in a position to do me or anyone else any harm.

---

[6] Letter from Wehrbereichsverwaltung IV, Az 39-90 G 72/68 dated December 4, 1968.

[7] See Rainer Pommerin (2016). The author writes about the German pilots who were sitting in the cockpits of nuclear-armed planes during the alert.

From that moment on, the unit operated with strict discipline. Two soldiers picked up the drunken private and loaded him onto the truck, and we drove to the road where we would take up our guard posts. The soldiers were stationed at 15-yard intervals along the road. I made sure that a drunk soldier stood next to a sober soldier who would hold the magazine for the drunk soldier's G3 rifle. He would reload the gun only when the NATO inspectors approached. The next morning, I received an official accolade as well as an extra day of leave because the unit had taken its positions so quickly and precisely. But if word had gotten out about what actually happened, my corporal buddy and I would have ended up in the brig.

Of course, I am not trying to justify this incident as an example of good leadership. But sometimes, volatile situations arise where subtle tactics simply will not work. These soldiers were not people to mess with. One of them once emptied the entire magazine of his sub-machine gun during his night watch. Fortunately, no one was injured. In any event, my time in the 33rd Fighter-Bomber Wing gave me leadership experience that would prove very helpful later in life.

What did we think when we saw an actual atomic bomb up close? To be honest, we did not think anything special. The ethics and purpose of our duty, and how we fulfilled it, never crossed our minds as young men. But looking back, this dismissive thoughtlessness frightens me. The bombs rolled by us on trucks as if they were harmless kegs of beer. I immediately thought of the philosopher Hannah Ahrendt, who escaped the Nazis in 1941 and coined the concept "the banality of evil" (Hannah Ahrendt 2011).

And how do I view these events from today's perspective? After the fall of the Iron Curtain and the breakup of the Soviet Union, someone found the attack plans of the Warsaw Pact in the defense ministry in Prague. Similar documents turned up in 2006 in a secret archive in Warsaw. As of 1969, the Warsaw Pact had a clear first-strike policy and felt that "the conflict should be comprised of massive nuclear strikes, almost from the start."[8] The logic behind the nuclear first-strike strategy derived from the Warsaw Pact's belief in its conventional military superiority. The Soviets believed that they would quickly penetrate the western front, leaving the West with no other alternative than nuclear retaliation. But if nuclear war was thus unavoidable, then the best strategy for the Warsaw Pact would be to strike first.

As I read those words several years ago, I saw the role of our Fighter-Bomber Wing in a different light. Perhaps the military deterrence—of which our Bomber Wing was an integral part—helped prevent the Cold War from becoming a hot one or a nuclear one. At the same time, it seems like a miracle

---

[8] https://www.welt.de/print-welt/article215588/Atomraketen-auf-Bremen-Die-Angriffsplaene-gegen-Deutschland-waehrend-des-Kalten-Krieges.html, accessed on March 20, 2017.

to me today that the decades-long confrontation between the heavily armed superpowers resolved itself without a single shot fired or a single atomic bomb falling from the sky.[9]

Flying Coffins

On our base, the primitive barracks that housed the guard units stood only about 200 yards from the runways. The remaining units of our Bomber Wing stayed about four miles away, so that they would be safe if the base came under direct attack. Whether night or day, our barracks shook when our Starfighters took to the sky. The thunder from the General Electric J79 engines sounded to us like the hiss from a wild, unbridled dragon. We were very proud of our Starfighters, which were referred to as a "missile with a man in it." To this day, I am proud that one of our Starfighters pays homage to this era at the German Technology Museum (Deutsches Museum) in Munich.[10]

Starfighter of Fighter-Bomber Wing 33 in German Technology Museum (Deutsches Museum) in Munich

---

[9] See also Jörg Link (2015). Professor Link wrote me a letter about this topic on November 11, 2016.

[10] The Starfighter was progressively replaced by Tornados and were for good removed from active duty on May 22, 1991.

But the Starfighter earned some sarcastic, dark nicknames such as "widow maker," "ground nail," "flying coffin," or "Sargfighter," a portmanteau of Starfighter and Sarg, the German word for coffin.[11]

One morning as our company mustered, an unusual sound suddenly drew our attention to the runway. A jet was taking off, but the engine sounded more like a sputtering cough than the throaty, uniform roar we were accustomed to. The Starfighter took off, and then began shooting flames. It turned out that the afterburner, which the jet needs to take off, had stalled.

The plane gained some altitude before it started coming back to earth in a parabolic arc. Then we saw a gigantic mushroom cloud about a mile away, the same form as the nuclear explosions we had seen countless times in movies shown in school and in the military. We immediately moved out to secure the accident site. The pilot had ejected safely and survived without any serious injuries. His first words when we found him were "go order up a keg of beer."

This crash was not the only one in my Wing and certainly not the only one in the German Air Force.[12] Out of 916 Starfighters, a total of 269, or 29.4 % of the fleet, crashed. These crashes killed 116 pilots (Hannsdieter Loy 2014; Claas Siano 2016). Nonetheless, the Starfighter enjoyed a good reputation among pilots for its climbing capabilities and its maneuverability. The only time the F-104s were in combat came during the Vietnam War, where they flew more than 14,000 combat hours. One account claims that the enemy was "especially reluctant" to get into their MiGs when the F-104s were flying their combat air patrols (Davies 2014). When I meet former pilots such as Erhard Gödert (record holder for a flight under sea level), Colonel Wilhelm Göbel, or General Andris Freutel, they rave about the F-104G.

Late in 1968, my time in the Air Force was coming to an end. My buddy (the boxer) and I treated ourselves to a going-away present: a trip to Paris. He had always dreamt of taking the train from Frankfurt all the way to Paris instead of getting off at the station in Büchel. We were about to make his dream come true.

At that time, Paris still had Les Halles, its huge fresh-food market in the very center of the city. Balzac had written a novel about it. We stayed in Paris for three days, partied day and night, and spent only one night in a hotel. But

---

[11] http://www.spiegel.de/einestages/50-jahre-starfighter-kauf-a-948207.html, accessed on March 20, 2017.

[12] Another Starfighter from the 33rd Bomber Wing crashed in Neuhütten in the Hunsrück region, not far from my wife Cecilia's parents' home.

we also saw the Mona Lisa in the Louvre, climbed up Montmartre, and conquered Paris by foot. That is the only way to truly get to know Paris.

At Les Halles, we hung out at a bar called Roi des Halles (King of the Halls), which we chose more for the people-watching opportunities than anything else. Every type of person was represented, from prostitutes to slaughterhouse laborers. You could feel the tension in the air. One wrong move or one careless comment could incite someone.

We sat down at a table with some suspicious characters who challenged us to arm wrestling. It was a challenge we could not refuse, seeing that they did not have a high opinion of Germans. Fortunately, my pal called on his boxing training once again and beat the French handily. That cleared the air, and peace now reigned at the table. Each side even sprang for a round of *Rouge Ordinaire*. My pal insists to this day that his arm-wrestling victories single-handedly marked the start of the French–German friendship!

On the day of my official military discharge, curiosity got the best of me again.[13] Due to the special role our Bomber Wing played in the Cold War, we had a high security clearance. I asked for—and was granted—permission to review my personnel file. In it, I found the background check for a different Hermann Simon. It appears that military intelligence is also just another bureaucracy. Without saying a word, I closed the file and put it back. It is probably still there today.

Above the Clouds—Later

Although my dream of becoming a pilot never came true, I did spend a considerable amount of my adult life above the clouds. I have no idea how many times and how far I have flown. The distance of two million miles, which I cited in Chap. 2, is just a rough estimate. To this day, it is an uplifting feeling whenever I watch a huge aircraft such as the Airbus A380 glide into the air. This giant of the skies weighs 560 tonnes at takeoff, which is the equivalent to a caravan of 14 tractor-trailers, each weighing 40 tonnes. The forces behind that thrust are incredible.

I am fan of Lufthansa. That applies especially to my return trips to Germany, and for one simple reason: as soon as I board a Lufthansa plane, I already feel

---

[13] Because of a sports injury that had not healed properly, I remained on the military payroll for an additional three months until I began my university studies in April 1969. On November 11, 1969, I was promoted in Bonn to lieutenant in the reserves.

like I am home. It is as if I have reduced the time away. One of my little rituals when I board is to set my watch to German time.

I have also had the privilege of flying many times in a private jet. This form of transportation has the odd name "general aviation" even though it is usually not accessible to the general public. I certainly do not have my own private jet. But if time is tight or the destination is in a remote area, then I will respond to a speaking invitation by saying "I can only do that if you make a private jet available."

Many companies, even mid-sized ones, have their own private jets or lease them, especially when they are located far away from a major airport. It also amazes me how many airports Germany has, and that is even more true for the United States. The country seems saturated with them, so much so that it takes no time at all to go from nowhere to somewhere.

One morning, I had a speech near Innsbruck in the Austrian Alps, followed by a meeting in the afternoon in southwestern Germany. A private jet brought me from one place to the other in 40 minutes. On another occasion, I had a speech in Paris that conflicted with a management seminar with BASF in southwestern Germany. A private jet, made available by BASF's CEO, ensured that I could take part in both events.

The Hidden Champion BHS Corrugated, the world market leader for machines to make corrugated cardboard, is located in the middle of nowhere in Bavaria. The trip there took barely six hours, including my speech, the dinner, and the round trip from Bonn and back via private jet. Had I attempted that same trip by train or car, I would have needed almost 20 hours and an overnight stay.

The flexibility of private air travel is unbeatable. One day a meeting in Stuttgart was running long, and at 2 p.m. I said that I needed to catch a train because I had another obligation in Bonn at 6 p.m.

"No rush," said the client. "We'll get you back on my plane."

Once we were in the air, I asked the pilot if he could drop me off at a local airport (Hangelar) outside of Bonn, instead of the original plan to go to the larger Cologne/Bonn airport. Otherwise, I might be late for my next meeting.

"No problem," the pilot said.

He let me off at Hangelar, and I made my 6 pm meeting even though I had not left the other firm's office in Stuttgart until 4 p.m. The distance between the two cities is 250 miles.

Private air transportation is even more important in developing countries with poor infrastructure. How did I get from Johannesburg to Victoria Falls in Zimbabwe? That was only possible by plane. The same is true for getting around in Papua New Guinea or the Fiji Islands. In the recent past, I have shied away from street traffic in some countries, preferring instead to rent a plane or ask my client to provide one. This makes sense both from a time and safety standpoint, but due to costs or other restrictions, private air travel is not always possible. Private air travel is an incredibly efficient mode of transportation that saves a tremendous amount of time. Whether it is environmentally friendly is another story.

But let us return to the Eifel and my shattered dream of becoming a pilot. Even today, I still see the American jets from Spangdahlem and the German jets from Büchel crisscrossing the skies above the Eifel. As I observe the jets merge with the horizon I indulge that old childhood dream once again and hear the closing verse of Reinhard Mey's "Above the Clouds" ringing in my head. It is practically impossible to translate the lines literally, but I hope my loose translation conveys the sentiment:

"High above, the jet beyond the horizon
No longer can I see it soar
But within me again, the child arises
Dreaming of the engines' roar."[14]

References

Hannah Ahrendt, *Eichmann in Jerusalem: Ein Bericht von der Banalität des Bösen*, Munich: Piper 2011.

Alfred Chandler, *Strategy and Structure: Chapters in the History of the American Industrial Enterprise*, Cambridge, MA: MIT Press, 1969, p. 13.

Peter E. Davies, *F-104 Starfighter Units in Combat*, Oxford: Osprey Publishing, 2014, p. 16

Jörg Link, *Schreckmomente der Menschheit: Wie der Zufall Geschichte schreibt*, Marburg: Tectum Verlag 2015, p. 32.

Hannsdieter Loy, *Jahre des Donners—Mein Leben mit dem Starfighter—Ein Zeitzeugenroman*, Rosenheim: Rosenheimer Verlagshaus, 2012, beginning with p. 111

Hannsdieter Loy, *Jahre des Donners—Mein Leben mit dem Starfighter*, Rosenheim: Rosenheimer Verlagshaus 2014

Peter Ochs, *Wir vom Jahrgang, 1947*, Gudensberg: Wartberg-Verlag, 2016, p. 5

---

[14] The German original verse is: "Meine Augen habe schon/jenen winz'gen Punkt verloren/Nur von fern' klingt monoton/das Summen der Motoren."

Rainer Pommerin, "Aus Kammhubers Wundertüte, Die Beschaffung der F-104 Starfighter für die Luftwaffe der Bundeswehr," *Frankfurter Allgemeine Zeitung*, November 15, 2016, p. 8.

Portrait "Erhard Gödert aus Wittlich—Starfighter-Pilot und Manager", in: Hermann Simon (Hrsg.), *Kinder der Eifel—erfolgreich in der Welt*, Daun: Verlag der Eifelzeitung, 2008, p. 67.

Portrait "Jürgen Bücker aus Großlittgen—Globaler Milchmann," *Eifelzeitung*, Week 9, 2009, p. 7.

Claas Siano, *Die Luftwaffe und der Starfighter. Rüstung im Spannungsfeld von Politik, Wirtschaft und Militär*, Berlin: Carola Hartmann Miles Verlag, 2016

Hermann Simon, *Was ist Strategie, in: ders. (Hrsg.), Strategie im Wettbewerb*, Frankfurt: Frankfurter Allgemeine Buch, 2003, pp. 22–23.

4

Getting Serious

Not All Fun and Games

If I had begun my university studies right after high school graduation, I would have followed in the footsteps of my slightly older cousin and neighbor Gerhard Simon. He majored in mechanical engineering at the Rheinisch-Westfälische Technical University in Aachen, which is Germany's leading institute of technology. Gerhard spoke enthusiastically about his studies in Aachen as well as his internships at some very good machinery companies. But my time in the military and the political awakening I experienced in 1967–68 had changed me.

After *Gymnasium,* I was fed up with learning. Had I not already collected a comprehensive base of knowledge during almost 14 years in school? Well, that attitude toward learning changed 180 degrees after my years in the Air Force, where the intellectual stimulation over 2½ years was not very high. The saturation effect—the feeling I already knew enough—had disappeared, replaced by a renewed appetite to learn new things. I could not wait for my university career to begin.

By that time, I developed a strong interest in economic, political, and social issues. Reading a selection of books had given me an initial overview of these fields. However, the language of the political scientists and sociologists turned me off. It was jargon: bloated, vague, and sometimes even meaningless. Maybe I did not understand everything. In any event, I ultimately chose to study economics at the Rheinische Friedrich-Wilhelm University in Bonn, which ranks today as one of 11 "Excellence Universities" in Germany. (For simplicity's sake, from now on I will simply refer to it as the University of Bonn).

© The Author(s), under exclusive license to Springer Nature Switzerland AG 2021
H. Simon, *Many Worlds, One Life*, https://doi.org/10.1007/978-3-030-60758-6_4

From my own subjective and naive vantage point, I could see many advantages to studying in Bonn. First, its economics faculty boasted many very well-known professors. To me, Bonn was more than the little city on the Rhine. It was Germany's capital at that time and was relatively close to my home village in the Eifel. I also preferred a smaller university. Although I enrolled in parallel at the University of Cologne—where 6000 students were pursuing degrees in economics—and earned several credits there, Bonn became my home base.

When I began my studies, a switch within me flipped. It was a complete metamorphosis that still amazes me today. Out of the carefree and often careless Hermann Simon—the one who was constantly pulling pranks or instigating his peers to do so—emerged a serious scholar. The people who knew me growing up no longer recognized me. The ones who first met me at the university were shocked and incredulous when they heard the stories from my past. I had frittered away five years in elementary school and had not taken *Gymnasium* seriously either. After my final written exams there, I skipped school with a buddy for several hours and blew off preparing for the oral examinations that followed. My final grades were average, probably because the teachers disapproved of my skipping school.

That all changed when I enrolled at Bonn. I never missed a lecture. I took every prep exam and did all my homework and seminar work meticulously. I did not waste time. Back then, the average student took 11.2 semesters to earn a diploma. I wanted to complete mine as quickly as possible and earned it in 8 semesters.

Of course, money was tight. I could not expect any support from home, nor did I want any. I had a good financial cushion, thanks to 7500 DM (or about $1900 at prevailing exchange rates) in savings from military service. I only took a job during the first semester break, but what a job it was! I worked 14 hours a day, six days a week, on the construction of the A48/A1 expressway (autobahn) in the Eifel. The job paid 5.11 DM (ca. $1.28) per hour, and over six weeks I accumulated 2500 DM ($625), a considerable sum. In addition, I received 320 DM ($80) from the government's financial aid program. Starting in the second semester, I got a job as a statistics tutor, which paid 125 DM (ca. $31) per month. One semester later, a professor of economic theory invited me to work for him as a tutor. It would have been hard to turn down that offer even though it was unusual for someone to serve simultaneously as a tutor in two subject areas.

Occasionally, I had other sources of income. One day, a representative from a publisher asked me if I would be interested in distributing catalogs. I said yes. It seemed easy enough. In the dining halls or in other common areas, there always seemed to be students handing out something. A few days later, the doorbell rang.

"Are you Mr. Simon?" asked a truck driver who was standing in the door.

I looked at the driver and did a double take. Then it dawned on me. The driver was the 20-year-old son of one of our neighbors. He now worked for a shipping company in Cologne. Then I did another double take as I watched him wheel in four palettes—with 20,000 catalogs!—into the hallway of the dorm.

What had I gotten myself into? I had absolutely no desire to stand at the entrance to the dining hall and hand out 20,000 catalogs. But I did have an idea on how to get the job done. The publisher paid me five cents per catalog distributed. I found students who would gladly hand out the catalogs for 2.5 cents apiece. The publisher tracked the effectiveness of the distribution via an insert card in each catalog, so I paid the students a small bonus for each card that got filled out. Our team achieved the highest response rate, which earned me an additional bonus. Everyone was satisfied.

Another side job opportunity arose by coincidence. As I was hitchhiking from Bonn back to the Eifel, a friendly driver stopped and waved for me to get in. He was on his way to Nürburgring, the famous Formula 1 racing complex which was about halfway between Bonn and my home. He was going to a hotel there to attend a training session on selling investment funds. This type of investment was very new to Europe, but had quickly become popular, thanks to an American named Bernie Cornfeld, who operated a firm in Geneva called Investors Overseas Services (IOS). That firm sold these investment funds so successfully that it had become known to the general public. German banks, of course, wanted to get a piece of this action. One of the first German banks to issue and sell investment funds was Herstatt, which was based in Cologne and had hired the gentleman who was driving me.

He invited me to take part in the training as well. I was not going to let that opportunity slip away. I was interested in sales anyway, and I felt well prepared after a couple of years of economics. The training focused less on the financial aspects of the funds, and more on sales psychology, a very compelling area that was new to me. The trainers gave me brochures and sign-up forms. In order to get investors to sign up, I would hold talks, but selling that way was painstaking. First, I lacked access to wealthy potential customers who had the liquidity and the willingness to invest in this new kind of fund. Second, Bernie Cornfeld and IOS, the flagship firm for this form of investment, ran into trouble shortly thereafter. Herstatt, whose funds I sold, went bankrupt in 1974. The investment funds were a special form of asset, so they were exempted from the insolvency assets. Nonetheless, their reputation was so tarnished that it took many years for them to re-establish themselves in Germany. I stopped selling the funds, but must say that I did learn a lot from the experience.

As a student I could not allow myself anything extravagant, but I also avoided financial trouble, thanks to these various sources of income. I believe that this freedom from financial worries is an important prerequisite to be able to concentrate on making it through a college or university program. It also gave me the luxury to indulge political activities, which I pursued in addition to my studies and my jobs. These exciting and time-consuming activities supplemented my formal studies in important ways by providing lessons in public speaking, rhetoric, and leadership. I will discuss them in more detail in the next chapter.

The economics program at Bonn was very quantitative and theoretical. At the beginning, it was quite a challenge for me to keep up with the required mathematics. It is hard for me to tell for certain whether that was function of the teaching and the curriculum at my *Gymnasium* or whether it was my lack of motivation as a student there. My hunch is that it is a little of both.

But over the course of my studies, my math skills caught up to such an extent that I later focused on quantitative classes, such as operations research. My professor was Bernhard Korte, Director of the Institute of Discrete Mathematics and a world-class mathematician. Together with his team, he developed the so-called Bonn Tools that IBM used to design its most advanced chips (Korte et al. 2018). The microchip for the chess computer Deep Blue was developed at Korte's institute.[1] He was involved in the development of the IBM mainframe processor "Bona," which made it into the Guinness Book of Records. The processor chip for the Power Mac G5, the first Apple computer with a 64Bit processor, also has its roots in the research of Professor Korte. His most recent achievement is the IBM chip "Isabel," named in honor of North Rhine-Westphalia's Minister of Science Isabel Pfeiffer-Poensgen. This chip drives the supercomputer "Summit" at the Oak Ridge National Laboratory. Summit went into operation in June 2018 with theoretical computing power of around 187 quadrillion processes per second.[2]

My favorite professor was the economist Wilhelm Krelle (1916–2004).[3] He was trained as a physicist, so it was not a big leap for him to view economics as another application area of principles and models from physics. I must

---

[1] "Warum 'Deep Blue' im Schach siegte," *General-Anzeiger Bonn*, February 27, 2007.

[2] "Spitzenforschung an der Universität Bonn: Mathematiker bringen schnellsten Computer der Welt auf Touren," *General-Anzeiger Bonn*, July 24, 2018.

[3] Krelle served on the staff of Field Marshall Erwin Rommel and was a board member of Krupp. These circumstances made him a target for left-wing attacks. Krelle did his dissertation in Freiburg under Walter Eucken. That is how he knew my uncle, Dr. Franz Nilles.

admit that those models appealed to me because they relied on clear, unambiguous assumptions and allowed one to use math to derive optimal solutions. Such solutions include optimal growth trajectories and the optimization of macroeconomic objectives.

Krelle's most ambitious project was an all-encompassing forecasting model that was meant to describe the entire economy on the basis of 70 equations. The idea was to predict the effect that changes in any key economic driver (e.g., interest rates, taxes, subsidies) would have on a range of macroeconomic indicators. The theory was elegant and exciting, but the results in practice left a lot to be desired. Every time there was an urgent need for forecasts from such models, they did not work. That was especially true for the first oil crisis in 1973 and the next one in 1978.

I do not know whether governments or central banks use these kinds of comprehensive models today. But one insight becomes clearer to me with every successive crisis: the lenses of the world of physics do not apply to the economy. In physics, there are natural constants. An established, measurable physical law yields the same result under the same conditions in every repetition. Such constants and such consistent outcomes do not exist in economics; in the real world, it is impossible to replicate identical conditions exactly. In some cases, we even encounter paradoxes.

Solely in terms of teaching, the most skilled professor was Franz Ferschl, who came from Austria. He loved statistics, and his enthusiasm was contagious. His exemplary lectures showed his rare gift, the ability to explain complex statistical concepts in an easy-to-understand way. His teaching paid dividends for me through my university career as well as later as a researcher. That is because statistics are ubiquitous. Ferschl frequently cited a simple sentence from the famous American statistician John Tukey, who said "Look at your data." I took that to heart then, and still live by it today. Whenever possible, I print out datasets and try to visualize them before I start conducting any formal statistical analyses. Of course, trying to visualize multidimensional datasets has its limitations. But I feel that even in this era of Big Data, people should still heed Tukey's recommendation.

At the University of Bonn, it was only possible to get a degree in economics, not in business administration. I only had two professors during my degree program that focused on microeconomics or business administration: Hans-Jacob Krümmel and Horst Albach. Professor Krümmel was a banking expert, while Professor Albach taught business administration in a broader sense, in that he covered all functions from production to marketing to organization. Albach, who would later supervise my dissertation, introduced case studies as a new teaching method. They were a welcome, practice-based contrast to the theory-laden approach traditionally taken by the economists. The case studies were almost irresistible to me, precisely because they were based on real-world examples. The lectures of adjunct professor Günter Klein, who owned an accounting and auditing firm, were likewise long on examples from practice. I took Klein's entire program not because I wanted to become an auditor or a certified accountant (although that was the career path that my uncle Dr. Franz Nilles had pursued), but rather to understand how all these concepts fit together in the real world.

Outside the Classroom

My social situation during my studies in Bonn was a pleasure from beginning to end. I received a spot in the newly established Cusanus dormitory, where I found myself in the midst of a very international group. Because everyone moved in at the same time, everyone was interesting in making acquaintances. On our floor we had students from Afghanistan, Libya, Burundi, Congo, Cambodia, and North America. Except for the French and American soldiers stationed in the Eifel, I had not met many foreigners prior to my studies. Now we lived on the same floor in the dorm, shared the same kitchen, and went about our daily routines together. I made friends with Dr. Sami Noor from Kabul and invited him to our humble farmhouse in the Eifel for Christmas. A friendship was born that endures to this day. He repeatedly invited me to visit Afghanistan. Time and again we wanted to make the trip, but every year we postponed it because the timing did not work. Then suddenly, it was too late. The Russians invaded and took control of the country at the end of 1979, and since then it has been too risky to undertake such a trip.

On one local holiday in 1971, when we did not have scheduled classes, my next-door neighbor in the dorm, an American student, had a young lady over to visit. He had helped her with an English translation and invited her to dinner at the dorm.

I entered the kitchen and saw him sitting there with his companion. Let us just say he was not the best looking guy around. Somewhat startled by seeing the pair together, I asked him "Harold, how did you end up with a beautiful girl like this?"

I no longer recall how he answered. I was known for being awkward around women. In any event, the young lady did not seem impressed by my remark. Several months later, though, she and I crossed paths at a Mardi Gras (Carnival) event, and we struck up a conversation. Later that evening, I drove her back to her dorm in my VW Beetle. Just by coincidence, my friend Sami

Noor had recently moved into the same dorm. I knew I could visit him any-time without drawing any attention, so he provided the cover for the true objective of my increasingly frequent visits: to run into that young lady again. Fortunately, that happened more often than not. So without the intervention of my Afghani friend Sami Noor, Cecilia Sossong would never have become my wife. We married in October 1973 in her home village in the Hunsrück region, across the Moselle River from the Eifel.

I look back fondly on my time as a student in Bonn. The coursework itself went smoothly, and I could enjoy the freedom of being a student without any financial worries. I did not learn all that much that I could apply directly later in life. But the demanding program taught me how to think. The ability to think and analyze was more important in my careers as a researcher and a consultant than any specific facts I could have retained. And I found my wife during college. What more could someone want?

Time as a Graduate Assistant

My college grades turned out better than expected. As a result, the professors Albach, Korte, and Krelle each offered me a position as a graduate assistant. These options saved me from having to think through my next career steps, but also confronted me with a very tough choice. I had written my diploma thesis with Albach, I took electives and passed the exams with Korte, and I had worked as a tutor for Krelle. Now I needed to let two of them down and had many sleepless nights as I agonized over the decision. Would I be able to keep pace in Korte's team, which primarily consisted of mathematicians and had launched the careers of numerous math professors? One of them was Achim Bachem, with whom I would later publish a paper (Bachem and Simon 1981). He became a math professor at the University of Cologne, and in his second career he was the Director at the Jülich Research Center, which employs 5800 researchers. I would not have stood a chance against mathematicians of that caliber.

The more difficult decision was between Krelle and Albach. Krelle was my favorite professor during my studies, in large part because I liked his quantitative approach. But in the end, I chose to work as a graduate assistant for Professor Albach. I had an inkling that business administration and management were more up my alley than economics. When I looked into the future, I saw myself best suited to be a manager, preferably in a large company. Due to his closer ties to the real world of business, Albach seemed to offer me the best development opportunities to realize that goal. Even though I had a degree in economics, I chose the business management track. That decision represented a life-altering fork in the road, and in hindsight I feel I made the correct decision.

Professor Albach held a chair for general business management and administration. He saw himself in the tradition of his father-in-law, Erich Gutenberg, who was the "wise old man" of business management teaching in Germany. Gutenberg himself had written three textbooks, one on manufacturing (Gutenberg 1983), one on sales (Gutenberg 1984) and one on finance (Gutenberg 1980). These books were standard textbooks and appeared in multiple editions. Gutenberg was like a grand lord of the old school, a very pleasant and unpretentious man. I never heard one of his lectures in person because he took on an emeritus role in 1967, but I met him on several occasions. I give him credit for one custom I continue to practice. Professor Gutenberg said "thank you" for every working paper or reprint someone sent him, regardless of how insignificant its contribution may have been. I sent him my first review from a German journal (*Zeitschrift für Betriebswirtschaft*) and recall how proud I was to receive a thank you note—several lines long— from this giant in the world of management. As best I could, I have adopted the same habit. But in the digital age—with its seemingly endless flood of emails—I cannot be sure that something occasionally slips through the cracks and goes unacknowledged.

What does it mean to be a graduate assistant to a professor? First and foremost, it means a secure source of income for three years. With my full-time position, I earned about as much as a student–teacher would. Back then, I felt like I could live like a king on that income.

But of course I also had to work for the money. I supported the professor by standing in for him during lectures, grading tests, and handling administrative tasks. Concurrently, I was also supposed to write a doctoral dissertation. One often hears that graduate assistants are exploited by their professors and need five years or even longer to complete their dissertations. It was more the opposite with Professor Albach. He gave us assistants as much freedom as possible and did not overburden us with work. We could work largely on our own to take care of the tasks he delegated to us. That allowed me to do the bulk of the work on my dissertation at home, where I could achieve a deeper level of concentration than at the university. Because our boss's activities kept him on the road frequently, we also received ample opportunity to take his place for lectures. There is probably no more useful form of practice than to teach. The French philosopher Joseph Joubert once said that teaching is like learning something for the second time. Peter Drucker had a habit of saying that he continued to teach into his old age because that was his best way to keep learning.

In 1975, Professor Albach let me organize the spring conference for Germany's association of business professors largely on my own. Completely naive and inexperienced, I threw myself into the task and was fortunate that the event came off more or less without a hitch. None of the 350 participating professors complained. My boss was likewise satisfied and even invited me to be co-editor of the conference proceedings, which had the title "Investment Theory and Policy of Private and Public Enterprises" (Albach and Simon 1976). That was the first book my name ever appeared on.

One of the most interesting facets of my years as a graduate assistant was the work on the expert witness analyses that Professor Albach carried out. This work was usually commissioned by large companies and covered aspects such as market power, pricing strategy, and whether market actions were in line with antitrust law. A project for the UK company Wellcome turned out to have a particularly strong influence on both the course of my research interests and the course of my career. This pharmaceutical company was known for several breakthrough innovations. In the 1980s, four researchers from the firm won Nobel Prizes. The most important product in the 1970s was the gout treatment allopurinol, marketed under the brand name Zyloric. After the patent on allopurinol expired, generic producers entered the market. These companies do not develop patent-protected products of their own, but rather offer the same treatments at much lower prices after patents on the original substance have expired. The European Commission alleged that Wellcome was abusing its dominant position in the market for these treatments.

Wellcome is also known for Zovirax (aciclovir), a groundbreaking innovation for the treatment of herpes. To this day, aciclovir remains one of the few compounds that is effective against the herpes virus. Glaxo eventually acquired Wellcome in the wave of consolidation within the industry, and the company was later absorbed into the GlaxoSmithKline group.

Why was this project so important to me? For the first time, I had the opportunity to apply econometric methods to empirical data. I acquired an innovative foundation of experience that guided not only my subsequent research but also led to the establishment of the consulting firm now known as Simon-Kucher & Partners. The report was highly regarded within the pharmaceutical industry and made it easier to gain access to other companies. The fact that Life Science is still the largest division within Simon-Kucher has its roots in this early work.

Research

My own research was far more modest by comparison. Because of the broad mandate and interests of Professor Albach, his assistants had the chance to work in different areas. One focused on accounting and finance, another on human resources, yet another on organization, and so on. I opted for marketing and devoted my dissertation to pricing strategies for innovations.

The wide range of topics covered in Albach's doctoral seminars meant that one needed to know a little bit about everything, but could not always find someone who could dive into deeper detail on specialized topics. The same applied to our library, whose supply of marketing literature and magazines was rather sparse. In some cases, I needed to borrow books from the agriculture department's library because they did have a marketing focus. In order to offset these shortcomings, I stretched out my antennae and started going to other universities and to conferences. The contact with the European Institute for Advanced Studies in Management (EIASM) in Brussels was a true eye-opener. I tried to make the best out of this situation, but it should come as no surprise that these circumstances were not fertile ground for groundbreaking work. I completed my dissertation in three years. It was published in 1976 under the title *Price Strategies for New Products* (Simon 1976).

Venia Legendi

The completion of my Ph.D. brought me to another decision point. It seemed clear that I would join the business world. I launched an ambitious job-hunting campaign, but it was unfocused and not very professional. Using the shotgun approach, I applied to companies in industries such as insurance, consumer goods, chemicals, mining and raw materials, and defense, just to name a few. I was flattered when a headhunter invited me to Munich. It was the first time I took a flight paid for by a company. I was close to accepting a position as an assistant to the board at the Cologne-based insurance company Colonia, which is now Axa. The salary offer of 52,000 DM, or roughly $13,000, struck me as very attractive.

Then the phone rang. It was Professor Albach.

"I'm offering you a post-doc position," he said. Technically speaking, he offered me a habilitation, which is the final step in the European university system to becoming a full professor.

"Hmm" was all I could muster as an initial reaction.

I had never seriously considered an academic career. Spending my life as a researcher, sitting at a desk with a bunch of books on the shelves behind me? No, I could not imagine myself doing that. I had just finished my dissertation, and could not envision producing that same kind of work again, never mind a habilitation thesis that must clear an even higher academic bar.

So I asked for some time to think about it.

It turns out that I did not need much time. I asked my perpetual advisor, Cecilia, what I should do, and her answer came almost immediately.

"Of course you're accepting his offer," she said.

My advisor apparently has more confidence in me than I do. And as a result, my life took another unanticipated avenue.

In my habilitation thesis, I expanded the scope of my dissertation—which examined only one product and one marketing instrument (price)—in two ways. First, I included advertising and sales as additional marketing instruments. Second, instead of looking at the optimal price strategy over the life cycle of one product, I looked at entire product lines. This meant that I needed to consider several products simultaneously. A revised version of my habilitation thesis was published in 1985 under the title *Goodwill and Marketing Strategy*. Goodwill is the store of trust or "trust capital" that a company accrues over time. It is generated through advertising and can be transferred to other products from the same company. In other words, good customer experiences with one product lead to increased purchase likelihood and willingness to pay for other products of the same company. The converse also holds true. Bad experiences can lead to a transfer of badwill to other products.

The approach I took is what made this study innovative. I tested my models empirically with data supplied by the companies Henkel and Hoechst. At the time, Hoechst was the largest pharmaceutical company in the world; Henkel remains a global consumer goods supplier known for its many strong brands such as Persil or Loctite. One of the biggest constraints for most marketing researchers at that time was the lack of access to empirical data. Nowadays in the age of Big Data, the opposite holds true. There is so much available data that the challenge lies in crafting an analysis that actually leads to relevant findings and insights. Yet four decades ago, I considered myself extremely lucky that I could get any data at all to work with. The fact that I found statistically significant relationships between the brands of the product lines can be described as an additional stroke of luck. Nonetheless, the faculty accepted my work[4] and I received the "Venia legendi," the right to teach business management at universities. That is a prerequisite for a full professorship.

---

[4] The work, which took more than three years to complete, covered over 300 pages.

A generous multi-year grant from the German Research Foundation (DFG) covered my habilitation and allowed me to focus full-time on my research as well as to spend a year on a post-doctoral fellowship at the Sloan School of the Massachusetts Institute of Technology. I will come back to my time there in Chap. 6.

In hindsight, how do I view my time as a graduate assistant and post-doc under Professor Albach? That time period expanded my horizons in more ways than I could have imagined. The collaboration with Professor Albach was extremely educational. That applies at least as much to aspects such as comportment, efficiency, appearance, and lecturing skills as it does to the actual content of my research. Albach deployed me in his executive seminars when I was a young and inexperienced assistant. I was frequently able to observe his teaching and speaking style. His high standards and the breadth of his competencies became standards for me to strive for although I could have never reached either of those levels. Last but not least, I learned from him what efficiency means within a university and a scientific organization. One example is dictation. The text that appeared in the original German version of this book was mostly dictated by me, not hand-typed. I have the impression that few people use dictation even though it is several times faster than writing by hand or on a keyboard. On the other hand, dictation requires a very high level of concentration and discipline. Without having witnessed Professor Albach in action, I would have never become a dedicated and effective user of dictation. We used to have to go to Albach's house to pick up the little cassette tapes and bring them to the institute for transcription. Today that process is much simpler. One can send the recordings directly to one's office electronically.

My personal relationship to Professor Albach is not easy to put into words. I had and still have tremendous respect for him, but I also always gave him my opinion. There was a certain, constant tension between us, something which did not escape the people who knew us. One colleague interpreted our relationship by saying "the two of you are just too similar." It was not uncommon for someone to approach me after a lecture and say that "during your talk I thought that was Professor Albach standing up there." I am somewhat embarrassed by those remarks because I value originality and am not a big fan of imitation. But when someone works year after year for a role model, it is unavoidable that some behaviors, mannerisms, and expressions will rub off and be internalized. This unconscious assumption and incorporation of certain behaviors is an important aspect of learning. It is similar to how kids imitate their parents.

I am thankful to Professor Albach for what he offered his staff and their families socially, not only academically. As a village kid, I was not familiar with a lot of sophisticated social formalities. Our department held a gala ball every year, to which both current and former colleagues were invited. Professor Albach was also famous for his hiking expeditions, which sometimes covered over 25 miles in a single day.

In short, I am very grateful to Professor Albach. Without the freedom that he granted me for my academic projects, I would not have become what I am today.

References

Horst Albach, Hermann Simon (Hrsg.), *Investitionstheorie und Investitionspolitik privater und öffentlicher Unternehmen*, Wiesbaden: Gabler 1976.

Achim Bachem, Hermann Simon, "A Product Positioning Model with Costs and Prices," *European Journal of Operational Research* 7 (1981), 362-370.

Erich Gutenberg, *Grundlagen der Betriebswirtschaftslehre, Band 3: Die Finanzen*, Berlin/Heidelberg: Springer-Verlag 1969, 1980 (8th edition)

Erich Gutenberg, *Grundlagen der Betriebswirtschaftslehre Band 1: Die Produktion*, Berlin/Heidelberg: Springer-Verlag 1951, 1983 (24th edition)

Erich Gutenberg, *Grundlagen der Betriebswirtschaftslehre, Band 2: Der Absatz*, Berlin/Heidelberg: Springer-Verlag 1955, 1984 (17th edition)

Bernhard Korte, Dieter Rautenbach, and Jens Vygen, *BonnTools: Mathematical Innovation for Layout and Timing Closure of Systems on a Chip*, http://www.or.uni-bonn.de/research/bonntools.pdf, 2018

Hermann Simon, *Preisstrategien für neue Produkte, Dissertation*, Opladen: Westdeutscher Verlag 1976.

5

Political Bystander

Politics in the Blood

My father served for 15 years as the mayor of our village and also represented the Christian Democratic Union (CDU) in our county assembly. As a result, I grew up from an early age in an environment where a certain kind of politics was omnipresent. It was not the politics of big ideas on the national or international stage, but rather the nuts-and-bolts practical issues a community faces. Ideology did not matter. The council was elected under the first-past-the-post system, which to this day I view as very democratic. But it works only under the assumption that everyone knows everyone. The voters wrote seven names on a ballot, and the ones with the most votes were elected to the local council. The council then chose the mayor.

During my father's tenure, there were two important events. The first was the construction of a new community center with a freezer, a washing bay, and public baths. This project represented not only progress—World War II had ended just ten years earlier—but also had a groundbreaking character. It made the lives of farm families easier in ways they could not have imagined in an earlier time. It also changed the way we lived by allowing us to store and conserve meat by deep-freezing it. The other major project was the building of a new church, an effort spearheaded by my father and the pastor.

My father led the community without much fuss. Together with a friend of the same age, he formed a team that guided the fate of the village. My father avoided polarization both in the council and in the village itself. Although he certainly had reasons to do so, he never said a negative word about his fellow citizens or fellow council members. I think this is an important point. In my own constellations

© The Author(s), under exclusive license to Springer Nature Switzerland AG 2021
H. Simon, *Many Worlds, One Life*, https://doi.org/10.1007/978-3-030-60758-6_5

later in life, I paid constant attention to preserving team spirit. Perhaps I learned more from my father in terms of leadership than I admit to myself.

This constellation from my childhood fostered a fundamental interest in politics. As a young man, I definitely had politics in my blood. As I described before, our history and civics teacher strengthened my burgeoning interest. He was a man with strong convictions and he knew how to get them across. He had the talent to become a politician and made some attempts to get involved, but his efforts eventually failed because he expressed his opinions too openly and forcefully. Nonetheless, his argumentation style motivated me because it resembled my own.

As a teenager, I went to campaign events and participated in the discussions, but did not join any political party. How does one come from the small-time politics of a remote village to the grander themes that were more compelling to me? One interesting person was the son of a teacher in our village. He was the only kid in the village who spoke High German. He did not do well at *Gymnasium*, perhaps because he was too non-conformist, so his parents sent him to a boarding school in Switzerland, where he graduated. He then studied history and political science at various German universities as well as in Paris and Amsterdam. He was well connected in European student political circles and knew many of the leaders on the left. He was a sympathizer and a member of the League of Socialist German Students (SDS), the most active and radical group on the left. In 1966, he took me to an SDS rally in Frankfurt, where I encountered a colorful mix of Marxists, Leninists, and self-appointed revolutionaries. Coming from my orderly rural world, I was shocked at both the ideas and the demands expressed at this meeting. I remember in particular an Iranian who demanded that the Shah be overthrown. This was a new and exciting world for me, but I had the feeling that it was not my world. I did not bite. My friend was disappointed.

His adventures led him to Munich, where he earned a Ph.D. and worked at the Institute of Contemporary History until he passed away at a relatively young age. I visited him once, but after that our paths never crossed again. So I did not turn into a left-wing revolutionary. But the right-wing radicals were just as suspect to me. And I soon had an opportunity to manifest that feeling in actions.

Storming the Danube Hall

The neo-Nazi party NPD had grown very powerful in just a few years after its founding in 1964. On April 28, 1968, the party drew 9.78% of the vote in state parliamentary elections in Baden-Württemberg. That is roughly the same share of the vote the right-wing AfD party is attracting today. The NPD was clearly a right-wing radical party. Many of its members back then were old Nazis who were still in the primes of their lives.

Ahead of that election, the NPD held a large rally in the Danube Hall (Donauhalle) in the city of Ulm on November 15, 1967. The hall holds more than 2000 people. At that time, I had completed my basic training and initial officers' training and was working as an instructor in an Air Force training regiment stationed in Ulm. The high school graduates in our company came from all over Germany and had a high level of interest in politics. This constellation foreshadowed 1968, which would become the Year of Revolution. The attitude in our unit was clearly against the neo-Nazis, and the announcement of their rally ignited an intensive discussion among us. Then one comrade threw out a suggestion: "Why don't we just storm the hall?"

The response from our comrades was unanimous: "Hey, why not?"

Between 80 and 100 of us agreed to go, dressed of course in civilian clothes rather than our uniforms. It was already cold out, so most of us wore winter coats or parkas, which proved advantageous in light of the brawling we anticipated. We broke up into small groups as we approached the different entrances to the hall. The doors were guarded by NPD operatives, who asked us for our tickets. But instead of giving them tickets, we gave each of them a pretty hard shove. As soldiers we were "combat ready," and the NPD bouncers did not really stand a chance against us. We cleared out the entrance ways quickly and then stormed the hall itself. Pandemonium ensued and we were amazed to realize that we were not the only uninvited guests. At that time, Ulm was the military's second largest garrison city in West Germany. Similar to us Air Force soldiers, recruits from the army, who were stationed at another barracks, had also independently decided to disrupt the rally. The left-wing students from the Ulm School of Design, not far from our barracks, also showed a strong presence.

The NPD leader and his top associates stood onstage and tried to shout over the noise and chaos. It took us only a few minutes to reach the stage, which was sealed off by more NPD muscle. But we outnumbered them and were well prepared for fighting in close quarters. We stormed the stage and the NPD leader fled. The rally was shut down and the police came and cleared the hall.

These events unfortunately had a tragic end. A reporter from a local newspaper was killed in the chaos, suffocated by the smoke bombs that were tossed as our attack unfolded. The next morning, an officer came into our room and held a newspaper to our faces. Unmistakable was a large picture showing me restraining one of the NPD bouncers.

Hermann Simon restrains an NPDz bouncer at the Danube Hall in Ulm, November 15, 1967 (Schwäbische Donau-Zeitung, 1967)

The caption read: "For his last assignment, our colleague concentrated on the altercation between demonstrators and the security guards. His picture— one of the last found in his camera—shows an NPD security guard approaching the photographer with hands raised." One week later, a report on the storming of the hall appeared in the national news magazine *Spiegel* together with the picture of me restraining the guard (NPD Geblähte Segel 1967a).

Citing sources within the criminal investigation, *Spiegel* reported that the smoke bombs did not come from the soldiers, but rather were "almost assuredly homemade bombs from the arts college students who disrupted the rally" (NPD Geblähte Segel 1967b). The bomb makers were allegedly from the "avant garde, non-conformist scene at the Ulm School of Design" according to *Spiegel*. I can say with certainty that no one from our company went to the action armed with smoke bombs. For several days, we lived in fear that the police would come knocking on our door, and thanks to the press photos, I would have probably been the first person they apprehended. Although we had nothing to do with the smoke bombs, they could have definitely accused us of trespassing. But nothing happened.

Our company commander also took no action. He never even asked once about what transpired in the hall that night. I suspect that he knew everything anyway, though, because he had a close relationship with the non-commissioned officer in our group with whom we had covertly planned our offensive. On the one hand, we were proud of the fact that we had disrupted the NPD rally and chased their leader from the stage. But the reporter's death, which was beyond our control, caused us to step back and reflect.

Against the Emergency Laws

During our service time in 1967–68, my military comrades and I turned increasingly political. Our discussions of the prevailing circumstances became more frequent and more critical. We were not immune to the effects of the landmark year 1968. We viewed Germany's state-of-emergency declarations as an attack by the government on our basic rights and freedoms. This body of laws amended the constitution and introduced an emergency constitution that preserved the government's right to take extraordinary measures in crisis situations such as natural disasters, revolts, or wars. We wanted to do something to protest this action. On May 11, 1968, we made our way to Bonn, then West Germany's capital, to join a huge demonstration.

This was also an entirely new experience for me. More than 60,000 demonstrators, the vast majority of them students, converged on Bonn's central park, where a giant stage was built. Heinrich Böll, who would win the Nobel Prize for Literature four years later, vehemently stated his opposition to the government's planned restrictions on our freedom. But the harshest criticism came from Karl Dietrich Wolff, who at the time was the head of the SDS. Wolff would later publish books by classic authors. In 2009, he received Germany's Cross of Merit for his significant contributions to publishing and literature and in 2015 he received an honorary doctorate from a Swiss University.[1] Such a transformation from radical student leader to a traditional cultural contributor was not unusual. I have encountered many former radicals at major business magazines as well as in iconic companies such as Procter & Gamble and McKinsey.

Proud that we had done something to stand up for democracy, we returned to our military routines at the airbase. We boasted about our political engagement as non-conformists to our comrades who did not participate, but at the same time we modestly fulfilled our duties within our Bomber Wing.

The demonstrations had little effect. The emergency powers were ratified on May 30, 1968, but they have not been applied since then. In subsequent

---

[1] http://www.frankfurt-live.com/front_content.php?idcatart=77925, accessed on March 23, 2017.

years, Bonn witnessed many large demonstrations, especially against the Vietnam War and the deployment of nuclear weapons.

Federal Elections in 1969

The federal parliamentary elections took place one year later. A clear spirit of optimism fueled an intensive election campaign. Willy Brandt was the hope of the Social Democratic Party (SPD). In my home village, our pastor organized a debate with parliamentary candidates from the major parties, and asked me to moderate. I was 22 years old and had just begun my university studies, but I also had no shortage of self-confidence and took on the challenging task.

Before the event began, I was nervous and anxious. But the moment I walked onto the podium in front of several hundred people, my nervousness evaporated quickly. Since then I have had a similar sensation on many occasions. As soon as I step into the ring, I can shake off the stage fright and focus 100% on the task at hand.

But in this case, the challenge involved established, experienced politicians. Hans Richarts (1910–1979) came from a farm in a neighboring village. As a candidate for the Christian Democrats, he had the Eifel voters in his back pocket. He consistently received over 60% of the vote, had been in the German parliament, the *Bundestag*, for 16 years and in the European Parliament for 11 years. No one could expect that a young man like me would read him the riot act, and perhaps he indulged me because he knew my father well. The libertarian-leaning party, the Free Democrats (FDP), put up Ferry von Berghes (1910–1981) as their candidate. He was also heavyweight and owned a castle in a neighboring village.[2] As a former minister in the state of Rhineland-Palatinate as well as CEO of the petroleum company DEA AG (now part of Royal Dutch Shell) in Hamburg, he had experience in both politics and in the private economy.

I do not know how I succeeded in moderating a debate among such experienced politicians. In any case, there were no complaints from the audience nor from the pastor who organized it. Such experience, even when it is acquired in the context of a small village, contributes enormously to one's self-confidence. I now trusted myself to hold my own in the political ring. I felt vindicated and encouraged to become more politically active. That is exactly what I did at the University of Bonn.

---

[2] It has to do with the castle "Haus Bergfeld," later purchased by the IT entrepreneur Thomas Simon (no relation.) The socially critical novel "Das Weiberdorf" by Clara Viebig is set in the village of Eisenschmitt.

One acquaintance who went all-out campaigning for Willy Brandt was Friedhelm Drautzburg, whom we called "Friedel." He came from Wittlich and also studied in Bonn. He got involved with the Social Democrats early on, and in 1969 he accompanied future Nobel-Prize-winning novelist Günter Grass on his major campaign trip throughout Germany. Grass stumped massively in support of Brandt and I am certain his efforts indeed played a role in the Social Democrats' eventual victory. Drautzburg even succeeded in getting Grass to make an appearance in Wittlich. After German reunification over 20 years later, Drautzburg became nationally known for founding a cult bar "Ständige Vertretung" in Berlin, the new (and old) capital of the re-united Germany. Our common Eifel heritage established a close bond between Drautzburg and me, stronger than the politics on which we largely disagreed.

Political Student

My most politically active period came during my time at the University of Bonn. When I began my studies in the spring of 1969, the political awakening of students in Europe—with its origins in Paris and Berlin—was gradually spreading to smaller cities and universities. Why did that happen in those particular years? Attempts to answer that question have filled entire libraries. For us students, and also for me personally, there was no doubt that one factor played a central role in this movement: the way that the Nazi period had been swept completely under the rug by our parents and teachers. Many of the people who raised us and who had taken on responsibilities in administration, business, and politics were entangled in that era in one way or another. But they preferred to keep their involvement a secret. It was not as if that generation was defending Hitler or trying to justify the Nazi crimes. But only rarely did we hear definitive condemnations of what happened.

Even as late as 1978, I encountered a harsh backlash when the series *Holocaust* aired on German television and exposed the extent of Nazi crimes and war crimes. I had returned home from the United States for a brief vacation and joined the traditional Sunday morning get-together of some contemporaries of my father (who had passed away a few years earlier). Everyone present had served in World War II and to a man they all repudiated the series as "slander" of the German armed forces, the *Wehrmacht*. They said they had only done their duties, and according to them, what was shown on television was the exception, not the rule. This attitude represents the kind of taboo we had grown up with.

At the end of the 1960s, the students finally wanted to free themselves from this repressed and hypocritical world in one fell swoop. A turbulent time began. The influence of the so-called extra-parliamentary opposition grew. At universities, it became an everyday occurrence for protestors to disrupt lectures, occupy buildings, damage public property, and stage demonstrations. A number of student groups were formed, most of them left-wing and more than a few of them on the radical left. The SDS was the most influential, but there were many splinter groups at that end of the spectrum, some with a Marxist-Leninist or Maoist orientation. On the conservative side, the Ring of Christian Democratic Students (RCDS) was the strongest faction. In between were the libertarians and the independents. This was fertile ground for charismatic, brilliant speakers to emerge and shine. At the University of Bonn, Hannes Heer stood out. Three decades later, he organized a very highly regarded exhibit about the *Wehrmacht* which was shown in all major German cities.[3]

Personally, I chose to remain independent and did not join any organized group. But on the student council level, we worked together with people who shared our views. One of them was Wolf-Dieter Zumpfort, who later became chairman of the Free Democrats in the state of Schleswig-Holstein and also a member of the German parliament. Our group won the student council elections several times. Years later, when I was a professor at the University of Bielefeld, I described this phase of my life by saying that "the spice was more in politics than anything else. Two years as member of the student council, including one year as chairman, during turbulent political times at the university made the formal studies seem trivial" (WiWi 1981).

In that role, I collected a ton of valuable experience. I was always holding speeches, usually in front of several hundred students. I led debates, campaigned for support, and fought left-wing anarchists. That was very intense. A flyer from one left-wing radical group blasted me as the "chief collaborator" and "betrayer of students."[4] Another group spoke of the "theoretically baseless pragmatism of Simon's provenance."[5]

---

[3] There were two traveling exhibits about the German *Wehrmacht*, both by the Hamburg Institut für Sozialforschung. The first one, which ran from 1995 to 1999, was titled "War of Extermination: Crimes of the *Wehrmacht* 1941 to 1944"; the second one, which ran from 2001 to 2004, bore the title "Crimes of the *Wehrmacht*. Dimensions of a War of Extermination 1941–1944." These exhibits drew broad public attention and led to controversial discourse around the crimes of the *Wehrmacht* during the Nazi era, especially in the war against the Soviet Union. After criticism of the first exhibit, the second one had a different tone but nonetheless reaffirmed the main message that the *Wehrmacht* took part in the Nazi war of extermination against the Soviet Union, in the Holocaust, and in the genocide of the Roma. Sources include: https://de.wikipedia.org/wiki/Wehrmachtsausstellung.

[4] Die Strategie des Fachschaftsvorstandes: Lüge und Privatabsprache, Flugblatt der Basisgruppe Volkswirtschaft, University of Bonn, July 1971.

[5] "Neue Fachschaft! Neue Fachschaft!" flyer distributed by an action group to dissolve the student council (led by me), University of Bonn, November 1971.

We produced newspapers and flyers and organized events and campaign activities. We needed to find fellow campaigners, motivate them, and keep them in line. As student council president, I had a seat in the faculty council, gained direct access to professors, and earned a certain level of recognition among students. That extended in some cases beyond the University of Bonn itself. I was sent as a student delegate to a committee at the newly established University of Bielefeld. That committee was tasked with building up the economics faculty. I remained active in committees in Bonn and Bielefeld after I became a graduate assistant. But I restricted myself to departmental issues and did not get involved in university-wide general policy. I think I was realistic in assessing the limits of my abilities in those areas and was well served by focusing on departmental matters.

To this day, I have a measure of pride that my generation was far more politically engaged than the students whom I later stood across from in my career as a professor. We did not submissively accept the conditions that ministries, professors, and administrators attempted to impose on us. We tried to effect change and we fought hard for it. Of course, I will not and cannot claim that change always leads to improvement. The popular and provocative motto from that time—loosely translated as "Under the robes is the mildew of 1000 years"—helped destroy traditions that we now long for today. One of those is the college graduation ceremony. After we completed our final exams at Bonn, we did not receive the pomp and circumstance of a graduation ceremony. Instead, the examination office handed us plain pieces of paper to certify that we had completed our diplomas. That was it. When I think back on the graduation ceremonies I experienced at foreign universities—Harvard comes to mind—I get a sting of regret about the traditions Germany has lost. If I compare the two ceremonies for honorary doctorates, one at a German and one at a Polish university, the events could hardly have been any more different. I believe that the ceremony in Poland, with professors in their robes and the collective voices singing "Gaudeamus igitur" ("So Let Us Rejoice") was significantly more moving than the event in Germany, which was totally devoid of symbolism and decoration.

The apex of such traditions, however, was an honor conferred by the Académie des Sciences Morales et Politiques of the Institut de France, which was founded in 1795. In 2013, I received their "Prix Zerilli-Marimo," a prize established in 1984 and endowed by the baroness Zerilli Marimo in memory of her husband, a correspondent of the academy. It is meant to reward work "highlighting the role of the liberal economy in the progress of societies and the future of man."[6]

---

[6] https://academiesciencesmoralesetpolitiques.fr/prix-et-medailles/liste-des-prix-par-classement--thematique/prix-zerilli-marimo/

At the ceremony, we entered the Institut de France through a row of graduates of the military academy St. Cyr, who were wearing historical uniforms.[7] The 40 members of the academy also entered in traditional historical dress, as shown in the picture with Bertrand Collomb, the president of the academy. The entire ceremony followed a strict protocol which has not changed in 200 years.

Award ceremony in Paris with Bertrand Collomb, November 18, 2013

To their credit, the German universities have made efforts over the last several years to revive some of the older traditions. But to some extent, one could compare my university years with the Cultural Revolution under Mao Zedong. In both cases, traditions were destroyed beyond repair.

What did the student revolts and activism of those years lead to? Altogether I would say not too much, especially when weighed against the enormous investments of time and energy among the students. We invested a lot of effort into political activities, and that inevitably came at the expense of going to class and studying. Having said that, I do not regret those efforts. The

---

[7] Napoleon founded St. Cyr in 1802.

experience that I gained went far beyond what one could acquire in lectures or from books. I see student politics—after my gang of friends, the example set by my father, and my time in the military—as another leadership school for me.

Home Game

During my time as a professor at the University of Mainz (1989–1995), I once again came into contact with politics. Having been born in the German state of Rhineland-Palatinate, I knew many of the state's political figures. Carl-Ludwig Wagner (1930–2012), who was serving as the mayor of Trier, became the state's prime minister.

Hanns-Eberhard Schleyer ran the state chancellery at time. He was the son of Daimler chairman and employer association leader Hanns-Martin Schleyer, who had been assassinated by Red Army Faction (RAF) terrorists. I discussed plans with him about the introduction of a management studies program at the University of Mainz. Dr. Alfred Beth, who came from my home county, was the new environment minister. Dr. Heinz Peter Volkert (1933–2013), whose dance class I attended in 1963, was the head of the state parliament. Heinrich Holkenbrink (1920–1998) still wielded influence at the state level even though he had resigned from his ministerial post shortly before that time for health reasons. He had been a teacher at our *Gymnasium*. He knew my father from their days working together in the CDU in the Wittlich district, and he had visited our home from time to time. I worked in a state commission, led by former EU Commissioner Karl-Heinz Narjes (1924–2015), which examined the effects and the opportunities for the state in the aftermath of the founding of the European Union, the so-called Maastricht Agreement. Although I was not a party member, I took part in formulating the economic program of the CDU. Dr. Werner Langen, who came from the Moselle region and whom I knew well from our college days together in Bonn, was the head of the CDU in the state.

The CDU offered me the position of economics minister in their shadow cabinet. Because at that time I had already decided to leave the University of Mainz and assume the role of CEO at Simon-Kucher & Partners, I did not accept their offer.

I always made the effort to interject original ideas into the political discussions. The Europe Commission had the task of preparing the state of Rhineland-Palatinate for a truly united Europe, which was a vision taken very seriously at that time. I suggested to replace the clunky and rather unloved

German name of the state, *Rheinland-Pfalz*, by the better-sounding Latin name "Rhenania-Palatina." My rationale: for Europe, we needed a suitable name for the state that would hold up internationally. The suggestion was discussed earnestly in the committee, but was not approved. Two additional suggestions had to do with the withdrawal of US armed forces, which had a very strong presence in Rhineland-Palatinate since World War II. For the airport in Hahn—now referred to as Frankfurt-Hahn—I suggested the concept of a freight hub, similar to Federal Express's base in Memphis, Tennessee, which I had seen first-hand several years earlier. This effort would have helped secure the long-term future of the airport, but the state government did not grasp the concept and did not seriously pursue it. Later, DHL established its freight hub in Leipzig and UPS established its own in Cologne-Bonn, creating thousands of jobs. The Hahn Airport came up empty. It is now owned by a Chinese company and faces an uncertain future.

The reduction of US armed forces had freed up a portion of the huge Baumholder military training area. I made the suggestion of introducing a herd of American buffalo to the area. I had two reasons for this. First, it would be a nice living memorial of the Americans, and second, it would create a new tourist attraction for an economically disadvantaged region. I had visited Yellowstone National Park shortly before that and was delighted by the buffalo herds there. I knew Goldman Sachs manager Bob Hormats, who in the meantime had taken up a post in the US State Department. I spoke with him about the buffalo, and he liked the idea. Several months later, I received his answer. It would be possible to give up several buffalo and fly them to Germany via jumbo jet.

But my rather exotic idea went beyond the limits of the imagination of the state's agriculture ministry, which shot it down because it would involve introducing a foreign species to the ecosystem. To this day, I am disappointed that the buffalo herds do not roam the grounds in Baumholder. I am certain they would have become a huge tourist attraction. Today, we see llamas from Latin America and ostriches from South Africa in the region, and they are certainly not indigenous animals. But in the 1980s, it was not possible to bring American buffalo to Germany. These crazy ideas and many others prove only one thing: I am not suited for politics.

Tilting at Windmills

From time to time, I still get involved in politics in my hometown. At the start of the 2000s, a plan emerged to install a large wind farm in our district. This plan divided the community, from the citizens themselves right through the local council. I joined the opposition to the project. In part due to my efforts, the decision on the project came down to a referendum. Ahead of the vote, I made sure that every household in town received a copy of the latest edition of the very influential national news magazine *Spiegel,* whose cover story dealt with wind energy and opposed turning Germany into a "countryside of asparagus stalks." Of the 427 eligible voters in town, some 379 cast a vote, a very high participation rate of 88.8%. The opposition against the windmills won with a slight majority (52.9% vs. 47.1%). The difference in absolute terms was only 22 votes.

The decisive session of the local council, which took place a few weeks later, saw a hefty debate. In the end, the council rejected the project, eight votes to five. This was my biggest political victory—a small issue in a small village.

Instead of the windmills, the town installed a solar park on a 100-acre plot originally planned for the wind farm. This installation is less detrimental to the landscape than the windmills would have been.

Although we no longer live permanently in my home village of Hasborn, Cecilia and I continue to participate in important village affairs. Occasionally, we support causes that are close to our hearts. We were very happy that Hasborn made us honorary citizens in 2020, the first ones in the small village's 800-year history.

Charitable Foundations

I have been able to gain experience as a trustee of four foundations. The operational activities of a foundation are carried out by an executive committee. This committee is overseen by a board of trustees that guides how the foundation's funds will be disbursed. My own four cases involved the foundation of a large German bank, the personal foundation of an industrialist in the consumer goods sector, a similar foundation of an industrial family from the Ruhr Valley, and the public foundation of the city of Wittlich.

My experiences with foundations—and my views about them—are mixed. Some founders believe they are immortalizing themselves through their foundation. My impression is that the activities of foundations are influenced very strongly by personal interests. That in no way means personal enrichment, directly or indirectly. Instead, it means that they steer funds toward their own personal preferences within the foundation's purpose and mandate. All committees and all organizations ultimately reflect the people who constitute them. The fact that someone is on a corporate board and charitable board does not mean they can suppress their human side. At the same time, it is not unusual for a foundation to actively seek out projects that make sense because they lack enough ideas internally. As a professor, I experienced that foundations would approach me with project ideas that were in some cases so ludicrous that I would have absolutely no interest in them.

Wittlich's foundation was established in 1991. The city had sold its electricity grid to RWE AG for 9 million euros. Instead of using the money for the budget, the city decided to roll the funds over into a public foundation aimed at promoting and funding projects in the areas of culture, sports, and the general social good. I have been on the board of trustees right from the outset. Dr. Hans Friderichs was the chairman until 2009. His career included time as Germany's minister of economic affairs as well as CEO of Dresdner Bank, then Germany's number-two bank after Deutsche Bank. Friderichs came from Wittlich and we share a strong and deep attachment to our hometowns. In 2009, I succeeded him as chairman of the board of trustees. In more than 25 years on the board, I have dealt not only with three mayors, but also with politics at the communal level. With only a few exceptions, however, ideology played no role in these interactions. Mayor Joachim Rodenkirch, who has served as the chief executive of the foundation since 2009, understands how to keep city politics focused on issues and relatively free of ideology. After his first eight-year term, he was re-elected with 91.7% of the vote.

The foundation has organized a wide range of interesting projects as well as meetings with important dignitaries from recent history. Even before the foundation was created, the artist Georg Meistermann (1911–1990) visited us a few months before his death, together with former German president Walter Scheel (1919–2016). After he was persecuted by the Nazis and after World War II, Meistermann received his first commissions from the city of Wittlich and maintained a close relationship with the city. He bequeathed several significant works to the foundation as well as the draft sketches for a large number of church windows. We have awarded the Georg Meistermann Prize, named in his honor, to a wide range of people to honor their contributions to democracy and society. The honorees include:

- Johannes Rau, former German President
- Charlotte Knobloch, the chairman of the Central Council of Jews in Germany
- Cardinal Karl Lehmann
- Hans Dietrich Genscher, the former German Foreign Minister
- Herta Müller, Nobel Prize winner for literature
- Jean-Claude Juncker, President of the European Commission

The award ceremonies are among the highlights in the lives of the 19,000 residents of Wittlich. Around 1400 people attend the grand events in the local hall. Another highlight for the foundation was the exhibit of an original piece of the Berlin Wall that Friedel Drautzburg, the founder and operator of the Berlin trend bar "Ständige Vertretung," donated to his hometown. Ben Wagin, an activist and environmental artist from Berlin, crafted the memorial, which was unveiled on October 2, 2010, exactly 20 years after the German re-unification. Politics—and even local politics—can also have their positive sides.

A Little Campaign Support

Now let us return to Bonn. In Germany's former capital city, Ashok Alexander Sridharan ran for mayor in 2015. The son of an Indian diplomat and a German mother, he grew up in Bonn and attended a local Jesuit school. His two predecessors as mayor, social democrats Bärbel Dieckmann and Jürgen Nimptsch, had led Bonn for a total of 21 years and left serious problems in their wake. The most prominent of those is the World Conference Center Bonn. When the German capital moved to Berlin, the United Nations offered to set up a department in Bonn under the condition that the city build a huge conference center for 5000 people. Dieckmann took up the challenge.

But under her administration the city was allegedly defrauded by a Korean businessman and ended up shouldering losses of hundreds of millions of euros.[8] By 2015, it was time for a change. I considered Sridharan to be the best-suited candidate for mayor. A few months before the election—and 48 years to the day after the demonstration against the emergency powers—I published a two-page article in the Bonn newspaper *General-Anzeiger,* in which I ruthlessly criticized the trends in the city and made ten recommendations for a re-orientation (Simon 2015). Two weeks before the election, the CDU ran an advertisement with my endorsement for Sridharan as mayor. The night of the election was extremely tense, but Sridharan avoided a run-off by winning an absolute majority of 50.1%. Who knows whether my modicum of support helped put him over the top?

Looking back at my numerous but small political adventures and my sporadic encounters with politicians, I must admit that I have remained only a bystander, an observer from the sidelines. I have never taken on any political leadership responsibilities, except for a few relatively minor roles as student

---

[8] "South Korean suspected of swindling Bonn Politicians is in custody," *dw*, January 19, 2011

council president or foundation board member. Had I been able to accomplish anything as a politician? Probably not! And I see several reasons for that. The very thought of having my existence depend on votes (a fact of life for career politicians) gives me the chills. Politics is the art of the possible, or said differently, the art of compromise. Compromises are not my strong suit. A third reason is that speaking openly and directly can damage one's political career, the lesson I learned from my history teacher. In my younger days, I seriously considered the option of entering politics. Today, I am happy that I did not venture down that path.

References

Schwäbische Donau-Zeitung, November 17, 1967, p. 9. The same photo appeared in *Der Spiegel* on November 27, 1967.

"Geblähte Segel," *Der Spiegel*, November 27, 1967a, p. 69.

"Geblähte Segel," *Der Spiegel*, November 27, 1967b, p. 70.

Hermann Simon, "Die Zukunft von Bonn," *General-Anzeiger Bonn*, May 11, 2015, pp. 8-9

WiWi, Mitteilungsblatt der Fachschaftsvertretung der Fakultät für Wirtschaftswissenschaften, University of Bielefeld, December 1981, p. 13.

6

Western Journeys: From Charles River to Silicon Valley

Dreams Come True

As a young man, I dreamed about America. My eyes followed the American jets in the skies over the Eifel. During my studies, I learned from American books. As a young researcher, I admired American scientists. My eyes and longings were directed to the West. Would I ever find my way into their sacred institutions?

Who would have thought back then that my dreams would come true far beyond all expectations?

Massachusetts Institute of Technology (MIT), Stanford, and Harvard Business School: I spent almost three years combined at these world-class institutions. They had a profound effect on me, even though I was already over 30 years old at the time. What do I recall from those years? To quote Julia Shaw from her book *The Memory Illusion*:

> *"Time-travelling through our memories, we may find that some events stick out more than others. If we think about the characteristics that these memories have in common, we may notice that the most vivid are the most emotional, most important, most beautiful or most unexpected events of our lives. We may also notice that our memories cluster. And they often seem to cluster around particular periods in our lives. This is a phenomenon called the reminiscence bump."* (Shaw 2016)

The years in the United States left many reminiscence bumps in my mind.

When I think back to my earliest days in Massachusetts in 1978, it is the seemingly small and insignificant events that spring to mind. On my first visit, I stayed at the Eliot Hotel on a noisy corner in Boston's Back Bay. As I was crossing the Harvard Bridge to get to MIT, someone in a passing car pelted me with a raw egg. It shattered all over my new leather jacket, probably the exact outcome the thrower intended.

"Oh, this could be fun in the US," I remember thinking to myself.

But that one event was the only such "surprise" I experienced in the United States over the years.

Much more unpleasant and frustrating was the recognition of how weak my English was at that time. Although I took English for nine years at *Gymnasium* and could read Shakespeare in the original text, the day-to-day conversation in American English quickly tested my limits. To this day, Americans hear the first sentence from my mouth and ask me "Hermann, are you German?" Cecilia, in contrast, is often asked if she is American. That is how different the language skills are in our family.

Several minor observations in Massachusetts were totally new for me. I will use two examples to illustrate this. First, at every time of day and everywhere I looked—in parks, on sidewalks, on the streets—I saw people running at a steady pace. This was called "jogging." At that time, the jogging habit not only did not exist in Germany, but was also virtually unimaginable. Back in my home village, people had already declared me crazy for running several miles through the streets in order to train for a cross-country championship. I ran under the cover of darkness on purpose so that fewer people could see me. The word "jogging" itself was completely unknown in Germany. I read it for the first time a year later in the news magazine *Der Spiegel*.

A second observation: many students and young people carried backpacks. That was also inconceivable in Germany at that time. Backpacks were for hiking and for the military. Nobody, especially a student, wore a backpack in the city. In contrast, we Germans were proud to parade around with our attaché cases, which had come into vogue a few years earlier. I finally exchanged my own briefcase for a backpack in 2017. That proved to be a wise decision because traveling with a backpack is much more comfortable and convenient than traveling with a briefcase that one needs to carry by hand or with a shoulder strap. But some people are still surprised today when I show up with a backpack.

These two observations show that trends frequently start in the United States and then take several years to make their way to Germany and elsewhere. I think this still holds true today and would argue that the internet may have even increased America's influence.

Immersing Myself at MIT

The contact to the Sloan School of Management at MIT came through Professor Alvin J. Silk, whom I had met at the European Institute for Advanced Studies in Management (EIASM) in Brussels. For me, EIASM became an early and important bridgehead into the world of international management studies, a nascent field in Germany at that time. The first university marketing chair in Germany was not established until 1969. Very little marketing literature was available to us there. Marketing magazines were a rarity, and finding sources for my dissertation and post-doc work was a struggle.

This extremely modest starting point was a stark contrast to the environment at MIT. The Sloan School of Management had seven marketing professors who were teaching and conducting research, including three tenured professors who enjoyed excellent reputations in the academic scene: Silk, John D.C. Little, and Glen Urban. Gary Lilien, who was likewise well known, was an associate professor, and there were three assistant professors. This team of seven marketing luminaries had offices near each other and formed a sort of "office commune." I received a desk in the office of an assistant professor, which put me right in the thick of things and allowed me to integrate myself into their open culture of discussion. In order to appreciate the significance of such marketing clusters, one should keep in mind that the first similar cluster in Germany did not come about until the late 1990s, around 20 years later.

In terms of methodology, Professor Silk was the most competent member within the MIT group. In his doctoral seminars, we wrestled for weeks with complex scaling techniques and statistically demanding market research designs. At that time, most marketing academics were unfamiliar with trade-off or conjoint analyses, but our team—led by Silk—was actively engaged with these methods. My colleagues and I benefited from this basis later on at Simon-Kucher.

Urban's primary area of interest was new products and how to market them. This area also attracted my interest because I had written my dissertation on price strategies for new products. The specialty of Little, the best-known professor in the team, was decision support systems. He also enjoyed an extraordinary reputation in the operations research community. Little's Law, considered an important tool for business efficiency and operations management, bears his name (Little 1961).[1]

---

[1] The long-term average number of customers in a stable system L equals the long-term average effective arrival rate, λ, multiplied with the average time a customer spends in a system, W, expressed in the algebraic formula $L = \lambda W$.

Little and Urban founded a consulting firm named Management Decision Systems. Their objective was to offer decision support to managers with the help of quantitative methods. Scanner data, which became available at that time, played an important role in their work. Thanks to this data, one could determine for the first time ever, without much effort, how much of a product had actually been purchased, and how much by individual customers. Little published a groundbreaking article on this topic in the *Journal of Marketing*. I translated the article into German and placed it in the *Zeitschrift für Betriebswirtschaft*, now *Journal of Business Economics* (Little 1979). Little's and Urban's firm was later purchased by Chicago-based Information Resources, a pioneer in the age of scanner data. A few years later, the firm entered the German market in cooperation with GfK (Gesellschaft für Konsumforschung). Their main product, called Behavior Scan, became popular in the consumer goods industry. The dissertation topic of Eckhard Kucher, my first doctoral student at the University of Bielefeld and later one of the namesakes of our firm, Simon-Kucher—emerged from this encounter with Little's scanner research.

How did I get access to a top-flight institution such as MIT's Sloan School? The personal acquaintance with Professor Silk played an important role. He gave me a contact person to send my request to. But more decisive was an article that I published in 1978 in the journal *Management Science*. One can hardly overestimate the significance that this journal, an A+ publication, enjoyed in marketing science circles at that time.

My article, titled "An Analytical Investigation of Kotler's Competitive Simulation Model," connected my own work to that of prominent marketing guru Philip Kotler. In 1965, he had published a seminal article on marketing mix in the product life cycle, based on an elegant mathematical model. I demonstrated that this model led to nonsensical results over time (Simon 1978). For example, it allowed a company to increase prices during the product life cycle at will, without harming volume in a meaningful way.

No one had exposed this implication before because uncovering it was relatively complicated mathematically. The fact that a complete "nobody" from Germany dared to criticize the famed Philip Kotler in the most renowned management journal did not go unnoticed in the relevant circles. In one blow, it created enough recognition for me to open doors that would have otherwise remained shut.

Kotler himself did not get upset about this "attack." In fact, he showed the opposite reaction. I visited him in January 1979 at Northwestern University in Evanston, near Chicago. At this first meeting, I showed him my research results on price elasticity during the product cycle. Full of self-confidence, I told him that my goal was to pursue research that would have real-world impact.

"Most scientific marketing researchers want to uncover something that has impact on day-to-day business," Kotler told me. "Few succeed."

He said that in the area of pricing, microeconomics was the dominant scientific area, and its relevance for practice was limited. And he was right.

On the same trip, I met Thomas T. Nagle and Robert J. Dolan, who were assistant professors at the University of Chicago. Nagle left the University of Chicago a few years later and founded the Strategic Pricing Group, which focused primarily on pricing training. Dolan later moved to the Harvard Business School, where I caught up with him again ten years later when I was a visiting professor there in the 1988/89 academic year. We began an enduring cooperation and published jointly.

My next stop after Chicago was Purdue University in West Lafayette, Indiana, where I met with Professor Frank Bass. Next to John D.C. Little, he was at the time the best-known quantitative marketing scientist. His name is most closely associated with the so-called Bass Model (Bass 2004), which explains the diffusion pattern of new products based on the interaction of innovators and imitators. It is a simple mathematical model that yields the development of sales volume according to the life cycle concept. Hundreds of researchers have worked with this approach, varied the model, and tested it with empirical data. My second doctoral student, Karl-Heinz Sebastian, later used the model to explain the diffusion of fixed-line telephones in Germany. He included advertising in the model, and it turned out to be a significant explanatory variable. Together we published an article on the topic in *Management Science* (Simon and Sebastian 1987).

With these meetings, I had visited the leading universities in my field in the Midwestern US and had personally met the most important marketing academics. I later made a similar trip to the US East Coast and visited Columbia and New York University as well as the Wharton School in Philadelphia. I also built up close contacts with the marketing professors at the Harvard Business School, which lies on the other side of the Charles River from MIT.

The personal side of my academic year in Massachusetts was rather difficult. I was nervous prior to moving to the United States. This was going to be my first extended stay abroad, and at a top university to boot. I was unsure how I would deal with day-to-day life there, never mind how I would handle the academic side. My initial idea was to go to the United States without Cecilia and our three-year-old daughter Jeannine. But Cecilia objected and said "We're coming with you." Looking back, that was clearly the right decision.

Finding an apartment in Cambridge proved difficult. In the end, I was able to rent only a very meager and overpriced place. The cities on both sides of the Charles River—Boston and Cambridge—were sellers' markets because of the waves of academics and students who flood the area every year. Day-to-day life also had its pitfalls. In many ways, Germany lagged far behind North America. In the late 1970s, hardly anyone in Germany had a credit card, whereas in the United States it was impossible to do many things, such as rent a car, without a credit card. Making international phone calls was extremely expensive and inconvenient. At the same time, many aspects of life in the United States were simpler and more easy-going than in Germany.

During my stay in the United States, I had planned to complete my habilitation on dynamic product line marketing.[2] That was very ambitious, in part because I wanted to conduct extensive empirical analyses. It is hard to assess *ex ante* how much time those analyses require. The only thing that helps is hard work. For two months, I was in the office every day except for one, my 32nd birthday. My family went back to Germany in the spring of 1979, several months ahead of me, so that I could concentrate fully on my work. But we used the time during Christmas and New Year's for a short vacation to Florida and a trip to Houston to visit some of Cecilia's relatives. In Florida, we rented a red Pontiac Firebird and drove over the hard sand beaches at Daytona Beach. I wonder if that is still possible today.

The highlight for Jeannine was Disney World in Orlando. Even the simplest motels there were comfortable for us. We indulged in the all-you-can-eat buffets, another American phenomenon completely unknown at that time in Germany. Jeannine also saw the Golden Arches of McDonald's from far away, so there was no way we could not turn in there. In Germany, the first McDonald's in our area had opened not long before we went to the United States.

In Houston, our rental car broke down, luckily only a few yards from our destination, the home of Bill and Elfriede Eck. Elfriede was my mother-in-law's cousin. Bill Eck had immigrated to the United States in 1929 and had worked in the auto industry in Detroit before settling in Houston, where he operated a small hotel. He was an enthusiastic fisherman, and on one of our outings, I caught a fish for the first and only time in my life. During the long drive, we experienced firsthand the huge expanse of the state of Texas. The Lone Star State is twice the size of the whole country of Germany!

---

[2] Habilitation is the process of becoming a university professor in German-speaking countries and in Eastern Europe. It requires a second thesis more advanced than a doctoral dissertation and a defense of a new theory.

The period at the Sloan School also gave me the opportunity to meet the famous scholars in the economics department, which was located in the same building. They included Paul Samuelson, who had won the 1970 Nobel Prize in Economics, and Robert Solow, who was widely known for his work on growth and innovation and also received a Nobel Prize. Several times a week, I had the opportunity to listen to the lectures of such giants. The University of Bonn had its own share of famous speakers, such as high-ranking politicians and ministry officials, thanks to the city's status back then as West Germany's capital. But of course they could not match the events offered by MIT and Harvard.

When I left the Sloan School at the end of the 1979 academic year, it was clear to me that I would be back, although at the time I could not have imagined the "how," "when," and "where." That first stay at MIT had laid the roots, and it took many years before they bore fruit. Some 17 years later, we opened the first US office of Simon-Kucher & Partners in Kendall Square, a stone's throw away from the Sloan School.

Flowers in Our Hair

As our plane from Hawaii smoothly touched down on the tarmac of San Francisco Airport on January 3, 1984, Scott McKenzie's famous song resonated in my head: "If you're going to San Francisco, be sure to wear some flowers in your hair."

Our family's extraordinary adventures in Japan, Hong Kong, and Papua New Guinea—which I will describe in detail in the next chapter—were behind us. Returning from the Asia-Pacific region, we were back in the West for my next American posting: a semester at Stanford University.

I had been to California a few times on speaking tours and consulting assignments. Staying for a whole semester at Stanford, however, promised to be an experience very distinct what from Asia and the US East Coast had to offer.

If you asked me to name the most beautiful universities, I would put Stanford at the top of the list, even ahead of her nearby "sister," the University of California, Berkeley. Stanford was founded in 1891 by the US railroad tycoon Leland Stanford. From the outset, the school has had a German motto: "Die Luft der Freiheit weht" ("The wind of freedom blows.")[3] The motto came under heavy attack during the Nazi era, but the university maintained it

---

[3] https://web.stanford.edu/dept/pres-provost/president/speeches/951005dieluft.html

then as it does to this day. From 1992 to 2000, Stanford even had a German president, the law professor Gerhard Casper.

The buildings in Spanish colonial style go on and on throughout a seemingly endless campus at the foot of the mountains that separate the Silicon Valley from the Pacific. In 1984, Silicon Valley still had many wide open spaces. The internet era and its building spree were years away. The leading light was Hewlett Packard, but semiconductor firms such as Intel were in rapid ascension. Apple was a young niche player. I remember the famous TV commercial which introduced the world to the Apple Macintosh during the Super Bowl in January 1984. Three decades later, an article about Steve Jobs looked back at the groundbreaking advertisement: "… the director Ridley Scott had created a commercial in which a young female athlete runs with a hammer toward a crowd under the control of an Orwellian 'Big Brother' force. When she shatters the projection system, the screen goes blank, as if a stroke of lightning had erased every memory of the dark, totalitarian past" (Burckhardt 2017). Everyone knew that the unnamed Big Brother in the commercial was IBM, which at the time held a level of market power that exceeds even that of today's internet companies. The ad made Steve Jobs a cult figure.

The academics I met at Stanford were of a similar caliber as those at MIT, but their fields of research were more diverse. The most important discussion partners for me were the professors David B. Montgomery, Seenu Srinivasan, and Rajiv Lal. Professor Lal was only 23 years old, had just completed his Ph.D. at Carnegie Mellon University, and was beginning his first year as an assistant professor at Stanford. Montgomery was on the same level as the professors at MIT, where he used to teach. Srinivasan was a methodology specialist. He made fundamental contributions to the development of conjoint measurement, which would emerge as one of the most important quantitative market research methodologies in the coming decades and would later play a vital role in the work of Simon-Kucher.

Lal was one of the most productive builders of quantitative models and published many papers in the newly established A+-journal *Marketing Science*. He later moved on to the Harvard Business School, where he turned away from theoretical quantitative research in favor of more practical work. We have remained friends and still meet regularly today.

The most important single impulse I received during my stay at Stanford came from Professor Robert Wilson, who published a groundbreaking paper on nonlinear pricing in *Marketing Science* (Oren et al. 1982). He explained the logic and the potential of the approach in a speech, and I was fascinated. It immediately triggered an idea for a doctoral dissertation topic, which I assigned to Georg Tacke. He ended up spending a semester as a visiting research fellow at Stanford and finished his dissertation on nonlinear pricing in 1988 (Tacke 1989). This paper provided the theoretical underpinnings for innovations such as the BahnCard program of Deutsche Bahn, Germany's railroad corporation. A team at Simon-Kucher, under Tacke's guidance, developed the program in the early 1990s together with Hemjoe Klein, the railroad's chief marketing and sales officer at the time. Cardholders pay an upfront annual fee for the BahnCard, which entitles them to a 50% discount on purchases of train tickets for one year. The program became wildly popular. Today around six million people have a BahnCard, and the program has generated billions of euros of revenue for Deutsche Bahn. One can thus draw a straight line from that speech at Stanford in 1984 to the launch of the very lucrative BahnCard in Germany in 1993.

California is far too beautiful to spend time sitting behind a desk. Every morning when I walked out the door, I was greeted by a clear blue sky and bright sunshine—a standing invitation to do something outside and blow off work. In Germany, if we do not take advantage of such nice weather, we have the feeling that we will miss out on something. After several weeks in California, that uneasy feeling subsided. We knew that if we missed an opportunity, there would be good weather the next day or on the weekend, and that rain would never wash away our plans.

We explored nearby San Francisco, to me the most beautiful US city, even ahead of Boston or New York. We drove out to Ano Nuevo on the Pacific Ocean and watched the hundreds of seals and sea elephants lying on the beach. In Monterey, we tried to reimagine the Cannery Row of John Steinbeck's time. I had read that novel and others by Steinbeck in school. We also traveled out to Yellowstone National Park and admired the beautiful landscape and the magnificent cliff formations.

I sometimes ask myself whether I should have stayed in California, not as a professor, but as an entrepreneur. This was the time when things in the Silicon Valley started to get going. Intel was the rising star. Apple, still an upstart, was making a lot of noise and attracting attention. This was long before the internet, and long before Google and Facebook, but signs of a new era were on the horizon. Many Germans were working in the Silicon Valley, especially at Intel. Some of the valley's most successful valley, such as Andreas von Bechtolsheim and Peter Thiel, are of German origin. My life would definitely have taken a totally different course if I had decided to stay in California.

In light of those thoughts, it gives me some comfort that I did return to California, albeit in a different form. In 2006, Simon-Kucher opened an office in Mountain View, and a second office followed in San Francisco in

2015. Both offices are extremely successful. Today, we have more than 30 West Coast unicorns as clients, among them Uber and other heavyweights whom we are not allowed to name.

But let us return to 1984. During our time at Stanford, we made many new friends, not only from the business school, but also from other departments and from the emerging Silicon Valley firms. It was an enriching, horizon-expanding experience for me, and I have extremely fond memories of our time in California. We had a nice house, Jeannine attended an American school without any difficulties, and Patrick also had a fun time there. I was much more relaxed than back in 1979 at MIT, when I was laboring in the midst of my post-doctoral process, the so-called habilitation. When we were in California, I was already established as a tenured professor and felt less pressure. Yes, Scott McKenzie found the right tone: "There's a whole generation with a new explanation; people in motion."

"Goin' Back to Massachusetts"—This Time to Harvard

Fast forward! This time, the opening line of another 1960s song kept ringing in my ears: "Feel I'm goin' back to Massachusetts," from the famous 1967 Bee Gees song. I played the song many times in our Bonn office before leaving for Harvard.

To sum it up in one sentence: the Harvard Business School is different! I sometimes claim that the differences between a typical German university and a typical American one are smaller than the differences between the Harvard Business School and other American universities.

HBS struck me as more of a corporation with a strong and idiosyncratic corporate culture. Founded in 1908, it is one of the oldest business schools in the world and also has one of the largest full-time, two-year MBA programs, with 900 students per year. HBS graduates make up by far the largest share of CEOs of the Fortune Global 500. A study published in 2012 claimed that 65 of the 500 CEOs had studied at Harvard, and 40 of them had an MBA from the Harvard Business School, four times as many as from Stanford. Without a doubt, HBS enjoys the highest name recognition and greatest reputation among business schools. But the school is also polarizing, and critical authors have taken aim at it (McDonald 2017).

HBS's campus along the banks of the Charles River is beautiful although it does not surpass Stanford, neither in terms of beauty nor weather. An open invitation to enjoy the great outdoors comes less frequently in Boston than it does in California. August in Massachusetts can be unbearably hot and humid. And I start to shiver the moment I think about the winters when the temperature would sometimes plunge below 0 degrees Fahrenheit (-17 Celsius) for weeks, and the infamous north winds of the so-called Montreal Express would drive the wind chill levels even lower. How I longed for the mild winters in Bonn during those cold snaps!

What has helped HBS carve out a unique status among the world's business schools? First and foremost, it is the enormous weight it gives to teaching. This is closely tied to its almost exclusive use of the case-study method. The approach flourished at HBS, which places a high priority on nurturing it. One could call the case-study method the heart and soul of the Harvard Business School.

In his book, *The Golden Passport*, Duff McDonald comments on the case-study method: "It is the foundation of their pedagogical approach. It is the object of their financial devotion, having consumed more research funds than all the rest of the School's efforts combined. The ability to write and teach cases effectively is the primary measure of faculty performance at HBS. It is also the primary means by which the School has spread the gospel of its thinking about business. Harvard swears by the case method."[4]

Around 80% of the cases used at business schools around the world either come from Harvard or are supplied by the Harvard Case Clearing House.[5] I was able to experience firsthand how intensively the professors prepare the case discussions. The 900 MBA students are divided into nine sections with roughly 100 students each. The sections work through the same case study in parallel. The number of professors is normally less than nine because some teach in two sections. After intensive individual preparation, the instructors gather for discussion under the guidance of the program director. The group reviews—which can last for several hours for each case study—are a forum for bringing up all possible questions about the case from all conceivable angles. This does not imply that the discussions in all nine sections follow the same routine procedure. The instructors have different styles and approaches. Nonetheless, they need to prepare for all eventualities in these intense discussions. The program director and several of the instructors are always battle-tested veterans, a design that helps transfer their experience to the younger professors.

The professors also have their own individual preparation time. I can not make any generalizations about how much time professors invest. What I do

---

[4] McDonald (2017), *The Golden Passport*. Harper Business. Kindle Edition, p. 46.
[5] McDonald (2017), Position 5418 in Kindle Edition.

know is that Bob Dolan would take about ten hours to prepare for a case-study discussion. He would make the commitment even though he had often written the case study in question and had already taught it numerous times. He wanted to have a fine-tuned awareness of detailed information, every number, and every conceivable direction for the discussion. Judging from the evaluations he received from students, this enormous investment of time was definitely worthwhile. Bob Dolan was always among the highest rated instructors, which is saying a lot considering the tough competition within that high-caliber faculty.

The preparation of the professors is matched by the level of preparedness of the students. They must have three case studies fresh in their minds each day. That demands extremely high concentration coupled with a huge time investment, with workdays often lasting deep into the night. A student must be top-fit the moment a professor enters the lecture hall. No one knows in advance who will be called on by the professor to "open the case." Once called upon, the individual student needs to speak around 15 minutes to lay out the case, analyze it, and put forward potential solutions. The students take their roles in these discussions very seriously because their performance makes up 50% of their overall grade. Last but not least, no one wants to embarrass himself or herself in this extremely competitive environment. One's reputation within a section depends heavily on how one performs in these case discussions.

Writing a good case study is a high art form. First, the author needs access to companies that are willing to release relevant information and then ultimately sign off on the case. That is by no means a sure thing because the case studies often deal with missteps companies have made. Such case studies are particularly instructive because one often learns more from missteps than from successes.

It is also a challenge for the author to describe a situation in such a way that a decision is not obvious. A case only becomes compelling when two or more alternative decisions could make sense. Such cases generate vigorous discussions, as advocates and opponents of the potential approaches or decisions defend and challenge arguments.

Why are so many case studies written by Harvard Business School professors? One reason is a question of corporate culture, which places considerable importance on them. At Harvard, they play a similar role to what academic publications in top-line journals play at other universities. The case studies are also a lucrative business for HBS. According to author Duff McDonald, Harvard generated $30 million in 2014 from the 12 million case studies sold.[6]

---

[6] McDonald (2017), Position 5418 in Kindle Edition.

The case-study authors receive an attractive royalty for every student that uses his or her case. That can be a considerable sum when a case study becomes a hit and gets used in hundreds of business schools around the world.

Many Harvard professors are also consultants and some have their own firms. The HBS faculty and student body are very international. At the same time, the internal spirit of the school remains very American. That is not necessarily a contradiction. Management thinking has traditionally emanated from the United States and continues to do so. No other country has such a significant global influence on management thinking and management teaching.

What McDonald says is true: "HBS had always been the dominant force in graduate business education at home. It dominated international business education as well."[7] Most of the business schools outside the United States that have established a strong international reputation are either offshoots or imitators of Harvard. These include INSEAD in Fontainebleau, the London Business School, or IESE in Barcelona, as well as several Asian business schools such as the China Europe International Business School (CEIBS) in Shanghai. It therefore comes as no surprise that Harvard students from outside the United States want to learn American-style management and are less inclined to bring the methods from their own countries to America. The same applies to a slightly lesser degree to the professors. Hirotaka Takeuchi, who worked closely with Michael Porter for many years, brought some ideas from Japan to the United States, but the flow of ideas in the other direction has been greater. Professors of German-language origin—and there are a considerable number in the United States—have generally adapted to the American system. I could not name anyone of the top of my head who has transferred ideas from the German-speaking world to the United States and implemented them successfully on a grand scale. The closest would be the late Peter Drucker, but he belongs to another generation.

Professors from India make up the greatest share of professors born outside the United States. One of them is Nitin Nohria, from 2010 to 2020 dean of HBS. Almost all of them practice "American style" management science and teaching. Two exceptions are the late C.K. Prahalad, the strategist who was one of the first to identify the massive economic potential in developing countries. He publicized it in his book *The Fortune at the Bottom of the Pyramid* (Prahalad 2004). Another is Professor Vijay Mahajan of the University of Texas at Austin, who has done intensive research in his homeland India and other developing countries (Mahajan 2008). North America is and will remain

---

[7] McDonald (2017), Position 4603 in Kindle Edition.

the El Dorado for management science. That applies to the universities and the A+ journals, and it applies to internationally renowned gurus such as Michael Porter (strategy) or Philip Kotler (marketing).

Interestingly, the influence of Harvard has remained lower in Germany than in most other countries. The management thinker Robert Locke commented by saying: "One searches in vain in Germany for the development of American-style business schools. Neither German firms nor German academia approached business studies in the same way, and hence made different educational demands than their American counterparts. Germans tended to view the firm as an organic whole with a life of its own. The American proprietary outlook harbored no such illusions. The firm was simply a money mill" (Locke 1999).

During this second stay in Massachusetts, this time at HBS, I spent less time behind a desk than I did while at MIT ten years earlier. I attribute that change to some advice Professor Theodore ("Ted") Levitt gave me right at the start: "Do in Harvard what you only can do in Harvard." This turned out to be very valuable advice.

I spent a lot of time in discussions and a lot of time listening. Levitt is only one of several people whom I got to know closely, but to whom I never spoke about their terrible experiences in Nazi Germany. From today's perspective, I do not know if it was the right decision to avoid actively discussing what had happened then. At the time it seemed too risky for me to potentially reopen old wounds. When I visited Professor Julian Simon from the University of Illinois in Urbana-Champaign, we took a walk around campus, and he seemed a bit downcast. All of a sudden, he spoke up.

"Hermann, you're the first German I've talked to," he told me.

Julian Simon was of Jewish descent. He was a multi-talent, having established a top reputation in both demography and in marketing. His position was Anti-Malthusian, meaning he was optimistic regarding the development of the world over the long term. In 1980, he made a bet with the famous Stanford biologist Paul R. Ehrlich, who had a rather pessimistic view regarding the world's future. Ehrlich claimed that the prices for five metals would increase in the next ten years. Simon wagered against that claim … and won. He probably would still be winning the bet even today, 40 years later, when one adjusts the prices for inflation. Julian Simon passed away in 1998, a few days before his 66th birthday (Wattenberg 1998).

The youngest star at HBS at the time was Michael Porter. In the early 1980s, he published his landmark books *Competitive Strategy* (Porter 1980) and *Competitive Advantage* (Porter 1985). In subsequent years, he devoted his attention to the competitiveness of countries and published a voluminous book *The Competitive Advantage of Nations* (Porter 1990). Before he turned 40, some simple concepts had catapulted him to worldwide fame. Those concepts include the Five Forces, under which competition is seen not only horizontally but also vertically along the value chain; the U-Curve, which recommends that one should be focused either on a very large market or on a small niche (but not in between); and the matrix of competitive advantage. Porter's strength is the ability to reduce complex issues to their bare essence. That also came across in his lectures. He had a knack for compressing problems down to a small number of attributes, often just two, thus capturing their essence. He also deviated from the typical Harvard blueprint, in that he only devoted about two thirds of the 75-minute classes to the case. In the remaining time, he gave a systematic European-style lecture. I found this combination very instructive and useful.

One clear measure of Porter's academic reputation is the extremely high Hirsch Index of 176 and his i10 Index of 862. The Hirsch Index gives the number of publications (n) of an author that have been cited at least n times. The i10 Index is the number of publications that have been cited at least ten times. Among the academics I know personally, only Philip Kotler has higher values of these indices (198 vs. 175 and 1214 vs. 747).[8] But Porter is 16 years younger than Kotler, almost to the day, and the Hirsch Index can only increase as an author gets older and his or her publications are cited even more often.

During my time at HBS, Porter focused on international competitiveness, at times collaborating with Hirotaka Takeuchi and supported by Christian Ketel. He took a close look at Germany and its industrial clusters. He was one of the few Americans who had a good understanding of Germany, or had at least "decoded" it to a certain degree. After a talk with him on March 8, 1989 I noted the following points on the competitiveness of a nation. It can be considered to have a strong position only when three conditions are met:

- The demand in the home market must be at a high level, qualitatively and quantitatively.
- The country has a strong industrial infrastructure.
- The internal competition is very intense.

It was Takeuchi in particular who transplanted these ideas to Japan. I recall his telling me that if the day came that only fewer than seven companies survived in Japan (thanks to intense competition), then those companies would conquer the world. Today that claim may sound astonishing or fantastical,

---

[8] https://scholar.google.com/citations, accessed on February 15, 2021.

but prior to 1990 it was accepted as truth. This Japan euphoria reached its peak with the publication of the book *The Machine that Changed the World* by Womack, Jones and Roos (Womack et al. 1990). Today, we know that things turned out very differently.

Germany was thought of as a weak "problem child" back then. Steven C. Wheelwright, the manufacturing expert at Harvard Business School,[9] once discussed with me in great detail the weaknesses of German industry. He emphasized a few points, namely that German industry:

– was too slow
– lagged in the amount and application of software in factories
– lagged in the amount of electronics in its finished goods
– held overly ambitious goals for software development because it focused on "grand schemes."

Similar to Japan, today we know that the future in Germany also turned out differently.

Another impressive figure at HBS was Professor Rosabeth Moss Kanter, who devoted herself to leadership issues with an emphasis on the psychological and sociological aspects. She had considerable influence in American industry and in politics. For example, she was in the inner circle of advisers to 1988 presidential candidate and former Massachusetts governor Michael Dukakis. Her 24 honorary doctorates attest to the extent of her academic reputation.

I met other well-known professors such as business historian Alfred Chandler, who coined the phrase "structure follows strategy" (Chandler 1969). His successor Richard Tedlow, who was both well educated and very friendly (and a Richard Wagner fan), created a furor in 2011 when he departed Harvard—his intellectual home for 31 years—and went to Apple University. I also held Walter Salmon in high esteem. He was a true expert in the field of retail, a research area where I have never really felt at home. His presence reminded me of how I felt around Otto Beisheim, the founder of the retail group Metro. When we celebrated his 70th birthday at the Kaufhof department store in Cologne, Beisheim, took us on a tour of the store and explained the merchandising strategy. He saw things I could not see.

---

[9] Steven C. Wheelwright later served as the ninth president of Brigham Young University Hawaii from 2007 to 2015.

A true original was Marjorie Salmon, Walter Salmon's wife. She was a psychoanalyst. She came into my office, whose furnishings and decoration could politely be described as Spartan.

"No sex appeal," she remarked brusquely.

That remark did not sit well with Cecilia. We bought some reasonably priced prints to decorate the walls.

My closest cooperation partner at Harvard was Bob Dolan. He had completed his doctorate under finance professor Michael Jensen at the University of Rochester before joining the faculty at Chicago.[10] Like myself, Dolan was interested in the topic of price management. Since our first encounter over 40 years ago, we have stayed in touch. Cecilia and Bob's wife, Kathleen Splaine Dolan, became good friends and we have all gotten together frequently over the years.

The collaboration between Dolan and me culminated in the publication of the book *Power Pricing* in 1996 (Dolan and Simon 1996). The book has aged remarkably well, and continues to sell so well that it was labeled as a best seller on Amazon.com in 2016. Unfortunately, we never wrote a second edition. Dolan became dean of the Ross School of Business at the University of Michigan in 2001 and held that position for more than ten years. It was a time-consuming job that did not leave him with enough free time to write books. When he left Michigan and returned to teaching at Harvard in 2012, his interest had shifted to other topics. In the meantime, I had also gone my own way and published *Confessions of the Pricing Man* (Simon 2015) and *Price Management* (Simon and Fassnacht 2019).

Dolan is a critical sparring partner who gets quickly and succinctly to the heart of a problem. But his true love is teaching at Harvard, and he often talks about the "joy of teaching." He has also provided expert testimony in legal conflicts between companies and gained some notoriety for his analysis on behalf of Polaroid in its patent battle with Kodak. The expert testifying for Kodak was the late Robert Buzzell (1993–2004), likewise a Harvard professor.[11] Polaroid had accused Kodak of violating its patents, and Kodak ultimately had to pay Polaroid $909 million in damages. Ironically, neither of these firms survived because they did not successfully make the leap into digital photography. Dolan also testified on the winning side in Honeywell's legal conflict with Minolta, which ended with the latter paying $135 million in damages. Dolan's testimony was credited with playing a decisive role in each of these wins, and his reputation rose accordingly.

---

[10] Michael Jensen later joined the Harvard Business School faculty.
[11] Buzzell first became well known as the main author of Buzzell and Gale (1987).

One of the many highlights at Harvard were the speeches by top managers, especially during the fall recruiting season. I was able to listen to speeches by the likes of Jack Welch, Michael Dell, and the CEOs of many other large companies such as Pepsico and Procter & Gamble. These top managers made personal appearances at Harvard in order to win over as many upcoming graduates as possible. In Germany, it is hard to imagine CEOs showing the same level of engagement. But the heavy concentration of high potentials makes a personal appearance at Harvard worth the while for even the most time-strapped CEO. In my time as the director of the German Management Institute, I witnessed the talks and discussions of many top managers, but the talks at Harvard were of a different and higher caliber. American managers are better trained in communication skills and get more practice at it. That gap has shrunk in the meantime in Germany, but Americans are still superior at close-quarters communication. They are more approachable, and after a speech there is usually a reception where one can comfortably engage the top managers in conversation.

I also had very interesting encounters on the other side of the Charles River at the Kennedy School of Government, which grants a master of public administration (MPA) degree. Speakers there included the prime ministers of many countries, as well as others with connections to politics, such as Sergei Khrushchev, the son of former Soviet premier Nikita Khrushchev. A few years later, Sergei immigrated to the United States and became a US citizen in 1999. At the Kennedy School, I also met researchers from the former East Germany for the first time. Two researchers from the Communist state—officially known as the German Democratic Republic (GDR)—had received special permission to spend several months at the Kennedy School during the 1988/89 academic year. When the two of them were together, their comments did not stray from the official Communist party line. But when I would go out for a drink with one of them separately, a completely different view of the world came to light. Let us just say that these one-on-one conversations made it clear to me that if nothing changed, the GDR would eventually fail as a state. When I returned to Germany in the middle of 1989 and assumed my professorship at Johannes-Gutenberg-University in Mainz, one of my first actions was to assign "GDR strategies for West German companies" as a dissertation topic. The doctoral student who accepted the assignment was overtaken by the events that unfolded in the second half of 1989, which culminated in the fall of the Berlin Wall and shortly afterwards in the German reunification. The student gave up on the project.

The unique culture at Harvard had many facets. One was the Faculty Club, where professors would meet for lunch and which also served as a venue for receptions. Unfortunately, this wonderful institution does not exist anymore. At the end of the fall semester, there was a gala ball at the Hotel Sonesta. In all my years, I have never seen anything comparable at another university. Another event I remember took place on October 5, 1988. Derek Bok, the president of Harvard University, had invited the visiting scholars, among them a number of Germans, including the two East German researchers I mentioned above.[12] The nametags of those guests included six different ways of describing my country: Germany, West Germany, Germany (West), Federal Republic of Germany, GDR, and East Germany. One year later, that problem no longer existed. There was only one Germany.

My official status at Harvard was "Marvin Bower Fellow." Marvin Bower was one of the three founders of McKinsey. The firm had donated the money for four visiting professorships at the Harvard Business School, and these would bear Bower's name. Within this program, Harvard would invite academics from different disciplines and countries to spend one year at the business school. The three other fellows in my cohort were from England, France, and Israel and specialized in logistics, finance, and organization. I was the marketing expert. We had the status of professor and were entitled to all faculty privileges. As a result, I became part of the US Social Security System and received a social security number. In Chap. 12, I will describe my personal encounter with Marvin Bower, who left an indelible impression on me.

America! America!

I have visited this enormous country over 100 times and lived there for almost three years. Every time I set foot on American soil, I am overcome by a strange feeling, an alchemy of amazement, uneasiness, skepticism, and an acute awareness of the country's strengths and weaknesses. On the one hand, one sees the nation's sheer economic power, its entrepreneurial spirit, its uncanny ability to innovate, and its top universities. On the other hand, one cannot overlook the run-down condition of many houses and cities, the crumbling infrastructure, and the social and educational contrasts. To this day, I cannot

---

[12] Derek Bok was the president of Harvard University from 1971 to 1991. He was 41 years old when he took up the office, the youngest president in the history of Harvard since its founding in 1634.

make rhyme or reason out of this polarity. I am intrigued, though, about how there are parallels between this polarity and what I observe in China, a country I came to know many years later.

The American business schools were not the only ones where I had the chance to learn, teach, and gain experience. Over the years, I also taught at business schools in France, the United Kingdom, South Africa, and Japan. All these contacts resulted in fruitful networks from which I have benefitted throughout my life.

Comme dieu en France

"Like god in France," that is how the French describe their wonderful country. And I could enjoy a little bit of "douce France" (sweet France) during my numerous stays in Fontainebleau, a picturesque French town south of Paris which was once the seat of NATO headquarters. The INSEAD business school in Fontainebleau was founded in 1957, making it the oldest school of its kind in Europe. INSEAD stands for Institut Européen d'Administration des Affaires, a French acronym in the spirit of how they write NATO (OTAN in French) or the UNO (ONU in French.). The school was established by General Georges Frederic Doriot and by Olivier Giscard d'Estaing, brother of the future French president Valery Giscard d'Estaing. Doriot was born in Paris in 1899, immigrated to the United States, rose to the rank of brigadier general in World War II, and eventually became known as the "Father of Venture Capitalism." The seed capital for INSEAD came from the Chamber of Industry and Trade in Paris. Harvard was the model for INSEAD, so one could say that INSEAD is an offshoot of Harvard Business School, similar to IESE in Barcelona, which was founded a year later than INSEAD.

The colleagues at INSEAD became aware of me through my publications and speeches in the United States and through European conferences. In 1980, I received an invitation to teach there on a part-time basis. Seeing a means to broaden my spectrum of experience, I did not want to let this opportunity slip away. Most of my teaching work was in executive programs. I also taught my specialty, price management, in the MBA program. Often I would fly in the morning to Orly, which is not far from Fontainebleau, and then return home in the evening. During the semester breaks, I would stay there for one or two weeks to teach straight through in the executive programs. I also got to know the leadership of the institute and the marketing group closely. The dean at that time was Heinz Thanheiser, who had grown up in

Vienna and had earned his doctorate at Harvard. He was an expert in business policy, an area which was increasingly interesting for me beyond the narrower confines of marketing. I would often teach together with Professor Reinhard Angelmar, who like Thanheiser came from Austria but had earned his Ph.D. from Northwestern.

Back then, Jean-Claude Larréché developed the famous marketing simulation "Markstrat," which I also used frequently in my own classes. The simulation was a valuable educational tool because it showed the effects of marketing decisions in a quasi-real market while also simulating what the competition would do. I considered this second aspect to be the more important one because the students learned that there is no such thing as an optimal decision in absolute terms. The answer to real-world business problems always depends on the competition.

INSEAD opened up an international network for me, one which would be hard to find anywhere else. Even in Germany, I got many interesting contacts through the German INSEAD organization. At that time, INSEAD also had its first feelers extended to Asia. Under the direction of Henri-Claude de Bettignies, the Euro-Asia-Center was established in 1980. He served as its general director for the next eight years. In this context I was invited, together with Professor Hellmut Schütte, to conduct executive seminars in Asia. From Jakarta, we had the opportunity to ride out to a small island that belonged to the former CEO of Hoechst Indonesia. The island had no running water, and the power generator ran for only a few hours per day. On the way back, I got seasick. That was my first adventure in Asia, but many more would follow, as the next chapter reveals. Schütte would later become dean of the China Europe International Business School (CEIBS) in Shanghai. I took advantage of another seminar in Kuala Lumpur to take a side trip with my family. We rode a nostalgic train from Kuala Lumpur to Singapore and spent a wonderful weekend there.

In contrast to its American "mother" Harvard, Fontainebleau aspired to be very international from the start. MBA students were required to speak English, French, and German, a standard they eventually had to abandon with the increased influx of Asian students. Nonetheless, to this day INSEAD lays claim to being the most global business school, with more than 250 professors and with locations in Singapore and Abu Dhabi. My collaborations at INSEAD offered me even greater access to the international business world than my stay at MIT did. I got to know many top managers from European and Asian countries.

During my stays, I learned to appreciate the vast forest of Fontainebleau, which covers almost 100 square miles. Fontainebleau itself is a small city with only 16,000 residents, but spread over a large area. The forest is famous. Giuseppe Verdi set his opera *Don Carlos* there. I jogged endlessly along its paths, where one must be careful to avoid getting lost. Occasionally, I ran across bizarre stones whose shapes resembled animals such as elephants, frogs, or crocodiles. The forest is also supposedly home to 3000 types of mushrooms.

After I was named academic director of the German Management Institute[13] in April 1985, I ended my collaboration with INSEAD because the institutions were competitors in the market for executive education. It would have been difficult for me to lead the USW and teach at INSEAD at the same time.

I have only been back to Fontainebleau twice, after 10 and after 30 years, and each visit left very different impressions. I was astonished to see how many of my colleagues had aged. It makes a big difference whether someone sees an individual or a whole group again after a long period. But in reality, I looked at myself in the mirror and noticed clearly that time had not stood still for me either. When I came back again after 30 years we were all more mature, more laid back, less stressed, and more self-confident. We did not have to prove ourselves anymore. The aggressiveness we once displayed had mellowed. This second visit was a nice encounter with the past.

Cape of Good Hope

The winters in Germany are not as harsh as in New England, but still quite unpleasant. Thus, it is a good idea to follow the migrating birds on their way south. I accepted invitations to teach marketing courses at the University of Cape Town. In this way, I could repeatedly escape the German winters for a few weeks. Overall, I have fond memories of my time in Cape Town, where I stayed in the cozy Vineyard Hotel. I recall the exceptional friendliness of the staff there. When I returned a year later, the doorman greeted me graciously by saying "It's a comeback." The team at the reception desk was just as cordial. No one is immune to the effects of that kind of flattering attention, regardless of whether it is organized or genuinely personal. My favorite place there was the wonderful garden, which resembled a park. It was peaceful to retreat there after work, enjoy a delicious orange juice, and look out onto Table Mountain.

---

[13] The institute was called USW at that time. Today, it is the European School of Management and Technology (ESMT).

South Africa is a marvelous country, rich in many aspects, but also with serious problems. When one looks at South Africa, one sees primarily the country's sunny side: the wealth, the cleanliness, the green spaces, the fit people, the beautiful landscape, and the wildlife reserves. But we also experienced the other side. Cecilia and I visited a friend in Durban who took us to areas that left us stunned and shocked. I also had mixed feelings as the business school moved from the quiet Rondebosch neighborhood in the southern part of Cape Town to a former prison on the northern side of the Table Mountain. I could never escape the aura of the building and the thoughts about what might have happened in those cells.

Business School Networks

At a board meeting of an insurance group, someone once said "every industry sector is like a village." This phenomenon equally applies to the global business school scene. Over the years, I have met many professors from a wide range of countries. In Europe, the European Institute for Advanced Studies in Management (EIASM) in Brussels opened the first doors for me. That is also where the European Academy for Advanced Research in Marketing (EAARM) was spawned. I always found that name somewhat clumsy, and when I took over as its president in 1984, I pushed to rename it the European Marketing Academy (EMAC), the name it holds to this day. The EMAC now has more than 1000 members from 57 countries.

The business school networks provided me with ample opportunities to speak at international academic and business conferences. These conferences, in turn, gave me the opportunity to meet well-known speakers and observe their speaking styles firsthand. On such occasions, I have met Tom Peters (see photo) and Robert Waterman, the authors of the blockbuster best seller *In Search of Excellence* (Peters and Waterman Jr 1982), Others included Michael Porter, whom I already knew from Harvard (see photo); Kenichi Ohmae, whose book *Triad Power* (Ohmae 1985) made him famous; C.K. Prahalad and Gary Hamel, who originated the concept of core competencies; Michael Hammer, the conceptual father of reengineering; Clayton Christensen, the inventor of the "innovator's dilemma"; and many other gurus.

Hermann Simon with Tom Peters, Berlin 1995

Hermann Simon with Michael Porter, Frankfurt 1993

In 1992, I became a visiting professor at the London Business School (LBS) and taught there on a part-time basis until 2002. In a talk about the productivity of German companies, I made a provocative statement about Germans: "When we work, we work." Professor Patrick Barwise, a colleague at LBS, responded with mock disdain by saying "you Germans are practicing unfair competition. You are actually working during working hours."[14]

I have turned down several offers at prominent business schools in Europe and the United States, as professor or in two cases as dean. I did not want to live and work abroad permanently. One reason is that I did not believe I would be able to establish the same kind of personal networks in a foreign country as I could within Germany.

Many of these early contacts have turned into long-term cooperations. In 1986, Dr. Danica Purg from Slovenia visited me. She had done her dissertation at the Sorbonne in Paris and presented me with a plan that at the time seemed like pure fantasy: to establish a business school within the sphere of Soviet influence. And I do not mean in the "previous sphere of influence." By the late 1980s, Yugoslavia—and especially the constituent state Slovenia— had begun to pull away from the grip of the Soviets. Tito, who was responsible for forcing parts of the western Balkans together into Yugoslavia, had died in 1980, and there were signs that the country could in fact disintegrate. In 1991, Slovenia became the first state of Yugoslavia to declare its independence. But in 1986, there was no way to make a confident forecast about the future developments in Yugoslavia, other Soviet satellites, or the Soviet Union itself.

This young woman's plan to launch a business school under such circumstances struck me as extremely ambitious and visionary. But Dr. Purg had so much determination that I felt compelled to take her seriously. In our initial conversation as well as follow-up ones, I gladly shared with her my experience from business schools I was familiar with.

Despite all the gale-force headwinds she faced, Professor Purg made her vision a reality. The International Executive Development Center (IEDC) became the first business school in Central and Eastern Europe. Today, it ranks among the leading schools in the region, which extends from Germany's eastern border to the Ural Mountains. Professor Purg also expanded her own sphere of influence far beyond the small country of Slovenia. She founded the Central and East European Management Development Association (CEEMAN) and has become a well-known figure in the global business school scene. I joined the international advisory board of the IEDC, which allowed me to visit Slovenia on a regular basis, including Bled, a resort town that is an absolute pearl. The IEDC awarded me an honorary doctorate in 2009.

---

[14] *Frankfurter Allgemeine Magazin*, April 23, 1993, p. 7.

I can also look back on a long cooperation with Kozminski University in Warsaw. Its founder, Professor Andrzej Kozminski, taught at Warsaw University. He was always a free thinker who suffered greatly under the Communist regime. When the Warsaw Pact collapsed, he seized the new-found freedom with gusto. In 1993, he founded a private university and named it after his late father, Leon Kozminski. Professor Kozminski and I were introduced through Professor Jerzy Dietl, who has been a friend of mine since the early 1980s. The grandson of Professor Dietl, Dr. Marek Dietl, later managed the Warsaw office of Simon-Kucher and in 2017 became the CEO of the Warsaw Stock Exchange. This shows how relationships can deepen over time and across generations. Joining the international advisory board of Kozminski University allowed me to lend them my experience. Professor Kozminski and I became friends, and the university he founded awarded me an honorary doctorate in 2012.

I have visited Warsaw more than any other city in Central Europe. Is the city's role in my parents' history a factor in that? I have never attempted to find the places where they worked. The odds are slim that I will detect anything remaining from their time there because the Germans completely destroyed Warsaw during the uprising in August 1944. Stalin's troops watched from the opposite shore of the Vistula River … and did nothing.

References

Frank M. Bass, "Comments on 'A New Product Growth Model for Consumer Durables The Bass Model'," *Management Science* 50 (12_supplement)/2004, pp. 1833–1840.

Dirck Burckhardt, "Das Genie der Masse," *Frankfurter Allgemeine Zeitung*, June 12, 2017, p. 13.

Robert D. Buzzell and Bradley T. Gale, *The PIMS Principles: Linking Strategy to Performance*, New York: Free Press 1987.

Alfred Chandler, *Strategy and Structure: Chapters in the History of the American Industrial Enterprise*, Cambridge, MA: MIT Press 1969.

Robert J. Dolan and Hermann Simon, *Power Pricing—How Managing Price Transforms the Bottom Line*, New York: Free Press 1996

John D.C. Little, "A Proof for the Queuing Formula: $L = \lambda W$," *Operations Research*. 9 (3)/1961, pp. 383–387.

John D. C. Little, "Entscheidungsunterstützung für Marketingmanager," *Zeitschrift für Betriebswirtschaft*, 49. Jg., Heft 11/1979, pp. 982–1007.

Robert Locke, "Postwar Management Education Reconsidered," in: Lars Engwall and Vera Zamagni, *Management Education in Historical Perspective*, Manchester: Manchester University Press, 1999, p. 149.

Vijay Mahajan, *Africa Rising: How 900 Million African Consumers Offer More Than You Think*, Upper Saddle River, NJ: Pearson Prentice Hall 2008.

Duff McDonald, *The Golden Passport, Harvard Business School, The Limits of Capitalism, and the Moral Failure of the MBA Elite*, New York: Harper Business 2017.

Ken-Ichi Ohmae, *Triad Power: The Coming Shape of Global Competition*, New York: The Free Press 1985.

Shmuel S. Oren, Stephen A. Smith and Robert B. Wilson, "Nonlinear Pricing in Markets with Interdependent Demand," *Marketing Science* 1(3)/1982, pp. 287–313.

Thomas J. Peters and Robert H. Waterman, Jr., *In Search of Excellence: Lessons from America's Best-Run Companies*, New York: Harper & Row 1982.

Michael Porter, *Competitive Strategy*, New York: Free Press 1980.

Michael Porter, *Competitive Advantage*, New York: Free Press 1985.

Michael Porter, *The Competitive Advantage of Nations*, New York: Free Press 1990.

C.K. Prahalad, *The Fortune at the Bottom of the Pyramid*, Upper Saddle River, NJ: Wharton School Publishing, 2004.

Julia Shaw, *The Memory Illusion: Remembering, Forgetting, and the Science of False Memory*, London: Random House Books, 2016.

Hermann Simon, "An Analytical Investigation of Kotler's Competitive Simulation Model," *Management Science* 24 (October 1978), pp. 1462–1473.

Hermann Simon, *Confessions of the Pricing Man—How Price Affects Everything*, New York: Springer 2015.

Hermann Simon and Martin Fassnacht, *Price Management—Strategy, Analysis, Decision, Implementation*, NewYork: Springer Nature 2019.

Hermann Simon and Karl-Heinz Sebastian, "Diffusion and Advertising: The German Telephone Campaign" *Management Science* 33 (April 1987), pp. 451–466.

Georg Tacke, *Nichtlineare Preisbildung: Theorie, Messung und Anwendung*, Wiesbaden: Gabler, 1989.

Ben Wattenberg, "Malthus, Watch Out," *The Wall Street Journal*, February 12, 1998.

James P. Womack, Daniel T. Jones and Daniel Roos, *The Machine That Changed the World : The Story of Lean Production*, New York: Free Press 1990.

7

Eastern Journeys: From Japan to the Edge of the World

Eastbound

Germany was a frontier state for the first 40 years of my life. Until 1989, our world effectively ended at the "Iron Curtain," the heavily fortified and guarded border between West and East Germany. That border cut right through my country, with West Berlin encircled by the Communist state of East Germany. Officially known as the German Democratic Republic, East Germany was anything but democratic. We did not know how people lived on the other side of the Berlin Wall or the Iron Curtain. We had no contacts, even in science and academia. Thus, it was natural that our interests and our journeys turned to the West, as I described in the preceding chapter.

But I remained curious. I wanted to know what was going on further east. I had been to Asia on a couple of short stints to teach executives in cities such as Jakarta, Kuala Lumpur, Singapore, and Mumbai. But the country that interested me the most—in part because of its spectacular economic rise—was Japan.

Strange Events

One of the most pleasant sides of life as a university professor were the sabbaticals, which one receives every three or four years. Professors are relieved of their teaching obligations and can devote themselves completely to research. I always spent these semesters abroad. In the spring of 1983, I received an invitation from Keio University in Tokyo that fit perfectly into my plans. I was to serve as visiting professor and lecture on marketing strategy during their winter semester.

The preparations were extremely hectic. Just a week before our departure, we had moved into our newly built house. Cecilia needed to manage the move more or less on her own. I did not return until the day before we would be embarking on a six-month trip and still needed to pack. After Japan, we would make a brief stop in Papua New Guinea, and then move on seamlessly to Stanford, where I would begin a three-month stay as a visiting professor. So far, so good. A half-year journey with two children aged eight and three requires some logistical effort. We ended up with seven suitcases.

At the height of the Cold War, flying to Japan from Germany would have required a time-intensive detour via Anchorage, Alaska. But in 1983, it had recently become possible to fly to Japan over the airspace of the Soviet Union. Instead of stopping in Anchorage, we would have a layover at the Sheremetyevo Airport in Moscow. On the plane, we met the businessman Torsten Griess-Nega, whom I knew well from INSEAD in Fontainebleau. He was on route to his dental factory in the Philippines. He cheered up our kids at the Moscow Airport by buying each of them two of the famous Russian Matryoschka dolls.

The long flight was torture for Cecilia. We sat in the first row behind the smoking section. The Japanese passengers directly in front of us smoked almost non-stop, and Cecilia suffered one coughing spasm after the next. When we finally landed in Tokyo, Professor Kazuyoshi Hotta and his family picked us up at the airport. He acted as our host during my stay at Keio University. The very friendly and heartfelt welcome launched a friendship that has endured over the decades.

We were quickly confronted with Japanese customs and behavior. The apartment that the university made available to us was close to the central Mita Campus right in the heart of Tokyo. My office was only a few hundred yards away. The apartment was typical of Japan. It had only around 400 square feet, and I had to duck to get my 6-foot-5 frame through the door. The bathroom had maybe 20 square feet. The "bedroom" comprised two closets. We slept on futons, the Japanese sleeping mats. This new, unaccustomed environment was exactly what I was looking for: new, non-western experiences.

An Emergency and a Subway Line

The next morning, however, we woke up to an unpleasant surprise that led to some non-western experiences none of us had anticipated. Cecilia's cough had worsened, and she complained of pain in her lungs. Professor Hotta took us to the emergency room on the Mita Campus, and the doctor there referred Cecilia immediately to the Keio University Clinic. We quickly packed up a few essentials and headed to the hospital, a trip that took over an hour by taxi. The doctors and nurses were extremely friendly and attentive, but the language barrier made communication very difficult. What we did understand, though, was that Cecilia had to stay in the hospital.

Completely unplanned and unexpected, I stood in the middle of Tokyo on a Monday morning with our kids. What to do?

The first thing I did was take the kids on the Yamanote Line back to Mita. This "green line" forms a large ring around Tokyo. The trains run every minute. During the next two weeks, we came to know the Yamanote Line much better than we would have liked. Every afternoon, I rode with the kids to see Cecilia in the hospital. I remember the names of the stations—Ebisu, Gotanda, Shinagawa, and Tamachi—to this day. When I come back to Tokyo and have some time, I ride the same stretch again and let my memories come back.

Jeannine was supposed to attend the German school in Omori.[1] To get there, she needed to go through an old part of the city to the Tamachi station. From there she would take a train on the Yamanote Line to the next station, Shinagawa. In that enormous train station, she needed to switch to another line and ride two more stops to her final destination of Omori. From there, it was only a short walk to the German school. That first week, while Cecilia was still in the hospital, I accompanied Jeannine twice on her way to school, but after that she had to make the way on her own. She was only eight!

That all worked out in the first few days, but one day at 9 a.m. she showed up back at our apartment. She had taken the wrong exit at Omori and did not find her way to the school. This could have turned into a nightmare, but luckily she figured out how to get back home. On the next day, I accompanied her again, and from then on the eight-year-old found her way to school every day without a hitch.

But what should I do with Patrick? The university proved very helpful. They found a Japanese student who spoke German. She was available right away to babysit Patrick and she turned out to be an invaluable help in this difficult situation.

After two weeks in the hospital, Cecilia returned home. That was a day to celebrate, for the kids just as much as for me. Her support freed me up to focus fully on work again. My plan for the research semester was to investigate the market entry problems of German companies in Japan. Because I cannot

---

[1] The German School is now in Yokohama.

speak Japanese, never mind read it, I had to rely on talks with managers, entrepreneurs, and academics as my primary research sources.

I met with all the important German firms in the Greater Tokyo area. In general, I was able to get a meeting with the CEO. I also spoke with top managers from other European countries and from the United States and learned that their problems and strategies for market entry turned out to be similar to those of the German firms.

Academics and Go-Betweens

At the same time, I used the opportunity to make contact with Japanese academics and universities. Especially instructive and enjoyable were the contacts with Sophia University, which is run by the Jesuits. At the time their faculty included Professor Robert Ballon, a Belgian considered to be an expert on internationalization. At Hitotsubashi University, I first met Professor Hirotaka Takeuchi. He had returned to Japan after 13 years in the United States and accepted a professorship at that renowned university. The readjustment to the Japanese culture did not come easy to him, but he went on to have an illustrious career over the next decades. His accomplishments included building up the business school at Hitotsubashi. In contrast to its mother institution, the business school lies in central Tokyo. The entire time he also worked closely with Michael Porter, and after his retirement in Tokyo he returned to Harvard where I encountered him again, as I described in the previous chapter. I always had the impression that his soul had remained stuck in the United States after his 13 years there. He maintains a house on Cape Cod, where he always spends his vacations.

I also got to know Professor Takaho Ueda of Gakushuin University, the school where the children of Japan's imperial family traditionally study. Professor Ueda and I developed a long-standing friendship. We still occasionally put on conferences together, and he has visited me in Germany several times.

At Keio University, I conducted a lecture series on marketing strategy. In this context, I worked closely with Professor Shoji Murata, who had become famous in Japan for his translation of Philip Kotler's marketing textbook. One could quickly earn status in Japan by translating the works of well-known American authors. That recalled the classical times of the nineteenth century, when German writers, philosophers, and scientists—who had already enjoyed strong reputations of their own—enhanced them by translating the works of foreign-language authors. Today, one could hardly score any points with such tasks.

Professor Murata was also known for another area of expertise. In Japan, as in Asia generally, many marriages are arranged. In such arrangements, the so-called go-between often plays a critical role. These intermediaries—who know many young people—introduce a young man and a young woman to each other when they believe the two are a good match. Shoji Murata was reputed to be a very successful go-between. Years later, I was in Japan as the guest of a Japanese medical technology entrepreneur. He had only one daughter, who was 27 years old and not in a relationship. He was very worried about succession. Finally, he turned to Professor Murata with the request to find his daughter a husband who would be able to take over control of his company. Years later, I learned that Murata's intervention had been successful. The entrepreneur's son-in-law had become a manager in the company. Professor Murata is said to have arranged over 200 marriages. He passed away in 2015.

The invitation to the private home of a businessperson is a small sensation and rarely occurs in Japan. Perhaps the invitation of the entrepreneur with the unmarried daughter came as a response to our having asked him to visit us at our house on the Rhine. In any event, it was an unforgettable experience for Cecilia and me. The entrepreneur's home is in the center of Tokyo, adjacent to a small park. For our first visit, we arrived a bit early and strolled around the park in the mild October evening air of Tokyo. Amidst the hubbub of that huge city, the park gave off a sense of calm that set us into a meditative state. The house itself had a Japanese garden straight out of a fairy tale. After supper, we sat out there. During our conversation, there were frequent pauses, not because we had nothing more to say, but because we were so enraptured by the tranquil atmosphere of the garden.

I had the opportunity to hold speeches at prominent universities such as Tokyo, Waseda, Hitotsubashi, Gakushuin, and Chuo. I also took trips to the Kansai Region, Osaka, and Kobe which allowed me to meet with professors who had visited us in Bonn or taken part in conferences or seminars in Germany. One highlight was traveling with the Japanese high-speed train Shinkansen, which had been in operation since Tokyo hosted the Olympic Games in 1964. Germany did not launch its own high-speed rail service (ICE) until 1991. In Tokyo, I spent my first night in a Japanese hotel, but it was only half-Japanese, not a fully traditional Ryokan. We would not enjoy the full Ryokan experience—something very unusual and almost alien for us—until years later in Nakutsugawa in central Japan.

What lessons and insights can I draw from the strange encounters in Japan? To prepare for my stay, I had read numerous books about the country and its culture. But the reality proved to be very different. Reading alone does not enable one to get a grasp of a country and its culture, never mind understand them. The most important insight I gained from my time in Japan was that people can organize a successful, smoothly operating society along completely different principles than the ones we are accustomed to in the West. I could not have come to that same realization in the United States or in other western countries because the predominant systems and principles are too similar to those of Germany.

No "no"

Other insights include the distinct non-binding nature of Japanese communication. Their conversations and speeches—whether written or verbal—rarely contain concrete statements. The Japanese do not commit or affirm. That holds particularly true for statements that would disagree with or contradict the view of others. In short, the Japanese do not say "no."

In subsequent years, I would sometimes receive no response to a request or a question. Not answering is an indirect Japanese method of saying "no." On several occasions, I have adopted that tactic myself, and I can say it works. But if someone happens to follow up, there is no way to avoid saying "no" directly.

In consulting, I see the tendency to avoid clear statements as a problem. But I have to admit that this opinion reflects my western perspective. Personally, I favor making firm statements, which could be precisely the wrong thing for Japanese ears. The consultants in our Tokyo office, who are all Japanese, likely know better than I how to communicate with their clients. Sometimes, they find my statements and lectures rather harsh.

What impressed me in Japan is how perfectly the systems work. The most obvious and easy-to-explain example is the railroad. All trains—from the long-distance Shinkansen to the local Yamanote Line—depart on the exact minute. They stop with remarkable precision at the corresponding marks along the train platforms. Boarding and exiting the trains, forming lines, and using the stairs in the enormous train stations is precisely regulated—and more importantly—followed obediently by everyone. In China, for example, in the Shanghai metro, one witnesses almost the exact opposite of that behavior.

The strict Japanese rules inherently run counter to the ability of a society to change and to innovate. I am often asked what has changed since my first visit to Japan almost 40 years ago, and invariably my answer is "nothing." This is not entirely true, of course, but it describes my general impression. The Yamanote Line looks exactly as it did in 1983. When I walk through the narrow alleys of the Mita District, with its endless number of overlapping buildings, restaurants, small shops, and Pachinko arcades, I feel taken back to the winter of 1983. Nowadays, Tokyo makes me feel as if the world and time have stood still.

After Cecilia was well again, we explored Tokyo and the surrounding area in our free time. We rode out to the huge Buddha statue in Kamakura, and we visited the vacation resort Nikko, where monkeys climb around the cliffs of a picturesque waterfall. And of course we did not miss the Ginza, the world's most expensive shopping mile, even though at that time there was hardly anything there that we could afford.

Stranded in Hong Kong

The months in Tokyo flew by, and it was soon time for the next phase of our six-month odyssey. Our plan was to board a US airline during its stopover in Tokyo on its way to Manila, where we would switch to an Air Niugini flight to Port Moresby, the capital of Papua New Guinea. But the arrival of the US flight was delayed by several hours, and we now faced the prospect of missing our connecting flight to Papua New Guinea. The problem was that the flight from Manila to Port Moresby departed only once a week! Had we reached Manila, we would have been stuck there for seven days. What was true then remains true today: the closer you get to the far edges of the world, the sparser the flight connections are.

Instead, the airline diverted us to Hong Kong, where we would catch a flight to Papua New Guinea three days later. A pleasant surprise was that the airline covered the hotel costs in Hong Kong for the three days of layover. So in the end, the cherry on top of our long, adventurous trip was a free stay in Hong Kong.

Naturally, we took full advantage of those three days to discover this amazing city, which at that time was still a British colony. Hong Kong impressed us in many ways: the hilly landscape, the skyscrapers, and last but not least the traditional market in the harbor. Back then "old" and "new" Hong Kong were wedged tightly together. And there was the unmistakable capitalist orientation. On city tours, the objective did not seem to be to show off Hong Kong's beautiful sites and the spectacular views of the hills. Instead, the guides constantly pointed out the homes or estates of rags-to-riches millionaires (there was no talk of billionaires back then) who had begun their careers as dishwashers and worked their way up to enormous wealth. The admiration for such success stories permeated the entire society. Perhaps it remains so today, despite the takeover of Hong Kong by China in 1997. China has not completely integrated the former British colony, but still allwos for a small measure of independence.

But at some point, the "Simon Caravan" needed to move on again. I was eager to fly with Cathay Pacific, which I was familiar with and which had a good reputation. It belonged to the Swire Group, whose owner I had met at INSEAD. In the middle of the night, we departed for the airport with our two kids and the seven suitcases. We were excited to find out what awaited us in Papua New Guinea, a real frontier country.

To the Edge of the World

In the light of dawn, the Boeing 747 touched down in Port Moresby. The country of Papua New Guinea had gained its independence from Australia only a few years earlier. Waiting for us was Brother Hermann, who operated the station of the Steyler Missionaries in Port Moresby. We knew him from his visit to Germany, so we immediately felt at home. We stayed in Port Moresby for one night and had our first encounter with termites.

On the next morning, we boarded a small plane that took us to Mount Hagen in the highlands. The other passengers were indigenous people who worked in Port Moresby and were traveling home for Christmas. They were loaded down with luggage and gifts. Some even had chickens in cages.

In Mount Hagen, my uncle John Nilles and a driver picked us up in a Toyota SUV. We had last seen John during his stay in Germany in 1976, some seven years earlier. He had aged somewhat, but was still very vigorous for a 78-year-old. He wore a wide-brimmed hat and rugged outdoor clothes. He looked more like a frontier man than a Catholic priest. He had the leathery skin of someone who has spent decades exposed to the subtropical sun. The Toyota seemed like a very solid vehicle. The driver was a seminary student in Port Moresby who was spending his Christmas vacation at home. We would end up having quite an adventure with him.

This is how my kids recounted the drive from Mount Hagen to Mingende at my 60th birthday party:

"We were picked up in a Jeep, which let us know a few kilometers later—with an enormous bang—that it suddenly had a flat tire. We thought we were completely alone in the middle of nowhere until we found ourselves surrounded by naked indigenous people with dog-tooth necklaces. They all looked on as we got the tire changed. Several hours later we finally reached the mission, totally exhausted and practically eaten alive by fleas and mosquitos."

To be honest, it was not that bad. But who knows how the eight-year-old Jeannine and three-year-old Patrick internalized that event back then. We must have seemed very exotic to the Papuas, who rarely encounter foreigners and may have stared at the kids. In any event, we arrived unharmed in Mingende, the mission station where John served as pastor until his semi-retirement, and where he still lived.

Uncle John

My uncle was a member of the missionary order Societas Verbi Divini (SVD), which is known colloquially as the Steyler Missionaries. That name is derived from the Dutch village Steyl, where the order was founded in 1875 by Arnold Janssen. Today, the headquarters of the order is outside Bonn in the city of St. Augustin. At the time of our visit, Uncle John had lived for over 50 years in Papua New Guinea.

What image does the phrase "mission station" conjure up? The center of the station is a church for several hundred people. In terms of style and materials, though, the church was very minimalist. Parts of the walls consisted of corrugated metal. This appearance did not dent the pride of both the missionaries and the Papuas that they had the largest church for miles around.

The mission station also included a large farm with a herd of cattle, businesses, and a workshop to maintain and repair tools and machinery. It also included a hospital with a maternity ward run by Sister Mirjam Morbach, who came from our home region in Germany. The technical leader of the station was Brother Theo, whom we also knew from a visit to Germany.

The station is the seat of the bishop of the Chimbu District. Bishop Kurz was a quiet, friendly man of Polish descent. He was later succeeded by a Dutchman named Henk Termassen. In this faraway part of the world, we had found a European enclave where we lacked nothing and where we needed to make a much smaller adjustment than in Japan. The station operated a guest house where we lodged comfortably. Only one thing disrupted that comfort. The climate and the remote, largely unspoiled wilderness surrounding the station made it impossible to protect ourselves adequately from the relentless onslaught of insects and pests. An occasional rat crossed our paths, and biting, blood-sucking bugs left their marks on our skin.

But these discomforts pale in comparison to the deep and lasting impressions the time in the highlands of Papua New Guinea left on us. Only Patrick, who was just three years old, has no recollection of the wonderful experiences there. He was too young. But I recall that he spent many happy days in the freedom of nature after months in the narrow confines of Tokyo. He became friends with a local boy of the same age named Henry.

The Big Pig Roast

It was a nice coincidence that we visited the Chimbu District during the Christmas season. They were holding a large pig roast, a tradition that takes place only every five years. Hundreds of locals from the whole region come to one location, many in war paint or colorful costumes. They dig holes and light fires to roast the pigs. The best pieces of meat are wrapped in banana leaves and laid in the ashes. A tempting, mouth-watering scent wafted over the plaza, as did a palpable mood of excitement. The people gathered could hardly wait to enjoy the roasted pork, if nothing else than because their day-to-day diet was short on protein. They lived mostly from fruits and vegetables that they grew in their own gardens and could harvest year round. Preserving or storing food was not necessary and therefore not practiced.

But the climate precludes the preservation of meat. When an animal is slaughtered, the meat must be consumed as quickly as possible. At the time of our visit, the typical families did not have refrigerators and freezers, similar to the situation 30 years earlier in my home village. Many of the more far-flung settlements in the area did not even have electricity. We never saw any wild animals because the local population had long ago hunted the forests bare. Even birds, an additional protein source, were a rare sight.

After several hours, the pork was cooked and ready to eat. Large portions were distributed to the now impatient crowd, which had a voracious appetite and showed no signs of being full. Some ate so much meat that they experienced a protein shock and needed medical attention or were admitted to the station's hospital. They also offered the roasted pork to us, and it was not easy to decline their offer. But it would have been extremely foolish for us to eat the meat that evening. The pork had not been examined for trichinosis or similar risks. There were no meat inspectors as we know them from home.

The Most Remote Village

From Mingende we undertook trips in the Toyota through the Chimbu province. Chimbu—also written as Simbu—is one of the 21 provinces of Papua New Guinea with a population of around 250,000, spread over a very large area. The provincial capital is Kundiawa, with 8000 residents. So it is more of a capital village than a capital city although it does have an airstrip where small planes land at an adventurously steep angle. Kundiawa is also home to businesses, bars, and a basic hotel—everything that residents from the surrounding area might need. The province is named after the Chimbu River, whose deep valley ends in Kundiawa. That is where we began our journey to Denglagu together with my uncle and his driver. There are certainly several places in the world that can claim the description "extremely remote" and Denglagu is no doubt one of them.

The drive was an adventure. An unpaved road carved its way along the steep cliffs of the Chimbu Valley. In some places, landslides reduced the road's width so much that it could barely accommodate one vehicle. The other issue is that we did not have complete trust in our driver. Although he was a seminary student in Port Moresby, he still retained one habit of his people. He regularly chewed betel nuts (also known as areca nuts), which are reputed to have a light numbing or narcotic effect. That did not bother John. He was used to this. But I kept a constant close eye on our chauffeur. At one point, I had seen enough and took the nuts away from him.

Along the way, we came to a cross erected in memory of an earlier missionary who had been murdered by the local people in 1934. The early missionaries evoked a sharp reaction in the indigenous population, who probably thought of them as hostile aliens from another planet. As they moved further and further into unchartered areas, the missionaries often carried rifles. Prior to the missionary's murder, a priest had shot and killed two pigs that belonged to the natives. A Steyler brother was also killed in 1935 by arrows.[2]

After several hours, we finally reached our destination: Denglagu Mission. The mission station, surrounded by several dozen huts, lies at the foot of Mount Wilhelm, which at 14,793 feet is the highest peak in Papua New Guinea. Occasionally mountaineers, seeking to add this peak to their "collection," appear in this isolated region. How John—left to his own devices—was able to build a mission station here in the 1930s was beyond my imagination.

We visited nearby settlements and huts. We were also invited to a traditional wedding. The people gave us a heartfelt welcome and we felt safe. The key to that comfort level was John himself. The tribe had named him an honorary chief. Without the umbrella of his presence, we would never have been able to get that close to the local people.

---

[2] John Nilles, "They went out to sow….," report about the early years of the Steyler Mission in the highlands of Papua New Guinea, Catholic Mission Mingende, 1984.

The "Children" of Papua

Never have I met people who were as open- and warm-hearted as the people of Papua New Guinea. But this emotionalism has a flip side. Traditionally, and even today, there are fights between the tribes that sometimes turn deadly. Many years later in Sydney, in 2010, Dr. Verena Thomas brought us together with a group of students from the University of Goroka, a city not far from the Chimbu district. At dinner at a harbor restaurant, the Papuas described their homeland. One said that he came from a small village, where the outhouse was located at some distance from the huts. It was dangerous for him to go to the toilet alone because at any time, someone from the neighboring enemy tribe could come out of hiding and kill him. So they used a buddy system, with the second person serving as a lookout and ready to sound an alarm.

The hostility between tribes stands in contrast to the deep social cohesion within the tribe itself. That was illustrated by an experience in Port Moresby. We were taking a tour of the city with a local driver who was from the highlands. Suddenly, he stopped the car and cried for joy. He called out "Wantok, Wantok," ran across the street, and wrapped up a man in a big friendly hug. What had happened? "Wantok" is pidgin English for "one talk" or "one language." Wiktionary defines a *wantok* as "a close comrade: a person with whom one has a strong social bond, usually based on shared language." It turned out that the other person came from the driver's village and spoke the same dialect. That is incredibly important in Papua New Guinea because the country has more than 700 dialects. A *wantok* then is someone from one's own village or tribe. The common idiom is the most important identifying trait that forges a bond. This is very similar to my own experience with dialects in the Eifel. The driver was completely stunned to see a *wantok* in the capital city.

The kindheartedness of the people is particularly evident around Christmas. Dozens of natives came to the mission station to offer gifts to John, their honorary chief. He was overwhelmed with fruits and vegetables from their gardens. They would touch him and hug him, refusing to let go. He was a kind of saint to them.

The Missionaries

The visit of a European family with two young children was an unusual event not only for the native people, but also for the missionaries. We stayed in the guest house, but ate our meals together with the bishop, the priests, and the brothers in a special dining room. The cooking was European, and lunch always consisted of three courses.

Our visit was a welcome change for the missionaries, but the encounter with a normal family caused some awkwardness. The priests and brothers were celibate. They had a good but modest life with everything they needed. But sharing their lives and sharing meals for a few days with a family with a young mother and two small children seemed to throw some of the missionaries off balance. Uncle John spoke openly with us about the topic. Celibacy, and especially childlessness, were a major sacrifice for him. Among ourselves we would sometimes wonder—more jokingly than seriously—whether there were a few little Johns in Papua New Guinea. When one thinks about all those lonely years in a remote location such as the Denglagu Mission, that would not be surprising, but to this day there is no proof.

Have the missionaries succeeded in permanently converting the indigenous people to Christianity and to "civilized" behavior in a Western sense? The question is justified. In the twenty-first century, a few activists among the indigenous peoples have developed a critical, if not hostile, stance toward the church. They have challenged how the church and the missionary orders ended up in their homelands in the first place. In the early years, the missionaries had used mussels, a form of currency in the native culture, as a means to buy land from them. Now there were demands for the missions either to pay an appropriate price for the land or to give it back.

At the time, Dr. Verena Thomas was producing a film on the life of John, who was her great uncle. The film entitled "Papa of the Chimbu" was scheduled for its premiere in Mingende, and we planned to travel there with the whole family.[3] But Bishop Termassen warned us urgently not to attend. He could not rule out that radicals might use the occasion for extortion attempts, and there was no way to prevent kidnapping or hostage taking. It was a difficult decision, but we did not make the trip.

In 2019 Dr. Joseph Sakite, who had been in Mingende since 1993 and had become the pastor, visited us in Germany. When I mentioned the extortion risk, he said that to his knowledge it was non-existent. Who knows what Bishop Termassen's motive was to keep us from returning to Mingende? Since our first trip to Papua New Guinea, none of us has returned there personally although teams from Simon-Kucher have done projects for banks there.

Papua New Guinea is becoming less and less safe, and its crime rate is among the highest in the world. On the list of the world's most unsafe cities, Port Moresby ranks number seven. To put that into context, one need only look at the other names on the list: Mogadishu, Grozny, Caracas, and Baghdad.

---

[3] Verena Thomas, Papa der Chimbu (Papa Bilong Chimbu), documentary, 54 minutes, 2008. The film was shown on German TV and has received numerous international awards.

Some rural areas are reverting back to pre-colonial times. But not everyone is scared off by these circumstances. Dr. Thomas has often returned to the adopted country of her great uncle and taught for several years at the University of Goroka. She is now a professor at Queensland University of Technology (QUT) in Brisbane, Australia.

Papa of the Chimbu

My uncle John remained among the missionaries and enjoyed a sort of celebrity status among the indigenous people. He lived in the remote Chimbu province for 54 years. During World War II, he was sent to an internment camp in Australia because he was German. He used that time to earn a degree in ethnology from the University of Sydney. He published articles, books, and dictionaries on the indigenous cultures and languages.

John became one of the founders of Papua New Guinea after the country gained independence from Australia. For several years, he was a member of parliament. His dual role as missionary and politician invited criticism. He sometimes came into conflict with the Vatican because he advocated a more liberal stance on marriage. It was hard for him to reconcile the rigorous laws and teachings from Rome with the reality of the indigenous people. But he also received his share of praise. The local people he cared for recognized him as their honorary chief. Pope John Paul II awarded him the order *Ecclesia et Pontifice* and he received the Order of the British Empire from Queen Elizabeth II.

John summarized his life as follows: "I was privileged to research the culture and customs of the Chimbu people before they were exposed to outside influence. I gave the best part of my life to the Chimbu people, who named me 'Papa of the Chimbu'. I am deeply devoted to them. My life was long and, I believe, fruitful. I thank both God and the people of Papua New Guinea for my religious, priestly, and missionary calling."[4]

At the age of 84, he returned to the St. Wendel Mission House in Germany, where he passed away in 1993. He is buried there. The native people he dedicated his life to, however, would rather have kept him in Papua New Guinea. The chief of the Chimbu was a close friend of my uncle's, and the chief's daughter, Elizabeth Gambugl, said after John's death: "You took him back to your home, and we don't know whether you have slaughtered a pig in his

[4] Kate Rayner, Papa Bilong Chimbu—A Study Guide, educational material to the film of the same name by Verena Thomas, p. 2.

honor. We are disappointed. We don't know if he received a proper burial and whether there was a celebration for him. We know nothing. All we could do was cry."[5]

Two New Year's Eves

As we headed east from the Far East, the calendar flipped from 1983 to 1984 for us not once, but twice. We left the highlands and landed on December 31, 1983 in Port Moresby, where we welcomed the New Year together with the priests and brothers at the mission station. After midnight we said our good-byes, wished them all the best for 1984, and returned to the airport. A few hours later, we boarded an old Air Niugini Boeing 707 and traveled ten hours eastward across the Pacific—and across the international dateline—before landing in Hawaii at around 4 p.m. on December 31. This gave us enough time to slide seamlessly into another New Year's Eve celebration. Along with a few smaller Pacific islands, Hawaii is one of the last places to greet a new year. It was there that we welcomed 1984 once again, 20 hours after our first celebration in Papua New Guinea.

Two New Year's Eves in 1983: Port Moresby, Papua New Guinea, and Waikiki, Hawaii

---

[5] Ibid, p. 7.

The journeys to the East are among the most unforgettable episodes of my life. I cherish those times.

8

University Life … And Beyond

"If we don't see each other in this world …"

Better known than the German city of Bielefeld itself is a saying about it: "If we don't see each other in this world, we will meet in Bielefeld." Starting in 1994, the city also garnered attention, thanks to the so-called Bielefeld Conspiracy, which claimed that the city actually does not exist. Since then, anyone who identified themselves as being from Bielefeld had to reckon with the accusation that "Bielefeld does not exist."

In 2019, the hype surrounding the Bielefeld Conspiracy reached a climax. The city administration offered a prize of 1 million euros for the proof that Bielefeld does not exist. More than 2000 proofs—logical ones and even mathematical ones—were submitted, including 350 from other countries. A committee of scientists from the University of Bielefeld examined the proofs, but none stood the test. On September 17, 2019, a large stone with the inscription "Bielefeld Conspiracy 1994–2019" was buried. The event made it to the international news, e.g. on BBC. Since that day, Bielefeld officially exists again.

What makes this city in the pastoral Eastern Westphalia region of Germany so polarizing? The residents rave about it. But passengers on the ICE bullet trains rarely get off when the train stops in Bielefeld. And when they do, they are often professors on their way to the city's young, large, high-caliber university. The University of Bielefeld ranked 166th in the world in the *Times Higher Education* rankings for 2020, and ranked 20th among young universities.[1]

I had a role in getting this university established, albeit a modest one. A new university obviously starts with no professors, no assistants, and no

---

[1] https://www.timeshighereducation.com/world-university-rankings/bielefeld-university 2020.

students. Where do they come from? To start the new university, the founders created a council staffed by representatives from other universities. I was a delegate to this council due to my role as student council spokesman for the economics department at the University of Bonn.[2] The original concept for Bielefeld envisaged a research institution that would have a smaller teaching load for professors than other universities. The goal was to attract top academics who would thrive in the relative peace and quiet of Eastern Westphalia because they could concentrate on their research without distraction. Professor Wilhelm Krelle, who was also on the faculty council, described the vision this way: "When the University of Bielefeld was conceived, the idea was to establish a relatively small research-driven university that would attract colleagues eager to pursue research in their chosen field."[3]

This ambitious project got off to a promising start. One of the first professors who answered the call was Reinhard Selten, who would later win the Nobel Prize in economics. Professor Carl Christian von Weizsäcker, likewise a renowned economist who had taught at MIT, joined some time later. Top-notch professors such as Niklas Luhmann and Franz-Xaver Kaufmann joined the sociology faculty. But the momentum from these early successes petered out. Several attempts to bring top German professors to Bielefeld—such as Wilhelm Krelle and Horst Albach from the University of Bonn—ultimately failed. Despite the peace and quiet, the location in the countryside was simply not attractive enough to lure a critical mass of top academics to realize the ambitious plan of a research university.

But for me personally, the work with the faculty council was instructive. I gained an entirely new perspective on the challenges a new university faces. I built up my network by connecting with representatives from many other German colleges and universities. Finally, the exciting pioneer spirit in this phase fueled my interest in academic research. At that time, the thought of eventually becoming a professor at Bielefeld myself never crossed my mind. But only a few years later in the winter semester 1979, I started teaching there and earned the title of professor.

---

[2] Other faculty members of Bonn University who were sent to the council at Bielefeld were Horst Albach, Wilhelm Krelle, and Carl-Christian von Weizsäcker. Besides me, there were three other students from different universities in the council.

[3] Letter from Professor Wilhelm Krelle, University of Bonn, on November 30, 1970, to Professor Carl-Christian von Weizsäcker, at the time at Heidelberg University. On July 5, 1971, this and other letters were published by the core economics group at the University of Bonn under the title "Wilhelm jetzt langt's! Geheimer Briefwechsel deckt Machenschaften auf" (English: "Wilhelm, enough! Secret correspondence reveals schemes").

What were the highlights of my time at Bielefeld? That question is not as easy to answer as it seems. Let us look at it this way: the ebbs and flows of life are not even. There are memorable phases that leave a permanent mark—positive or negative—on one's life. Then there are occasional calm phases in life where little of note happens. The fuzzy memories of those times, to the extent they exist at all, seem to blend together. In contrast to my time in the United States—which clearly falls into the first category—I would put my time in Bielefeld in the second category.

My life comprised the typical list of "professor" duties: I taught, conducted research, graded papers, and listened to oral exams. I assigned thesis papers, and guided and advised doctoral students. There were some successes, large and small, such as publishing articles in top journals and magazines, the publication of my first German textbook *Preismanagement* (Simon 1982) (*Price Management* in English) and the book *Goodwill und Marketingstrategie* (Simon 1985) (*Goodwill and Marketing Strategy*). The successes also included the completion of dissertations by Dr. Eckhard Kucher and Dr. Karl-Heinz Sebastian, who would later join me as the founding partners of the firm Simon-Kucher & Partners.

What offset those successes? Far less fun and interesting were the mundane administrative tasks, the endless meetings, and my stint as dean of the economics department. In the German system, the deanship is a rotating task, where you serve as vice-dean for one year and as dean for another year. But these duties are part of the job. I think that a good balance is achieved when 70% of work is fun and only the remaining 30% is considered a burden.

The economics department at Bielefeld had an extremely quantitative focus. This focus had positive and negative consequences. One positive aspect was the self-selection of the students. Students who did not feel they could "handle the math" at Bielefeld did not even apply in the first place. And the ones who had difficulties with the math during their undergraduate years switched to other universities for their graduate studies. There was a strong winnowing process in the first few years. This meant that a smaller number of students actually majored in economics and business, but they were well above average. Due to our high quantitative standards, we produced many strong graduates.

One of the less positive effects was that the curriculum was very heavy on theory and modeling. Production and finance were reduced—too much in my view—to mathematically based planning methods. The focus inherently limited the "real world" element and practice orientation that I had come to appreciate during my time in the United States.

But overall, the quality of the teaching and research was high. We also achieved a measure of international recognition, even though the university was still very young. I was the first marketing professor there and was able to send all of my doctoral students to top US universities for six months. Kucher went to the University of Chicago, after he had already spent a year at the University of Georgia. Sebastian spent time as a research fellow at UCLA, as did Klaus Hilleke. Georg Tacke conducted research at Stanford.

We also frequently welcomed international professors to Bielefeld. They included John D.C. Little, John Hauser, Richard Schmalensee, and Gary Lilien from MIT, Frank Bass from Purdue, and many others. The quality of our graduates is underscored by the successes they later enjoyed in their professional careers. Hartmut Ostrowski became the CEO of the large media conglomerate Bertelsmann. Burkard Schwenker led the largest German consultancy Roland Berger for many years. Leonhard ("Lenny") Fischer became the youngest board member of a large German bank and later CEO of a large Swiss insurance company. Numerous CEOs of Germany's *Mittelstand* and Hidden Champions graduated from Bielefeld. Bielefeld graduates also played vital roles in the start-up and scaling-up of Simon-Kucher & Partners.

One special aspect of the University of Bielefeld was its campus concept. The idea of a "reform university" called for intensive interdisciplinary cooperation. To facilitate and encourage this, all departments were housed in one huge building, one of the biggest in Germany. The common central area was a giant hall with a glass ceiling. It resembled the kind of central market square one would find in a city of the Middle Ages. And this marketplace did indeed offer everything one needed in day-to-day life, including stores, restaurants, a post office, and even a swimming pool. One could directly reach the lecture halls from this market square.

The first floor of this vast building contained the department libraries. Above that rose ten stories of offices and seminar rooms. That is about as efficient as it can get. From my office on the 10th floor, I could quickly reach the lecture halls, the library, a pharmacy, or a restaurant. I could take care of what I needed in a matter of minutes. There was no waste of time in reaching something. Is such an arrangement humane or does it have a negative effect on its occupants? I will leave that determination to history.

I recall one story from the 1980s that seems silly in today's context, but was taken very seriously back then. At that time, there were all kinds of initiatives to improve the role of women, including making academic titles gender-neutral, or creating female equivalents for terms and titles that traditionally took only a male form. One example that ignited a controversy was the idea to expand the formal name of the business degree we had awarded from (loosely translated) "Diploma Businessman" to "Diploma Businesswoman" for female students.[4] Some professors in the economics department were adamantly opposed to the extension. The heated discussion went on for months.

What can one learn from such controversies? One should withhold judgment when a significant change or innovation comes along, especially when that judgment risks being driven by emotions. The reason is that passionate opposition to change usually arises not from rational consideration of the pros and cons of the issue at hand, but rather from a desire to cling to the status quo. This withholding of judgment has served me well because I have avoided knee-jerk resistance to new ideas, but have also escaped the risk of jumping on every new trend. A sound approach is to take time to weigh the arguments in a rational way. Even better is to view the change from a future perspective. What would people think about this change in five or ten years? Will the change inevitably happen anyway? Fighting against ideas which are destined to eventually succeed is a futile waste of time and energy.

So what happened with the businessman vs. businesswoman controversy? It soon became standard practice, so much so that a few years later, one could not imagine that once upon a time the only designation for business graduates was exclusively "Diploma Businessman," even for women. Another 20 years later, the gender-neutral master's degree was introduced Europe-wide.

During my time in Bielefeld, I took several leaves of absence. This included a three-year hiatus to lead the German Management Institute (USW) at Castle Gracht outside Cologne. The university also granted me a year off to accept a visiting professorship at Harvard Business School. Like most other things in life, these leaves of absence were not liked by everybody. A student from Bielefeld made the following statement in a national business weekly. "Why is Professor Simon teaching at Harvard when the Americans don't need any help in marketing? Mr. Simon should return to his chair at Bielefeld. More than a thousand students would welcome that" (Patzelt 1988). From the students' perspective, this is understandable.

---

[4] In German: "Diplom-Kaufmann" und "Diplom-Kauffrau."

Lord of the Castle

Who has not dreamt of residing in a castle at some point? For three years, my professional home was actually within the walls of a medieval castle. It would be virtually impossible to find a greater contrast between the home building of the USW and the home building of the University of Bielefeld.

Castle Gracht is one of the most impressive moated medieval castles in the Rhineland. It consists of an outer bailey with three wings and a residence with two wings. The garden, originally inspired by French chateaus, was relandscaped in the nineteenth century to mirror an English garden. The grand castle belonged for 400 years to the very influential Wolff-Metternich family, which resided there until 1945. Several prominent people were born in the castle. One was Carl Schurz, who started as a freedom fighter in the German revolution of 1848 and had to flee from his home country. He then immigrated to the United States, where he became the first German-American elected to the US Senate and later became US Secretary of the Interior (Draeger and Draeger 2006).

How did I come to work in such a wonderful historic environment? I was appointed academic director of USW. The USW was formed in 1969, thanks to the initiative of my academic advisor Professor Horst Albach. The institute was sponsored by an association of 110 large German corporations. The academic director was always a university professor who served a term of three years.

Similar to the executive programs of business schools such as Harvard or INSEAD, the USW aimed to provide management and executive education for high-potential business leaders. Special emphasis was placed on business training for managers with technical or science backgrounds. This group formed the backbone of German management, but typically had not received any business training. An equivalent to the MBA did not exist in Germany. After German reunification, USW became the executive education department of the newly founded European School of Management and Technology (ESMT) in Berlin. The school now appears throughout as ESMT.

I assumed my duties as academic director of the USW on April 1, 1985, not long after my 38th birthday. That made me the youngest academic director by far in USW history. Because of my release from university duties, I could devote myself fully to the work at USW. The role was challenging, but at the same I felt myself fit for it due to the rigorous training I had received under Professor Albach. He had me running or supporting executive seminars when I was a young teaching assistant in my mid-20s. That meant standing before experienced international managers, many of whom were a decade or two older.

The easier part of the job was the lectures, which I could plan and prepare in advance. These lectures provided welcome and relevant content for the technical- and scientific-oriented executives. In their day-to-day work, they were continually confronted with business challenges—from accounting to cost calculations to finance to pricing—but they lacked a basic, systematic training to cope with these issues. The USW training succeeded in addressing that need.

Far more difficult for me than the lectures were the case-study discussions. Case studies are most effective when they lead to controversial discussions. The moderator needs to memorize all of the information in the case study, but more importantly, must be able to moderate a discussion while maintaining full command of the content. The case-study session must then close with clear conclusions or lessons. When I presented at my first-ever seminar under the direction of Professor Albach, I admitted openly that I was filling that role for the very first time. Seated across from us were 30 highly educated, experienced managers from Hoechst AG, which at that time was Germany's largest chemical company and the largest pharmaceutical company in the world. Many of these managers had doctorates in chemistry, physics, or engineering and had worked abroad. Many later advanced to C-level positions. On average, they were 18 years older than I was.

Professor Albach confessed to me that his heart nearly stood still the moment I introduced myself as a completely green beginner. This seminar, a true baptism by fire, lasted two weeks. I survived not only without any damage, but with flying colors. This most demanding exercise generated a set of contacts that would help provide the initial leads for the business of Simon-Kucher & Partners some ten years later. Hoechst became our firm's biggest customer in its early days.

The experience I had gained in these early executive seminars would prove immensely valuable, and I had deepened that basis further through my teaching activities at INSEAD. The most important insight for me was that in contrast to theory, there are no clear-cut solutions in practice. One always needs to weigh the pros and cons of various viable alternatives. A critical aspect is to understand the motives of the people involved. That may sound simplistic, but it became a fundamentally important part of my later work as a consultant. The line of argument differs depending on whether there is a scientist, a salesperson, or a finance expert making the decision.

These experiences, reinforced by what I learned at MIT and Stanford, gave me a solid foundation for my role as director at USW. When I took over, the institute had a very German focus. One of my personal goals during my three-year term was to make the USW more international. But I fell short of that goal. I discovered that the barrier to internationalization was mental more than anything. To overcome the inertia and internal resistance to internationalization, I would have needed to replace the bulk of the staff and the lecturers. That would not have been feasible within the short period of three years. I did manage to introduce a couple of seminars in English, and we also held some seminars in Asia. But most other efforts to internationalize our activities failed. One example was the attempt to set up a subsidiary in China. Our German board of supervisors refused to approve this project, arguing that it would distract us from our focus to transform German engineers into business managers.

My lesson drawn from these failures is that it is very difficult to internationalize an organization whose team and internal structures are accustomed and confined to a domestic market. This applies even more strongly to services than to products because with services one needs to "internationalize" individual people.

Professionally speaking, the three years at USW are among the most wonderful and impactful years of my life. Though I was unaware at the time, that tenure sent me down a path that would alter my future. What did I learn and what made these three years so special? It was the first time that I had to manage a substantial, somewhat complex organization. USW was a non-profit, but we needed to cover our costs. The staff of around 50 people included a business manager who handled matters such as administration, infrastructure, and hotels. Beyond the core academic staff, we needed to coordinate and compensate dozens of professors from several universities who came to teach. The upkeep and operation of the castle itself was not a trivial matter. We were after all a business. It was a pleasure both to lead it and to develop it further.

Right from the start, I sensed new opportunities and felt the drive to grow awaken within me. We had a solid portfolio of existing seminars, but these offered little additional growth potential. They were usually fully booked, and there was little room to raise prices. That was not due to demand, but rather due to the fact that the owners of USW were often also its customers. The committee that represented the owners merely wanted to cover costs. If costs rose, they would see the justification for price increases. But at the same time, they themselves would need to bear higher prices when they sent their managers to the open or the company-specific seminars. The net result is that any price increases we could implement were modest.

This left the creation of new programs as the logical growth path. I introduced new seminars for the pharma industry and for retail, as well as an extension to the general management seminar. We also started to emphasize company-specific seminars, a move that allowed us to win over companies such as General Motors as key accounts. I met the top leadership, including the CEOs, of Deutsche Bank, General Motors, Siemens, Bayer, Bosch, BASF, Nestlé, Swiss Bank Corporation, and other large multinationals. During my three-year term, we almost doubled our revenue. This growth gave me some consolation after my failure to implement the desired internationalization.

During this time, I also learned how to deal with difficult people. This category included the administrative director. He had already made life difficult for some of my predecessors. These conflicts did not escape outside observers. The national business weekly *Wirtschaftswoche* wrote: "Hermann Simon maintained the upper hand in this uneven battle. The marketing professor from Bielefeld let every little accusation bounce off him. He orchestrated his own public image and that of the USW" (Seifert 1989). Being a manager is never easy.

USW and Its Network

The networks I was able to cultivate were a very inspiring aspect of USW. They fell into three categories: the board of trustees, the speakers, and the executive students. My direct boss was Professor Herbert Grünewald, then CEO of the pharma and chemicals conglomerate Bayer AG. He served as the association chairman, assisted by Horst Burgard, a board member of Deutsche Bank, and Erhard Bouillon, a board member at Hoechst. All three were grand gentlemen from the old school, and working under and with them was a joy. They waved through almost all of my recommendations. Only the internationalization ran into a brick wall with them, as I mentioned above. That is somewhat amazing because Bayer and Hoechst were truly global organizations at that time.

The board of trustees was led by Otto Wolff von Amerongen (1918–2007), one of the most significant figures in the German economy, and later by the CEO of Deutsche Bank, Dr. Alfred Herrhausen (1930–1989). It was filled with high-profile leaders from throughout German industry, and these top managers actually showed up to the meetings and events.

Herrhausen was the uncontested number one in German industry and one of the most impressive people I have ever met. He was also keenly aware of his status. Security was a very relevant topic in those days. When he attended a meeting or gave a speech at USW, his security detail would come a day ahead and inspect the castle. He was the only leader allowed to drive over the bridge into the castle's inner courtyard. This resembled the way the lords of the castle had entered for centuries.

Herrhausen's grand entrance stood in sharp contrast to how Walter Frehner, the CEO of the Swiss Bank Corporation (SBC, later acquired by UBS), approached the castle.[5] At that time, SBC was larger than Deutsche Bank in terms of assets under management. Frehner arrived in a Volkswagen taxi and got out in front of the building. He carried a small briefcase, rang the doorbell, and when I received him he said "My name is Frehner. I'm supposed to give a speech here." No one recognized this modest man or had any clue about the role he played.

Herrhausen did not suffer from a lack of self-confidence. He was friends with Augustinus Heinrich Graf Henckel von Donnersmarck (1935–2005), a member of the Catholic Order of the White Canons, who regularly gave remarkable lectures on ethics at USW. One evening at dinner, the discussion turned to Cologne's Cardinal Joseph Höffner (1906-1987). Father Augustinus said that Höffner had earned doctorates in four fields: theology, philosophy, economics, and law. These were not honorary doctorates, but earned ones, an extremely rare accomplishment. Herrhausen's response was: "Augustinus, if we had wanted that, we could have achieved it too."

The high security ultimately could not protect Herrhausen. He was assassinated on November 30, 1989, allegedly by the Red Army Faction (RAF) terrorist organization. When it happened, I was in the office of Günther Wagner, a board member of MTU (now MTU Aero Engines) in Munich. Wagner's secretary came in, walked over to him and said "Herrhausen has just been murdered." We were stunned speechless.

The second network group at Castle Gracht were the speakers. This group included both academics and practitioners. We also had a range of academics on staff. In particular, I remember Karlheinz Schwuchow, who earned his Ph.D. under my supervision and today runs the Center for International Management Studies in the northern German city of Bremen. He became an authority on human resource development. For more than 25 years, he has published an annual handbook on the topic. The 2018 edition is entitled *HR Trends 2018—Strategy, Culture, Innovation, Concepts* (Schwuchow and Gutmann 2017). Sabine Rau was also an assistant at Castle Gracht during my tenure. Later, she became a professor at various German and British business schools and the founding director of the Hidden Champions Institutes (HCI) at ESMT.

---

[5] In German, USW stands for "UniversitaetsSeminar der Wirtschaft" (University Seminars of Business). In English, I use the denomination German Management Institute. After the German Reunification, the USW became the executive education department of the newly-founded European School of Management and Technology (ESMT) in Berlin. In 2018, it was fully merged with ESMT and the USW logo was retired.

Many university professors from inside and outside Germany taught at USW as part-time lecturers. But the majority of speakers were experienced, high-ranking practitioners. In this way, I became acquainted with hundreds of top managers from Germany and other European countries, including dozens of CEOs, board members, and division or function leaders from multinational and large *Mittelstand* companies. I got to meet C-level executives from Siemens and Bosch, from BMW, Daimler, Volkswagen, from the leading chemical and technology firms such as Mannesmann (now Vodafone) and ThyssenKrupp—a true cross-section of the German economy. The leaders from the *Mittelstand* included Professor Berthold Leibinger, owner-CEO of the world's leading machine-tool and laser company Trumpf. He arrived once in a helicopter that blew off part of the castle's roof when it landed in the courtyard. Leibinger and I always laughed about that when our paths crossed. He passed away in 2018. Berthold Leibinger remains for me the epitome of a Hidden Champions leader.

The speakers—especially the practitioners—were the backbone of the USW. They guaranteed real-world relevance. An article in Germany's leading business monthly *Manager Magazin* cited a survey of 500 managers responsible for training at German companies. The comment: "What apparently matters is the practical relevance of the seminars. That is why USW is so highly regarded among German training experts. This puts it ahead of even the famous elite schools such as INSEAD, St. Gallen, and Harvard" (Lentz 1988). Here, I would add the caveat that the survey was limited solely to training leaders and experts within German companies. The assessment certainly did not apply internationally.

The executive students were the third pillar of the extensive USW network. During my three years there, I personally led the flagship course at USW, the General Management Seminar. In its original form, it was a ten-week seminar designed by Professor Albach. This mammoth program made its debut in 1969 at a cloister in St. Augustin, outside of Bonn. The atmosphere in the cloister was symbolic of the hard work in those ten weeks. In addition to the content itself, the goal was to unite a group of managers who were on career paths to C-suite roles. One expressly stated goal was that working together so intensively over several weeks would create friendships for life. But ten weeks turned out to be too long, so we cut the seminar back to six weeks. Yet within those six weeks, the program remained extremely intense. It would begin with exercise in the morning, ahead of the first learning session at 8 a.m. The sessions continued through the early evening. After dinner, there was an evening lecture at 8 p.m. On most days, neither the seminar participants nor I would make it to bed before midnight because we all had case studies to prepare for the next day. I was personally present at all sessions during these six weeks.

The name "general" in the title of the core USW seminar was correct in the literal sense. The program covered all areas that a top manager would confront. We had around a hundred active speakers. They included not only top business managers, but also politicians such as federal ministers, heads of federal agencies, and military officials. We also had talks by theologians, sociologists, and artists. I supervised three of the General Management Seminars, each with 30 participants, but among them was only one woman. At that time, top management in Germany was solely a male arena, and to a large extent it still is today. Many of the participants rose to C-level and CEO positions. These contacts proved invaluable in my later career as a consultant.

Looking back from today's perspective, how do I assess the USW seminars? First, they were very different from the case-study-driven programs offered by Harvard and the other business schools I knew. The USW essentially offered "living case studies" in that active corporate leaders acted as teachers. Altogether I witnessed 458 lectures in my three years at USW, with 345 of them held by top managers and 113 by university professors. Out of all those numerous talks, which could hardly have been more diverse, I learned one great lesson: the person is more important than the content. To be honest, I have not retained very much of the content from all those speeches. But so many of the speakers left unforgettable impressions. At the reunions, a story about Gerhard Ackermanns usually makes the rounds. He founded the German supermarket chain Allkauf, which became the Real chain after he sold it to the Metro Group. Ackermanns then entered the new field of private television in Germany by founding Pro7, which later became ProSiebenSat.1 after a merger with Sat1.

When he was asked about the genesis of the name "Allkauf," he said the origin "was very simple. It is the place where 'all go to buy'." The compound word formed by "All" and the German word for "buy" forged the simple name. I have seen other companies form their names in a similar fashion. But the kind of character such as Ackermann's was more common among the *Mittelstand* than among larger companies. I encountered many Ackermann-like leaders during my later research into Hidden Champions.

Castle Gracht was an oasis of calm. The moment one crosses the moat and enters the courtyard through the heavy oaken doors, one says goodbye to the distractions of the outside world. The ring-shaped bailey and the main building create their own idyllic enclosure. The wide moat protects the gaps between the buildings. The photo shows Castle Gracht.

View of Castle Gracht

The complex was simply ideal for the kinds of retreat-like seminars that Castle Gracht became synonymous with. There were no distractions. The seminar participants could focus their attention fully on learning and the communication among themselves. In the three years there, I only traveled once with a seminar group for an evening to Cologne. It was the Thursday before Karvenal, the Mardi-Gras-like season that turns Cologne into a massive, frenzied party. Even though the participants did not return until right before dawn, the next day's sessions began promptly at 8 a.m. German discipline reigned at Castle Gracht.

My own workplace was like a dream—a room in the corner tower with a view of both the moat and the castle's park (shown in the right front of the photo). It was there that I saw a heron for the first time. Today, these large birds are no longer a rarity, but in the 1980s there were just starting their comeback in Germany. A water landscape such as Gracht's offered inspirational working conditions. From the office, a wooden spiral staircase led to an unused room above. It was exactly as one would imagine the homestead of a lord or baron. The seclusion of Gracht had a strong influence on the working atmosphere as well as the people themselves. In contrast to almost all other stations in my adult life, the atmosphere was rarely hectic. The students and the speakers came to us, and we did not need to travel far or often. At the time, there was no internet and no one had a mobile telephone. The cutting-edge communications tool of that era was the fax machine. Even personal computers were not a standard part of a manager's or leader's toolkit. They were just being introduced during my tenure.

Upon my departure, the USW presented me with the painting "Hommage à Schloss Gracht" by the artist Otmar Alt, who was a frequent lecturer at USW. The picture hangs today in my home office as a daily reminder. What else did I take home from the three years as "lord" of Castle Gracht? I took away lasting memories of a wonderful working environment and enriching encounters with hundreds of inspiring people. I took away a cornucopia of insights into corporate management. I wrote those insights down in a bound booklet that I still consult often today. The most important learnings generally came from entrepreneurs and top managers, not academics. Finally, I established a network of hundreds of contacts covering all industries, politics, culture, science, and the military. This network proved to be extremely valuable in the ensuing years, especially in setting up our firm Simon-Kucher & Partners.

My Time with Johannes Gutenberg

Johannes Gutenberg (1400–1468) invented the printing press. The ensuing printing revolution, a milestone of the second millennium, ushering in the modern period of human history. In 1989, I moved from Bielefeld to Johannes Gutenberg University in Mainz. The two universities and our departments could hardly have been more different. While Bielefeld was an ultra-modern "reform university," Mainz was more of a traditional university with well-established structures. It was originally chartered in 1477 by Diether von Isenburg, the Archbishop of Mainz, who was also a prince-elector and arch-chancellor of the "Holy Roman Empire of the German Nation."[6]

Before I joined Mainz, the department of law and economics had only offered a degree in economics, not in business. In my negotiations with the minister of science of Rhineland-Palatinate, I made my transfer to Mainz conditional on the establishment of a business program and degree. Fortunately, the minister was eager to cooperate because he also wanted Mainz to offer a business degree track.

But the professors of economics did not share our enthusiasm. Traditionally, they outnumbered the few business professors and were stronger in terms of sheer power and influence. They saw my demand as a frontal assault against their supreme authority. They showed up in person at the ministry and asked the minister to withdraw my job offer.

---

[6] Teaching at the University of Mainz ceased during the turmoil of the French Revolution and did not resume until 1946, when the university was reconstituted under the name of Johannes Gutenberg. Cologne and Trier—two other major universities established in the Middle Ages by Archbishop or Papal decree—suffered a similar fate.

The minister arranged a meeting between me and representatives of the economics department, but that meeting got off to an auspicious start: I showed up two hours late. Think about that for a moment. The person who is the subject of such a critical meeting lets the assembled professors and ministerial staff sit and wait for two whole hours. That was neither a calculated nor malicious move on my part although I cannot rule out that some of the participants may have interpreted it that way.

What caused this embarrassing delay? I wanted to drive to Mainz by car from our house in Königswinter, but a snowstorm struck as I was heading down the autobahn. Getting to Mainz under those weather conditions was out of the question. I turned back and drove instead to the train station in Bonn and took a train to Mainz. The net result is that I arrived at the science ministry two hours late.

This delay may have had a slight silver living, though. The two-hour gap was so long that the initial anger of the representatives of the economics department had begun to subside. They had no other choice but to discuss the situation with the ministry officials, who—with the minister's blessing—were strong advocates of introducing a business program. My job offer was upheld.

Shortly after I assumed my professorship, we launched a full degree program in business. The university was granted five new professorships in business, thus changing the balance of power between economics and management within the faculty. As expected, within a year around 80% of the students selected business as their major instead of the classic economics track. This did not make me popular with the established economics professors.

Accompanying and supervising my team of assistants with their doctoral and post-doc work was the most enjoyable part of my job at Mainz. Kai Witlinger undertook a dissertation on implementation problems in price management, at that time a totally unexplored area (Wiltinger 1998). Martin Fassnacht devoted himself to price differentiation in services (Fassnacht 1996). Christian Homburg completed his post-doc work on customer loyalty (Homburg 2000). All three became professors. Homburg, now at the University of Mannheim, ranks as the most prolific and internationally recognized German in marketing science. As of September 2019, his Hirsch Index stands at 100, far and away the highest value among management academics in German-speaking countries. Georg Wuebker wrote his dissertation on price bundling and later led the global banking division at Simon-Kucher. Martin Moehrle became chief learning officer at Deutsche Bank and UBS. Eckart Schmitt made it to CEO of a Hidden Champion.

During my tenure, we were able to reach an agreement with the business department of the French Université de Bourgogne in Dijon on a joint study program. The fit seemed good. Both universities were of similar size. Bourgogne had 30,000 students, while Mainz has around 33,000. Even the cities fall into the same category. Mainz has a population of 213,000 and Dijon 155,000. Both are situated in wine-growing regions. Since this agreement began, many students have been able to get a French-German dual degree.

The faculty in Mainz was significantly more conservative than its counterpart in Bielefeld. But that had little influence on my own work. Mainz had the advantage of being in a more central location than Bielefeld. The close proximity to the major international airport in Frankfurt made it easier for us to bring in high-profile guest speakers. I organized events with speakers such as Jürgen Schrempp, CEO of Daimler; Daniel Goeudevert, CEO of Ford Germany; Rolf Breuer, CEO of Deutsche Bank; Bayer CEO Manfred Schneider, and many others of the same caliber. We had many international speakers from Europe, the United States, Russia, Poland, Japan, India, and South Korea. The most interesting speaker in all those years was Dr. Gerhard Neumann, the former CEO of General Electric Aircraft Engines and the "Father of the Jet Age." Our lecture hall's capacity of 1200 was not large enough to hold the audience that wanted to hear him speak. I will have more to say about this extraordinary man in Chap. 12, "Encounters."

At that time, I was beyond busy. I was active in five endeavors though my time was not spread evenly across them. First, I was teaching as a university professor. Second, I got involved in the state politics of Rhineland-Palatinate. Third, I was speaking frequently at management conferences. Fourth, I was working in the firm founded by me and my first doctoral students Eckhard Kucher and Karl-Heinz Sebastian. Fifth, I was a non-executive director of several corporations and foundations. The time commitments for all five activities were becoming unbearable. Even today, I get dizzy when I look back at my appointment calendars from back then.

More and more often, I asked myself whether it would be better to concentrate on only one activity. After all, I had said that only focus leads to world-class. Should I choose teaching or consulting? Being a university professor had distinct pros and cons. The research and the freedom of the position afforded me opportunities to remain mentally fit and engaged, to allow ideas to ferment and come to fruition, and to read, to write and publish. I appreciated the lively discussions with students, doctoral candidates, and scientists. But the ever-expanding demands for administrative tasks at the university (committees, deanship, etc.) got on my nerves, as did the endless faculty meetings, the time-consuming examinations, and the inescapable routines of teaching. As my alienation from the university increased, consulting became more and more a matter of the heart. I started to broach the decision—professor vs.

consultant—carefully in discussions with people I could trust. Augustinus Heinrich Graf Henckel von Donnersmarck, the monk of the White Canons who had delivered so many inspiring lectures at Castle Gracht and who had known me well for a long time, wasted no time in making a sharp and accurate diagnosis. He bluntly told me: "Your heart doesn't belong to the university." As it turned out, he would be prescient.

On September 19, 1994, at a meeting near Düsseldorf, I informed my consulting partners that I would be leaving the University of Mainz and assume the roles of CEO and chairman in our firm. The message struck like a bomb. My partners were surprised, to say the least, but the reaction was positive. We agreed to strict confidentiality, and the partners did indeed keep an airtight lid on the news. I knew I could rely on them.

Effective at the end of 1994, I gave up my tenured professorship and resigned from the Johannes Gutenberg University in Mainz. My university assistants were shocked. But they did not have to worry about a disruption to their degree programs. I accompanied the doctoral candidates and the diploma candidates until they had all completed their degrees. These commitments took several years to fulfill, before I could finally close that chapter of my life for good.

On January 1, 1995 I assumed my new roles in the consulting firm, which we renamed Simon-Kucher & Partners, the name it has had ever since. At the time, the firm had only one office, which was located in Bonn. I was determined to change that.

German Marketing Science Goes International

The end of my university career induced me to take stock of my time as an academic and of the general state of marketing science in Germany. During my years as a researcher at the University of Bonn 20 years earlier, I had already recognized that marketing scientists must not confine themselves to the "Island of Germany." My impressions from international conferences and my stays abroad reinforced this insight. As a young researcher, but not yet a professor, I had published an article on the international perception of German marketing science. My goal was to challenge established professors to become more active internationally and publish in English, the *lingua franca* of science (Simon 1979). This article did not win me many friends among the tenured professors. How dare a young kid—who has not even earned the right to call himself a professor—call out the established professors for not being present on the international stage? How dare he challenge them to publish in English, for crying out loud?

I cannot rule out that this article alone disqualified me from being considered for some professorships. Years later, I followed up that original article with a more nuanced one under the title "German management science in international competition: a black hole?" (Simon 1993) My central claim was that while the German academics read English-language journals, they did not publish in them. Analogous to a black hole, the Germans constantly sucked in information, but emitted none of their own. The consequence was that German management scientists were unknown and had zero impact outside German-speaking countries.

But I went a step further and argued that German management journals should switch to publishing in English. Many colleagues considered that idea to be pure heresy. A well-known professor of the Free University of Berlin wrote: "I raise objections to Hermann Simon's suggestions. His suggestion that German journals publish English-language contributions is inappropriate. He also demands more English-language publications from German management scientists. That would make things easy for the Americans and the British, but why don't they undertake the effort to learn German? Simon places the burden of overcoming language barriers solely on the shoulders of Germans. He apparently has no interest in preserving German as a language of science."[7] From today's perspective, such views sound strange. But that was the reality of German academia in the 1980s.

Today, many German-based management journals have been renamed—such as *Journal of Business Economics* (formerly *Zeitschrift für Betriebswirtschaft*), or *Schmalenbach Business Review* (successor to the *Zeitschrift für betriebswirtschaftliche Forschung*) and *Marketing ZFP—Journal of Research and Management* (originally *Marketing—Zeitschrift für Forschung und Praxis*). And these journals publish predominantly or exclusively in English. The international reputation of these journals, however, is still not where it could and should be. One clear reason is that they were latecomers to the world of English language publishing. The situation is better in fields such as operations research or economics, which made the conversion to English much earlier.

What has radically changed for the better, however, is the presence of German marketing and management academics at the international level, both at conferences and in journals. Professor Alfred Kuss of the Free University of Berlin writes: "In the last few years one could observe a dramatic increase in the number of German contributions to leading international

---

[7] Text by Professor Walter Endres "Betriebswirtschaftslehre nur englisch?" from 1994; author has copy. Professor Endres (born 1917) had the chair for business studies at Free University Berlin from 1969 to 1985.

journals" (Kuß 2013). Kuss notes, however, that a small number of authors are responsible for that increase. They include Christian Homburg (University of Mannheim) as well as Sönke Albers (Kühne Logistics University Hamburg, formerly University of Kiel) and his students Bernd Skiera (University of Frankfurt/Main) and Manfred Krafft (University of Münster), to name just a few. In the leading *Journal of Marketing* the share of articles from German authors more than doubled in ten years, from 6.2% to 12.6% (Kuß 2013, p. 44). This development is extremely gratifying. Today, the Germans are the second-strongest group of authors in this field, trailing only the Americans. The process took time, but the outcome today far exceeds my expectations from 1979. I could not have conceived of such an outcome when I presented my original provocative demands 40 years ago.

There is no way to deny, however, that most authors who are native German speakers (including myself) have to accept that the native English speakers have a clear and significant advantage. Even when someone has relatively good mastery of English as a foreign language, one is unlikely to reach the level of a well-educated native speaker. This problem is by no means new. Cusanus (Nicholas of Cusa, 1401–1464), who came from my home region[8] and was one of the most outstanding scholars in the late Middle Ages, obviously wrote in Latin, the *lingua franca* of all scientists at the time. In 1440, over 50 years before Copernicus and around 200 years before Galileo, he wrote "*Terra non est centrum mundi*" ("The earth is not the center of the world"). But in his own perceptions, he felt about Latin the same way many Germans feel about English, namely that native English speakers have a big advantage. He wrote: "Only with the greatest effort, as if one must fight against one's own nature, is a German capable of speaking Latin correctly" (de Cusa 1994). Cusanus complained about his own unpolished writing style, but admired the ease and elegance with which the classically educated Italians wrote. Many Germans, including me, feel the same way about our writing relative to our American and British colleagues. This problem is, of course, not confined to Germans. It is even more serious for people who grew up as a native speaker of a Romance, Slavic, or Asian language.

Becoming an Author

During my school years, I never thought that one day I would become an author and spend a significant part of my life writing books and articles.

---

[8] My *Gymnasium* is named after him ("Cusanus-Gymnasium").

Writing essays in school—whether in German or in a foreign language—was one of my least favorite assignments, a distaste clearly visible in my grades.

But when I was 17, I co-founded the first student newspaper at our school. It was a sensation right from the start. In the first issue, we published an interview with Wolfgang Leonhard, who was considered a leading expert on the Soviet Union, East Germany, and Communism. From 1935 to 1945, he lived in the Soviet Union after his mother took him there for indoctrination when he was 13 years old. After World War II, he returned to Germany as member of the Ulbricht Group, which ultimately founded the Communist government of East Germany. But in 1949, he become a Soviet critic and later joined the faculty at Yale University, where he gained a reputation for his powerful talks in his unmistakable German-Russian accent. He is considered to have had a strong influence on former US President George W. Bush, one of his students at Yale. Leonhard's famous book *Child of the Revolution* became an international bestseller and has appeared in multiple languages.

How did we, as young high school students in the rural Eifel, get access to such a world-renowned author? The answer is simple. He came to us. He had recently moved to the nearby town of Manderscheid (population 1400), where he lived until his death in 2014. In 1974, he married Dr. Elke Leonhard, who later became a member of the German parliament and life-long president of the German Parliamentarian Society. She still lives in the small town. On August 30, 2014, we celebrated Wolfgang Leonhard's life with a dignified funeral service at Himmerod Abbey. Many high-level politicians attended, including the late Hans-Dietrich Genscher, Germany's most famous foreign minister after World War II. Genscher played a key role in the fall of the Berlin Wall and the Iron Curtain as well as in German re-unification. In recognition of Genscher's achievements, the foundation of my hometown Wittlich awarded him the Georg Meistermann Prize for services to democracy.

My primary interest at the newspaper was the business side, though, and not the editorial side. I served as sales manager. Was that an early indicator of my interest in marketing and sales? My first publication did not come until a few years later in 1968, when I published an article about my home village. It appeared in the booklet for the dedication of the new church (Simon 1968). I collected all kinds of facts and statistics about the local population, education levels, mobility, jobs, and the economy, and analyzed the data. I developed my own simple statistical methods. To my surprise, I would encounter some of these methods later in my university studies. The article's title—"A Critical Look"—applied not only to the article's content, but later also to its reception, which was not universally positive.

For several years after that first amateurish publication, nothing else that deserved the term "publication" appeared under my name. The work on my dissertation and the ensuing post-doctoral thesis was more of a burden to me than a pleasure. But at the same time, every aspiring professor must be aware of the age-old mandate: "publish or perish." I discovered that the more I wrote, the more fun I had at it. One contributing factor was that after all those years sitting behind a desk, I no longer needed to write to pass a test or earn a grade. I had become a writer by choice, not by obligation.

The result? Over the decades, I have either written or edited more than 40 books. Counting all translations (into 27 languages) and all editions, over 180 book versions have either sole authorship or significant contributions by me. But these exact counts do not say much because not all of the books are entirely new. While some have a lot of new content, others are follow-up editions or have overlap with their predecessors.

The amount of time and effort to write these books has varied considerably. My "fastest" book took only six weeks. That intense speed was essential because the book, *Beat the Crisis: 33 Quick Solutions for Your Company,* came out in the depths of the Great Recession (Simon 2010). One needs to act swiftly in times of crisis because no one knows when the crisis will end or when interest in the topic will wane. The timing and the rush proved very effective. Within less than a year, the book had appeared in 13 languages. Whenever a new crisis pops up in a country, there is renewed interest in this book.

The longest period came for the second edition of *Price Management,* published in German under the title *Preismanagement* (Simon 1982, 1992). That project lasted six *years*, not six weeks. Writing such an exhaustive book is more like running a cross-continent race, not a mere marathon. Today, I would no longer have the endurance to conceptualize and write a book like that. The most recent English-language edition of *Price Management* was published in 2019 by Springer Nature New York (Simon and Fassnacht 2019).

Which books were the most fun to write? I would be inclined to say the *Hidden Champions* books, primarily because of the research into the topic. It allowed me to get to know some of the most impressive corporate leaders I have ever met.

None of my books have been blockbusters. But the term "best seller" depends on the basis of comparison, and in that regard some of my books have reached that level. In Germany, the book *Hidden Champions of the 21st Century* made it to number two on the list of best-selling business books. That book's resonance in Germany and internationally was huge. In terms of volume, my books have sold very well in China, with some books selling more copies than in Germany. Books in China are inexpensive, and the Chinese market is simply many times larger than any other country's market.

My books appeal to a specialized readership rather than the general public, and therefore tend to be relatively expensive. My primary goal is not to sell as many copies as possible, but rather to reach the right target group. I have succeeded in that to some extent. One does not earn much money directly from selling textbooks or business books. But the indirect benefits can be significant. Bestsellers may increase an author's recognition, but specialized books—when done well and marketed to the right audience—are indispensable for building a reputation. They are also very effective in generating leads for speaking engagements. To this day, I am somewhat baffled by the fact that the compensation for one single speech can exceed the entire royalty income from the book that led to that speech. I still have no convincing explanation for that phenomenon. But the music business has a similar dynamic. Successful musicians today earn far more from touring than they do from their recorded music.

Writing academic articles brings different challenges than writing books. The processes that I experienced in my early years to get articles published in top US journals were nerve-wracking. If the more recent reports of my younger colleagues are to be believed, the situation is even worse today. It takes an extreme level of patience to endure all the hurdles: multiple revisions, battles with editors and reviewers, and the uncertainty of whether the article will be accepted at all. But those efforts are often worthwhile. Without articles in American A+ journals, I would never have become internationally known. When I left academia, my ambition to undergo these tedious, protracted processes ebbed away. That was due in part to the fact that my target group had shifted as well, from academics to practitioners.

For that target audience, I wrote a column for 25 years in *Manager Magazin*, Germany's leading business monthly. This magazine has an almost 100% reach in Germany's top management circles. The opportunity to write this column came about during my stay at Harvard in 1988. I reached out to the editor-in-chief of *Manager Magazin* and suggested I could write a monthly column called "Report from Harvard." The column would introduce German managers to the ideas and insights I was gaining there.

Manager Magazin was the optimal medium for that purpose and that audience. It was founded by the legendary news magazine *Der Spiegel* in 1971. Its first editor was Leo Brawand, a streetwise and battle-tested *Spiegel* journalist. He was once a speaker at Castle Gracht on the topic "Press and Business—an Uneasy Relationship." Shortly before that talk, the prime minister of the German state of Schleswig-Holstein, Uwe Barschel, had been found dead in a hotel in Geneva. A press photographer had taken photos of the dead body before the police arrived, and these photos were actually published. The participants in the General Management Seminar at Castle Gracht thought that taking and publishing the photos was serious journalistic misconduct and wanted to confront Brawand about it. But he immediately defused the situation by beginning his talk with a clear statement: he would have acted the same way that the press photographer had. He said that no journalist lets such a chance go by. The way he began his speech taught me a lesson that I often applied as a consultant. If there is an issue, address it yourself and address it immediately, before the client does. That is by far the most effective way to defuse a conflict-prone situation.

For 25 years, my column appeared regularly in *Manager Magazin*. I covered a very eclectic range of topics—some hot and current, some basic and fundamental—and along the way I acquired skills that are very important for an author. The first was learning to write within sharply defined space constraints. The column had a limit of 4000 characters, which meant that I needed to pack whatever I wanted to say—regardless of the complexity—onto no more than two pages. In most cases the first drafts were much longer than that, and like most authors, I am reluctant to discard any text I have written. But the constraint was binding. It forced me to focus on the essence of my arguments and to keep the writing simple and clear. In the first few years, some of *Der Spiegel*'s experienced journalists would polish my drafts. I was not always pleased with that process, but I must admit that in most cases, they improved the text. That was especially true for headlines. Some things should be left to the professionals.

But over time, practice makes perfect, as the saying goes. The more columns I wrote, the less the editors needed to change, until the entire editing process became superfluous. I believe that this experience as a columnist changed the way I write books today, compared to my years in academia. If one wants to reach an audience of practitioners, one needs to adopt the appropriate writing style. The same applies to speeches. Unfortunately, many highly qualified professors fail to connect with practitioners because of their writing or presentation styles. They are unable or unwilling to change their styles to meet the preferences and the needs of practitioners.

After all those years and close to 200 columns, the opportunity had finally run its course for me. I was relieved that I no longer needed to deliver a column on a regular basis. But this series had raised my profile among the readers of *Manager Magazin* more than any other activity I can think of.

In an interview in 1990, a journalist asked me about what I had planned for my retirement years. At the time, I was just 43 years old. I told him I would write a book about how I personally experienced the transformation from an agrarian society to a global service society.[9] I was very amazed when I found that quote in my files in the summer of 2017 because in 2016 I had pretty much written exactly that book. It bore the title *The Gardens of Lost Recollections* (in German: *Die Gärten der verlorenen Erinnerung)* and described the incredible changes that took place in the first two decades of my life (Simon 2017). That I had had the idea for such a book already in 1990 came as a true surprise to me. But I have seen that the ideas we set our minds to often become reality later in life. During my time as an assistant, I kept a notebook with ideas and topics for academic articles. When I leaf through the notebook today, I realize that almost all of the ideas eventually led to a publication, even if it took ten years. Writing ideas down seems to be very effective. It prevents them from becoming fleeting or ephemeral.

A Step Toward Practice

During my time as a university professor, I served on seven corporate boards as a non-executive director and on the boards of trustees for four foundations.[10] I found myself as a naïve rookie on these boards, which comprised established businesspeople and professionals. I learned the most from my service as a board member for Dürr AG, a company with a revenue of around $4.5 billion in 2018. The years on the supervisory board of Kodak AG, Kodak's German subsidiary, were also very instructive. Both companies were headquartered in Stuttgart. I also learned quite a bit as a board member for IhrPreis.de AG, a start-up built around the "name-your-own-price" concept.[11]

Dürr is the world market leader in car painting systems. The company went public in 1989, but Heinz Dürr, who would later become CEO of Deutsche Bahn, remained the primary shareholder together with his family. The board included German business luminaries such as Rolf Breuer, CEO of Deutsche Bank; Walther Zügel, CEO of the state bank of Baden-Württemberg; and Tessen von Heydebreck, a board member of Deutsche Bank. I learned how a

---

[9] *w&v*, November 2, 1990, p. 180.

[10] The German system has two boards, the executive board ("Vorstand" in German) and the supervisory board (non-executive directors). In the supervisory board meetings, the members of the *Vorstand* usually participate but have no voting rights. For companies with more than 2000 employees, both the shareholders and the trade unions name an equal number of board members. This system is called co-determination ("Mitbestimmung" in German). In case of a tie between shareholder representatives and union representatives, the chairperson of the supervisory board has a double vote. The chairperson always comes from the shareholder side.

[11] Today Dürr AG is based in Bietigheim-Bissingen. IhrPreis.de no longer exists.

publicly listed company functions from the perspective of the board, including the role of a majority shareholder, the interaction between the executive and the non-executive directors, and the always well-attended annual shareholders' meetings. As with the supervisory boards of most large companies, Dürr's included more bankers and lawyers than people who represented the operational side of the business. To that extent, one needed to trust the executives, who fortunately were very close to the day-to-day business. In that regard, I had full trust in Reinhart Schmidt, the CEO of Dürr AG at that time. His successor, Hans Dieter Pötsch, came into the company from the outside and was not as deeply familiar with the peculiarities of building paint shops. Pötsch later became chairman of the supervisory board of Volkswagen.

Even though Dürr was the global market leader in its field, its total market share was less than 25%. The market was an oligopoly. In my opinion, the best option would have been to focus completely on that core market and avoid diversification. Instead, Dürr AG took over Carl Schenck, a highly diversified auto industry supplier. This led to problems, and ultimately Heinz Dürr needed to get personally involved to steer the company back on the right course. After I gave up my professorship and assumed the CEO position at Simon-Kucher, I decided to let my board mandate at Dürr expire at the end of the 1990s. As I explained the decision to Mr. Dürr: "You named me to the board as a university professor, not as the CEO of a consulting firm. Because my position has changed, I would like to give up my mandate." He accepted, and later became an important client of Simon-Kucher & Partners when he was CEO of Deutsche Bahn.

My experiences at the German subsidiary of Kodak were completely different than what happened at Dürr. In order to understand why, one must keep in mind that the shareholders and the trade unions both have the right to name an equal number of board members when a company has more than 2000 employees. This system is called co-determination, or "Mitbestimmung" in German. In case of a tie vote between shareholder representatives and union representatives, the chairperson of the supervisory board—who always comes from the shareholder side—has a double vote. Kodak AG had more than 2000 employees. Thus, its supervisory board included representatives of Kodak Inc. (the sole shareholder) and representatives of Germany's most powerful trade union, IG Metall. I was on the shareholder side.

Prior to the full board meetings, the representatives of the shareholders would meet to discuss and define their basic positions on strategic issues. The full board meetings with the trade union representatives were therefore more of a formality, but we still had frequent standoffs with the labor side. I had the impression that the IG Metall representatives used these meetings to raise their own personal profiles. I also recognized that the board of the German subsidiary of this American corporation had little say. The division leaders from Kodak's headquarters in Rochester would intervene directly and sometimes present the German board with a *fait accompli* instead of options. I witnessed a similar relationship between General Motors and its German unit Opel although in that case I was involved as a consultant, not as a board member.

In my opinion, a lack of insights and foresight was not behind the ultimate demise of Kodak. Prior to joining the board, I had conducted numerous executive seminars for the company. Kodak did recognize early on that digital technologies posed a threat. In 1983, the company redefined its business as "imaging," independent of the technology used to create the images. That was undoubtedly the right approach, but knowing something is not the same as actually doing it. Kodak's workforce, over 100,000 strong, was steeped in the classical camera technologies and chemical films. Compounding this was the decades-long preeminence of Kodak in its market, which fostered a pronounced arrogance and a reluctance to change. The combination of technical challenges and corporate culture makes it very difficult to transform a large corporation and develop a new business, especially one that will inevitably destroy the existing one.

Kodak did attempt some diversification. It entered the pharmaceutical industry and bought Sterling Drug, which owned the rights to the Bayer Aspirin brand in the United States but otherwise was not among the R&D leaders in the industry. When an industry outsider buys a middle-of-the pack company in an industry, it is often unable to challenge the industry's leaders. That happened with Kodak in this case. This failure turned out to be a stroke of luck for Bayer, though. Thanks to the problems resulting from the Kodak-Sterling combination, Bayer, the German chemical and pharma multinational, was able to swoop in and re-acquire the US rights to its own name and the Aspirin brand. These rights had been expropriated after World War I.

Professor Herbert Grünewald, CEO of Bayer from 1974 until 1984, often told me of the resentment that festered in the United States because the German parent did not own the US rights to its own name as well as to Aspirin, one of its most famous brands. Often, when a product with the Bayer brand logo appeared unintentionally in the United States, Bayer was dragged to court and Grünewald had to testify. He told me that he often found these negotiations unfair. In the 1970s and 1980s, Bayer was repeatedly reproached for Germany's political past. Currently, one can get the impression that similar reproaches are still lurking in the background in the context of Bayer's acquisition of Monsanto and the lawsuits involving glyphosate. But at least the issue of the brand logo has been resolved in the meantime. Under CEO

Dr. Manfred Schneider, Bayer bought back the rights to the Bayer logo and Aspirin brands in 1996, purportedly for $1.6 billion. In my opinion, that was a very good deal for Bayer.

I later broadened my experience by serving on the supervisory boards of the insurance group Gerling; the machine tool company Hermann Kolb AG; and the German market leader in bitumen, Deutag AG. Most of the board meetings I attended were dominated by formalities. In my view, supervisory boards in Germany do not generally make a meaningful contribution to the strategic development of a company. I increasingly found the meetings to be boring. My learning curve had flattened out, and when I took over as CEO of Simon-Kucher in 1995, I let all my board mandates expire. Management consulting and supervisory board activities are not compatible. First, it seems a bit shady when a company commissions consulting engagements with a firm whose CEO is a member of the company's board. Second, potential conflicts of interest mean that the consulting firm is effectively excluded from working for other companies in the same industry. After stepping down as CEO of Simon-Kucher, I again received numerous invitations to join supervisory boards, but have turned all of them down. Working on boards is not my vocation.

Having said all that, the experiences at the start-up IhrPreis.de AG were truly unique among all my times as a board member. This internet company was founded in 1999 by graduates of WHU Beisheim School of Management, Germany's leading private business school. I joined the supervisory board from the very beginning. Board members included some high-level politicians, including Dr. Günter Rexroth, the former federal minister of economic affairs. The business idea was built on the so-called name-your-own-price model, under which a customer offers a price and the seller then decides whether to accept it. The US firm Priceline.com has pioneered this idea.

Name-your-own-price, also known as customer-driven pricing or reverse pricing, rests on the assumption that customers will reveal their true willingness to pay for a product or a service. The customer's price offer is binding. As soon as the customer's bid exceeded a minimum price known only to the seller, the customer won the bid and paid the named price. Payment was ensured and processed via credit card or direct bank withdrawal.

The founders undertook this project with a high degree of professionalism. The work in the supervisory board was exhilarating, due to the constant stream of new ideas and approaches. With its initial financing in place, the platform succeeded in bringing in prestigious corporations as investors and suppliers.

The business got off to a promising start, but over time it became clear that too many customers were not only low-balling, but making unrealistically low bids. Either the platform was a magnet for bargain hunters, or customers were reluctant to reveal their true willingness to pay and instead wanted to see whether they could get desired products at unrealistically low prices. Despite its intriguing potential from a theoretical standpoint, the name-your-own-price model did not meet expectations. After around two years, IhrPreis.de shuttered the platform, thus suffering the same fate of so many dot.com business models in that era. But I do not regret my time at this start-up during the excitement of what is now called the internet bubble. I learned a lot in that short time and even exited with a small profit from my investment.

Dr. Rexroth and I became well acquainted when we served on the board of IhrPreis.de, but I associate him with a sad recollection. It was a situation in which I was lucky and he was less fortunate. In May 1996, we coincidentally visited the Victoria Falls in Zimbabwe at the same time. He was making a private side trip while visiting Zimbabwe on political business, while I was giving a speech at a conference held by the South African firm SAPPI, the world market leader in casting and release papers. On the evening before my speech, we went on a tour to the Zambezi River and concluded the outing with a barbecue on the shore. A South African asked me by chance whether I had malaria prophylaxis. I said no, citing my German doctor, who had considered such preventative measures unnecessary for a visit of only one day.

"Are you insane?" the South African asked.

He gave me some malaria tablets when we returned to the hotel, and I took them right away. In the weeks after I returned to Germany, I watched anxiously for any signs of malaria, but none ever materialized. Dr. Rexrodt was not as lucky. He contracted *malaria tropica,* the most dangerous form of the disease, in the same place and the same week. One month later, he was admitted to Berlin's Charité hospital. He never fully recovered and died of its effects a few years later.

Tempting Offers

Thanks to the exposure from many activities—Castle Gracht, management seminars, speeches, the *Manager Magazin* column and other publications—I had achieved a certain level of recognition in the business world. As a result, the CEOs of two of Germany's 50 largest companies approached me separately while I was at Harvard Business School. One headed a publicly listed company in electronics. The other was co-owner of a pharmaceutical firm. He came to Boston to recruit me and introduced me to the family that owned the firm. I had several talks with each of them, and these meetings culminated in offers to join their executive teams. These offers were a huge temptation for me. At the time, I was in my early 40s and the option of becoming full-time CEO of my own firm, Simon-Kucher & Partners, was not yet on my horizon. The firm had only 12 employees. So I faced a very tough choice. I could continue my academic career with a consulting practice on the side, or I could opt for a career in industry with a large corporation, starting at the C-level. The electronics company was substantially larger, but I preferred the offer of the family-owned firm. In my view, the company was more attractive and offered me better development opportunities.

But I also had a couple of concerns. First, while I knew all of the firm's top managers and expected I could work with them at eye level, I thought my lack of both industry and leadership experience could be a disadvantage. Second, I had the sense that the chemistry with the family owners was somewhat off. That made me nervous because such chemistry is a prerequisite for success in a family-owned business.

In the end, I turned down both offers.

Sometimes I ask myself—with a slight undercurrent of regret—what would have become of me had I accepted one of these tempting, attractive offers. But at the same time, dwelling on such questions is pointless. One can only go one way. When I look back, I believe that the way I chose was the right one for me.

References

Nicolai de Cusa, *De Docta Ignorantia/Die belehrte Unwissenheit*, Hamburg: Verlag Felix Meiner, 1994, p. 240.

Marianne Draeger and Otto Draeger. *Die Carl Schurz Story. Vom deutschen Revolutionär zum amerikanischen Patrioten*, Berlin: Verlag Berlin-Brandenburg 2006.

Martin Fassnacht, *Preisdifferenzierung bei Dienstleistungen: Implementationsformen und Determinanten*, Wiesbaden: Gabler, 1996.

Christian Homburg, *Kundennähe von Industriegüterunternehmen: Konzeption—Erfolgsauswirkungen—Determinanten, 3rd edition*, Wiesbaden: Gabler, 2000 (1st. ed. 1995, 2nd ed. 1998).

Alfred Kuß, *Marketing-Theorie, Eine Einführung*, 3rd ed., Wiesbaden: Gabler 2013, p. 44.

Brigitta Lentz, "Votum für die Praxis," *Manager Magazin*, 1/1988, pp. 150–153.

Dieter Patzelt, "Rückkehr gewünscht," *Wirtschaftswoche*, November 11, 1988, p. 104.

Karlheinz Schwuchow and Joachim Gutmann (eds.), *HR-Trends 2018—Strategie, Kultur, Innovation, Konzepte*, Freiburg: Haufe Lexware, 2017.

Bruno Seifert, "Böser Spuk im Schloss," *Wirtschaftswoche*, July 28, 1989, pp. 72–74.

Hermann Simon, "Hasborn—kritisch betrachtet," in: *Kirchbauverein Hasborn (ed.),* Hasborn, 1968, publication celebrating the occasion of the inauguration of the new church, pp. 32–37.

Hermann Simon, "Zur internationalen Positionierung der deutschen Marketingwissenschaft," *Marketing-Zeitschrift für Forschung und Praxis* 1 (2/1979), pp. 140–142.

Hermann Simon, *Preismanagement,* 1st ed., Wiesbaden: Gabler, 1982.

Hermann Simon, *Goodwill und Marketingstrategie,* Wiesbaden: Gabler, 1985.

Hermann Simon, *Preismanagement,* 2nd ed., Wiesbaden: Gabler, 1992.

Hermann Simon, "Die deutsche BWL im internationalen Wettbewerb - ein schwarzes Loch?" *Zeitschrift für Betriebswirtschaft. Sonderheft: Die Zukunft der Betriebswirtschaftslehre in Deutschland,* 03/1993, pp. 73–84.

Hermann Simon, *Beat the Crisis - 33 Quick Solutions for Your Company,* New York: Springer, 2010.

Hermann Simon, *Die Gärten der verlorenen Erinnerung,* 2nd ed., Daun: Verlag der Eifelzeitung 2017.

Hermann Simon and Martin Fassnacht, *Price Management–Strategy, Analysis, Decision, Implementation,* New York: Springer Nature, 2019.

Kai Wiltinger, *Preismanagement in der unternehmerischen Praxis—Probleme der organisatorischen Implementierung,* Wiesbaden: Gabler, 1998.

9

The Seductive Power of Price

Hog-Tied By Hog Prices

Already in my childhood, I had visceral firsthand experiences with the power of price. When our hogs were ready for slaughter, my father would bring them to the local wholesale market, where they would be auctioned off to butchers or traders. The sheer number of farmers who brought their hogs to market, matched by the large number of butchers and traders on the "buy" side, meant that no individual buyer or seller had a direct influence on the price of the hogs. We were at the mercy of the local cooperative, which cleared the transactions. They would tell my father the price he would receive, and thus determine how much money he could take home to our family.

The same applied to milk, which we would deliver to the local dairy. We had absolutely no influence on the price. The dairy, again part of a cooperative, told us what the price would be. The milk price would fluctuate based on supply and demand. The market for young hogs had a similar dynamic. That market was held every two weeks in Wittlich, and we would go there on our horse-and-wagon. In times of oversupply, prices would plunge.

In every market my father went to, we were "price takers." We had to accept the set price, whether we liked it or not. It was an extremely uncomfortable position. As anyone with a similar experience will attest, money is tight on a farm. These sales were our only source of income.

I absorbed all these impressions as a boy and I must admit, I did not like them. Decades later, I would explain in interviews that these lessons taught me something that has guided me in running my own business and helping

© The Author(s), under exclusive license to Springer Nature Switzerland AG 2021
H. Simon, *Many Worlds, One Life*, https://doi.org/10.1007/978-3-030-60758-6_9

others improve theirs: never run a business in which you have no influence on the prices you charge.[1]

I will not claim I articulated those thoughts exactly that way in the 1950s as a young boy. But I have that same visceral feeling today whenever I think about the price of pork or buy a gallon of milk. I am rather certain that these childhood experiences shaped my opinions about how businesses operate. To this day, I do not think much of a business that does not make money.

Despite my remarks about prices for our hogs and our milk, money played a secondary role in our lives during my childhood. Self-sufficiency was the priority, neighbors helped neighbors without any formal "price" mechanism in effect. The money-based part of our economy was small. Nowadays, prices are pervasive. They are inescapable. You see them everywhere, sometimes in unexpected or troubling roles. An important question we all wrestle with is how much these market forces—and with them, prices—will take over even more aspects our lives. This makes it all the more important for us to understand how prices and pricing mechanisms work.

The Magic and Mystery of Price

Prices are the central hinges of a market economy. Everything revolves around prices. Prices help balance supply and demand. In typical industrial constellations, price is the strongest profit driver. But at the same time, no other marketing instrument is better suited to increase sales volumes quickly and effectively than price cuts. In highly competitive markets, price is a manager's weapon of choice, the most frequently used form of aggression. That is why price wars are the rule rather than the exception in many markets, often with devastating effects on profits.

Discounts and price promotions—two standard forms of price cuts—are an everyday occurrence in retail, but they seem to occur with increasing frequency and depth. In one of the world's largest beer markets, some 70% of all beer sales at the retail level take place on promotion, with discounts as high as 50%.[2] Managers tend to have a fear of prices, especially when they need to increase them. The fear has one legitimate source: one can never know with absolute certainty how customers will react to a price change. If we raise prices, will customers remain loyal or will they run in droves to the

---

[1] "Hier ist meine Seele vergraben," interview with Hermann Simon *Welt am Sonntag*, November 9, 2008, p. 37.

[2] "Brauereien beklagen Rabattschlachten im Handel," *Frankfurter Allgemeine Zeitung*, April 20, 2013, p. 12.

competition? If we cut prices, will they really buy more? Such questions make managers very uncomfortable. When in doubt, they will keep their hands off the pricing lever and turn their attention instead to something more tangible and more certain: cost management, or more precisely, another round of cost-cutting. But I have never kept my hands off of pricing. Pricing became my calling and my life's work.

How Price Seduced Me

Price would become my lifelong companion. In college, I was fascinated by Professor Wilhelm Krelle's lectures on pricing theories. They were mathematically elegant and often very complex. These challenging lessons gave me a solid set of ways to think about price problems, structure them, and solve them. They would become one more essential building block to my understanding of how pricing works. But I would have never for a moment thought that this knowledge would have some kind of practical application.

Pricing became an emotional experience when I met Professor Reinhard Selten, who would go on to win the Nobel Prize in Economics in 1994 for his work on game theory. Prof. Selten conducted a pricing experiment in class with real money at stake—a true innovation! He offered a prize of $100. One "A" player and four "B" players could divide this money up among themselves if they could form a coalition that lasted at least ten minutes.

Player A could form a coalition with two B players or the four B players could join together. I was Player A, and after a lot of back-and-forth with shifts in the coalitions, I managed to get one that lasted the required ten minutes. Two B Players each received $20 and I pocketed the remaining $60. This vividly clear experiment taught me that price is always about how people divide up value.

Eight years later, I became a colleague of Prof. Selten at the University of Bielefeld. To this day, he remains the only German to win a Nobel in economics. His experiment was one of the highlights of my studies.

After passing my exams, my university studies continued seamlessly, with price becoming a common thread. It turns out that my dissertation *Price Strategies for New Products* changed the course of my life (Simon 1976). During my time as Prof. Albach's assistant, I worked on several expert analyses that dealt with pricing-related issues. That work gave me my first glimpse into how pricing works at large companies. It struck me that there was a lot of improvement potential.

During my time as professor at Bielefeld (1979–1989) and Mainz (1989–1995), I assigned many master's theses and dissertations in that field. Every area of price management we explored seemed to generate more questions. All of this work combined to advance and expand the base of knowledge around price management. In addition to my teaching activities at Bielefeld and Mainz, I conducted classes and gave talks on price management at universities, business schools, and management conferences throughout the world. It was as if pricing was slowly but surely awakening from a deep sleep.

When I visited Philip Kotler at Northwestern University, he referred me to someone in Chicago named Dan Nimer, who called himself a "price consultant." His work was practice-oriented and he seemed to be making a good living at it. The thought of a "price consultant" in that sense was a completely foreign concept to me at the time. Nimer sent me some of his articles, and the differences between his publications and the theoretical papers I had read and written in my academic career could not have been more striking. The scientific papers on price in the academic world were long on theory but devoid of practical advice. In his early years, Nimer formulated a sentence whose validity has stood the test of time: "The job of pricing is not to earn back costs, but to capture the perceived value of a product" (Smith 2015).

I would see Nimer on occasion in the ensuing years. In 2012, members of the pricing community honored this visionary of pricing with a voluminous book of almost 400 pages for his 90th birthday (Smith 2012).[3] But he was by no means retired. He still lectured on pricing and advised clients. Dan Nimer passed away on January 9, 2015.

I also had many interesting discussions about pricing with the world-renowned management thinker Peter Drucker, who encouraged me in my pursuit of the goal of finding practical applications for pricing theory and research.

"I am impressed by your emphasis on pricing," he once told me. "And I think it will be a while before competitors catch up with you. Price is totally neglected in marketing. Pricing strategy today is little more than guesswork."[4]

Pricing intrigued Drucker from an economic and also from an ethical perspective. He understood profit to be the "cost of survival" and sufficiently high prices to be a "means for survival." Drucker always tried to strike a clear ethical balance. He warned against the abuses of market power. He commented on price transparency and advocated fair behavior. Shortly before his death in 2005, he provided a testimonial for *Manage for Profit, Not for Market Share*, a

---

[3] My own article in this reader has the title "How Price Consulting is Coming of Age," pp. 61–79.
[4] Personal letter from Peter Drucker from June 7, 2003.

book which I co-wrote with my partner colleagues Frank Bilstein and Frank Luby: "Market share and profitability have to be balanced and profitability has often been neglected. This book is therefore a greatly needed correction."[5]

Since my dissertation, I have remained true to the topic of pricing and concentrated my research on it. For the title of my first textbook, published in 1982, I coined a new term: price management (Simon 1982). I had dwelled on potential titles for a long time. At the time, the term "price management" was unique in German as well as in English. As far as I could tell, no one had used it before, but it also did not trigger a lot of spontaneous acceptance. Up to that time, the common terms in the pricing vernacular were "price theory" and "price policy." Price theory was the field that I learned, thanks to the theoretical emphasis at the University of Bonn. Price policy covered the more practice-oriented content, but it was qualitative, akin to an oral history passed down from generation to generation. Such qualitative statements do not provide much to go on. At the end of the day, a price is a number, which means it is a quantitative term. With the term "price management," I aspired to integrate these seemingly incompatible worlds by making the quantitative, theoretical concepts accessible and useful, so that businesspeople could make better pricing decisions.

The first edition of my textbook was quite the tome, with 483 pages. The second edition in 1992 reflected a complete overhaul of the content as well as the addition of a subtitle: "Analysis—Strategy—Implementation." The book's size grew accordingly to 740 pages. A few years later, I shifted away from the textbook format and collaborated with Bob Dolan on a trade publication aimed primarily at managers. We jointly published the book *Power Pricing* in 1996 and it continues to sell well to this day (Dolan and Simon 1996).

In 2008, I published the third edition of *Preismanagement* with Professor Martin Fassnacht as co-author. His involvement would ensure that the book reflected the current state from the academic side, which I was no longer as close to as in the past. He and I formed a rare combination for textbook authors because we merged the practical side—where I had spent the previous 13 years—with the academic side. In 2011, the third edition won the Georg Bergler Prize in Germany for the best marketing textbook. In 2016, we prepared the fourth edition, which explored the effects of digitalization much more thoroughly than the previous three editions, and in 2019 the updated

---

[5] Personal e-mail from Peter Drucker's wife Doris Drucker from November 2, 2005. She writes: "I am sorry to tell you that Peter is very ill. Before his collapse, he dictated a letter to you. The secretary just brought it here for his signature," followed by the quoted text. I received the letter only after Peter Drucker's death on November 11. We had planned to meet at his house in Claremont, CA, near Los Angeles, on November 12, 2005.

and expanded English-language version *Price Management* was published by Springer, New York (Simon and Fassnacht 2019). My various pricing books have been translated into more than 20 languages.

Imitation is the sincerest form of flattery, as the saying goes. But when imitation crosses the line legally and ethically, it is not very flattering. We experienced that feeling firsthand in 2010, when a well-known German publishing house released a book with the same name, *Preismanagement*. The author was an established professor in Germany whose name I will not mention.

Due to the comprehensive "overlaps" with our book, the copycat book was removed from the market at the end of 2010. Its publisher recognized our rights to title and agreed to refrain from publishing or distributing any books that violate those rights. My lawyer also sent a cease-and-desist letter to Amazon's German operations because the book was still available there. Amazon complied immediately.

Pretium—the Legacy of the Ancient Romans

People have asked me countless times to name the most important aspect of pricing. I answer with one simple word: "value." More precisely, the answer is "value to customer." The price a customer is willing to pay, and therefore the price a company can achieve, is always a reflection of the perceived value of the product or service in the customer's eyes. If the customer perceives a higher value, his or her willingness to pay rises. The converse is equally true: if the customer perceives a lower value relative to competitive products, willingness to pay drops. "Perceive" is the operative word. When a company tries to figure out the price it can achieve, only the subjective (perceived) value of the customer matters. The objective value of the product or other measures of value, such as the Marxian theory that value is defined by the human labor time invested, matter only to the degree that the customer thinks they matter and is willing to a pay a price in return.

The Ancient Romans understood this connection so well that they incorporated it into their language. In Latin, the word "pretium" means both price and value. Literally speaking, price and value are one and the same. This is a good guideline for businesses to follow when they make their price decisions. It leaves managers with three tasks:

- **Create value:** The quality of materials, performance, and design all drive the perceived value of customers. This is also where innovation comes into play.

- **Communicate value:** This is how you influence customers' perception. It includes how you describe the product, your selling proposition, and last but not least the brand. Value communication also covers packaging, product performance, and shelf or online placement.
- **Retain value:** What happens post-purchase can be decisive in shaping a lasting, positive perception. Expectations about how the value lasts will have a strong influence on a customer's willingness to pay for luxury goods, consumer durables, and cars. The price of Porsches or Ferraris may actually increase over time.

Sellers should start the process of setting prices only after they are clear about the perceived value of the product or service. At the same time, customers must also develop a keen awareness of value. The customers' best defense against getting ripped off or overpaying is to understand the value of what they are buying. Knowledge of value also helps the customer avoid buying a "lemon," which is a product that appears to be a bargain at first glance but turns out to be a bad deal.[6]

The wisdom of the famous Spanish philosopher Baltasar Gracian (1601–1658) captured that sentiment perfectly: "Better be cheated in the price than in the quality of goods" (Gracian 2009). It is very frustrating to pay more than you should have. But the anger over this form of "rip off" often fades if the product gets the job done well. Worse is the situation when the product is flawed. The frustration stays with you until you finally use up the product or get rid of it. The moral here is that one should not lose sight of quality in pursuit of a better deal. Admittedly, that is easier said than done. The price itself usually has one dimension, or a small number, whereas the quality of a product or service is a function of many variables and is therefore harder to assess.

The French have a similar saying to Gracian's: *"Le prix s'oublie, la qualité reste."* Loosely translated, it means that the quality you bought endures long after you have forgotten the price. Prices are often ephemeral and quickly forgotten, while impressions of value and quality last much longer. Who has not hastily celebrated capturing a bargain or paying a low price, only to find out later that quality was poor and the bargain an illusion? Conversely, who has not at least once complained about paying a high price and then been pleasantly surprised when the quality turned out to be

---

[6] The term "lemon" for a bad product was first used in a widely read article of the American economist George A. Akerlof in which he examines the signals of prices in the used-car market. George A. Akerlof, The Market for "Lemons": Quality Uncertainty and the Market Mechanism, The Quarterly Journal of Economics, August 1970, pp. 488–500. Akerlof received the Nobel Prize in 2001.

excellent? The English social reformer John Ruskin (1819–1900) described this insight succinctly: "It is unwise to pay too much, but it is worse to pay too little. When you pay too much, you lose a little money—that is all. When you pay too little, you sometimes lose everything because the thing you bought was incapable of doing the thing you bought it to do. The common law of business balance prohibits paying a little and getting a lot—it cannot be done. If you deal with the lowest bidder, it is well to add something for the risk you run, and if you do that you will have enough to pay for something better."[7]

I must confess that I learned this lesson the hard way. The farms in my home village were so small that two or three farmers needed to share a reaping-and-binding machine. That also meant that we all needed to help each other with our harvests. When I was 16, I had had enough of this time-consuming routine and decided to do something about it. My family would become independent. Without asking my father, I spent $600—almost $5000 in 2019 dollars—on a second-hand reaping-and-binding machine. The price seemed very reasonable, and I was proud to have found such a bargain! Then we used it for the next harvest and quickly made a frustrating discovery. The machine used a new and unfamiliar system, which proved unreliable in practice. The damn thing kept breaking down. So much for my bargain! The frustration dogged us for two years, before we scrapped the machine for good. I had learned my lesson.

I wonder if governments and their agencies—who generally award contracts to the lowest bidder—are aware of that French saying or Ruskin's comment. I am reminded of a remark that Alan Shepard—the first US astronaut in space—once made when asked about whether he ever felt fear in a space capsule. He admitted that he once thought to himself "My God, just think, this thing was built by the lowest bidder" (Thompson 2005).

When Prices Come First

For innovations, it can be advisable to flip around the conventional wisdom of price setting. Instead of developing the product and then deciding the price, companies should first think about the achievable price. This "first the price" process is the core idea of the book *Monetizing Innovation* by my partner colleagues Madhavan Ramanujam and Georg Tacke (Ramanujam and Tacke 2016). They recommend that the product be developed around the

---

[7] www.iposs.de/1/gesetz-der-wirtschaft; accessed on Jun 6, 2017.

price in order to avoid the fatal errors that doom new products in the market. One such common error is what the authors call "feature shock," which occurs when too many features are crammed into the product. The attempt to offer everything to everybody leads to two consequences: nobody gets the product they truly desire, and the resulting prices end up unacceptably high. The "Fire" smartphone offered by Amazon illustrates this. The phone had four camera lenses in order to enable facial recognition. The product was launched in July 2014 at $199, and just four months later Amazon cut the price to 99 cents. Thanks to this flop, Amazon incurred a write-down of $170 million.

Another fatal error is to make a product from the outset that no one really needs, and even worse, compound the error by charging an expensive price. Many technological marvels fall into that category. One prominent example—perhaps the poster child for this kind of product—is the Segway personal transporter. When the innovation first hit the market, inventor Dean Kamen anticipated selling 50,000 units in the first year. Six years later, sales had totaled 30,000 units. That is not per year. That is the absolute total for the six years. In other words, the Segway missed its original forecasts by 90%. One root cause was the horrendously high price. The base version cost $5000, while other versions cost as much as $7000. Apparently, the perceived value of the product was significantly lower. The launch of the Segway ignored the principle of the Latin word "pretium."

In my view, companies that really do start their product development process with the price are still the minority. A pioneer in the area, however, is Porsche. Few companies in the automotive industry, never mind other industries, probe the consequences of price before they invest in the development of a new product. In their book, Ramanujam and Tacke describe the process for the development of the Porsche Cayenne: "Long before the first concept car rolled out of the Engineering Group center in Weissach, the product team conducted an extensive set of surveys with potential customers, gauging the appetite for a Porsche SUV and evaluating prices to find an acceptable range. They were pleased to find that customers were enthusiastic. Analysis showed that customers were willing to pay more for a Porsche SUV than they would for comparable vehicles from other manufacturers. The potential for a hit was there" (Ramanujam and Tacke 2016, p. 4). It is no coincidence that Porsche is the most profitable carmaker, and also one of our most interesting experiences in pricing and product development.

Pricing Power is Critical

As Warren Buffett has said: "The single most important business decision in evaluating a business is pricing power".[8] Pricing power determines whether a supplier can achieve its desired prices. It also determines the degree to which a brand can earn a premium price. The flipside of pricing power is buying power: to what extent can a buyer get the desired prices from his suppliers? In some industries, such as car manufacturing, purchasing power is high and buyers wield significant buying power over suppliers. Likewise, retailers can exert their buying power over suppliers when market concentration is high. In Germany, some 85% of the revenue in food and grocery is concentrated in the hands of four retail groups: Edeka, Rewe, Aldi, and the Schwarz Group, which operates Kaufland and Lidl.

An unusual interpretation of price, one which emphasizes the importance of pricing power, comes from the French sociologist Gabriel Tarde (1843–1904). He considered every agreement on prices, wages, or interest rates to be equivalent to a military truce (Tarde 1902). This is often evident in the wage negotiations between unions and employers. The peace lasts only until the next round of fighting begins. In a business-to-business negotiation, the agreement on a price reflects a power struggle between supplier and customer. Fortunately, it is not a zero-sum game. But price plays a pivotal role on how a pool of money gets divided up between a supplier and a customer.

In reality, the pricing power of most companies is relatively modest. Simon-Kucher & Partners interviewed over 2700 managers in 50 countries for its "Global Pricing Study"[9] and found that only 33% of respondents felt their companies had a high level of pricing power. The remaining two thirds admitted that their companies are not able to implement the prices they need in the market to achieve an appropriate return.

At the same time, the survey revealed that pricing power was 35% higher in companies whose top management was involved in setting the framework for pricing decisions instead of delegating that authority. Companies with dedicated pricing departments had 24% more pricing power than companies without such departments. The key lesson is that it pays for top managers to make a strong and serious commitment to better pricing and to invest time and energy into this endeavor. This sparks a positive spiral, as higher pricing power leads to sustainably higher prices and higher profits.

[8] From the transcript of an interview of the Financial Crisis Inquiry Commission (FCIC) with Warren Buffett on May 26, 2010.
[9] The study was conducted in 2012.

Price Moves into Unchartered Waters

In the past, many goods and services had no prices. The use of streets was free, going to school cost nothing, and many services came with an all-inclusive price. Governments, churches, and charities delivered goods and services at no charge because it would help others or because charging a price would be considered immoral or taboo. But that is changing rapidly.

In his book, *What Money Can't Buy: The Moral Limits of Markets*, Harvard philosopher Michael J. Sandel reports that prices are creeping into all realms of our lives (Sandel 2012). The airline Easy Jet charges passengers $16 to be among the first to board the aircraft. It costs a foreigner $14 to enter the United States. That is the price of an entry into ESTA (Electronic System for Travel Authorization.) In some countries, you can pay extra during rush hour to travel in exclusive lanes, with the prices dependent on the current traffic.

The so-called market designers recommend general traffic pricing systems that apply to all roads. They estimate the cost of the current levels of traffic congestion at $1 trillion. Modern technologies make it possible to monitor and price the usage of roadways based on real-time scarcity. Some authors see this as "an inevitable future" in order to make the usage of roadways more efficient. According to their study of expressways in Singapore, the introduction of such a system increased the average speed from 19 to 42 miles per hour (Cramton et al. 2018). The prices vary according to the traffic situation.

Other areas where prices have made inroads range from the creative to the unexpected. For a fee of $1500 per year, some doctors in the United States offer a dedicated cell phone access number and 24/7 availability. In Afghanistan and other war zones, private companies paid mercenaries between $250 and $1000 per day, with the price based on qualifications, experience, and the mercenary's country of origin. In Iraq and Afghanistan, these private security and military companies had more people on the ground than the US armed forces did (Miller 2007; Glanz 2009). Moving further along the moral spectrum, one can pay a surrogate mother in India $6250 to carry a baby to full term. If you want to immigrate to the United States, you can purchase that right for $500,000. Some universities are auctioning off scarce opportunities to enroll.

Someday many more things will have a price tag attached to them, as more and more of our lives and routines come under market and pricing mechanisms. This creep across moral and ethical boundaries is one of the most significant economic trends of our time. Sandel commented on this development. "When we decide that certain goods may be bought and sold, then we decide—at least implicitly—that it is appropriate to treat them as commodities, as instruments of profit and use. But not all goods are properly valued in this way. The most obvious example is human beings" (Sandel 2012; Kay 2013).

The valuation of companies also poses a challenge and can lead to very high prices. In this context, I encountered the highest price I have personally experienced in my entire career. It was March 2, 2000 in Ludwigshafen, Germany. I was sitting in the office of Max Dietrich Kley, at that time the CFO of BASF, the world's largest chemical company. BASF had recently sold its pharmaceutical unit—which it had bundled into the company Knoll AG—to Abbott Laboratories. Kley's secretary came into the room and handed him a piece of paper. He looked at it and said "this is the confirmation, the purchase price for Knoll AG, 6.9 billion Deutschmark, has been deposited into our account." That sum corresponded to US$3.6 billion, an amount that no one would look at twice in today's environment for mergers and acquisitions. But at that time, it was a gigantic sum of money.

The Philosophy of Price

After having spent my whole life dealing with prices, the idea arose to illuminate the concept of price from a philosophical point of view. We hardly ever link price-related activities to philosophy. What does philosophy have to do with price? Why should we look at something as ubiquitous and mundane as price from a philosophical standpoint?

It turns out that viewing price through the lens of classical philosophy reveals some very practical insights that can prevent us from making mistakes, both as buyers and sellers. What I refer to as the "philosophy of price" can:

- deepen our understanding of price and its effects
- keep us humble (many seemingly modern pricing concepts were first articulated by ancient philosophers)
- help us to solve difficult ethical pricing issues, such as in health care.

In the remainder of this chapter, I offer some intriguing insights—drawn from classical philosophers—that remain surprisingly relevant for twenty-first century price decisions.

Socrates and Aristotle on Price

The eternal equation "price = value" begs the question: "What is value?" The first known answers to this question come from the Greek philosopher Socrates (469–399 BC,) who said "happiness does not come from ownership, but from the use of a product."[10] In contemporary terminology, we speak of "value-in-use" (Pfisterer and Roth, 2018). We can therefore consider Socrates to be the father of a very modern concept, the sharing economy.[11] In the sharing economy, one does not own a car, a bicycle, or an apartment; one uses it, often only for a defined period. The increasingly widespread implementation of the sharing economy is radically transforming entire industries.

Why was this revolutionary Socratic idea not implemented earlier? The answer is obvious. Transaction costs of sharing were too high prior to the arrival of the internet. Selling a car at $30,000 is one transaction. Sharing it in hourly increments means thousands of transactions over the life of a car. Offering a car on a per-hour basis or a bicycle on a per-minute basis requires an extremely efficient transaction process and the ability to bring together a critical mass of buyers and sellers. Neither is possible without the internet.

We owe more sophisticated insights on value and price to the Greek philosopher Aristotle (384–322 BC). He observed that value-in-use can vary among individuals. This is the basis for the ubiquitous price differentiation or price discrimination we experience today.[12] Aristotle also noted that the value-in-use declines as the quantity of goods increases. This fundamental law is now known as Gossen's Second Law, formulated in 1854 by Hermann Heinrich Gossen (1810–1857) (Gossen 1854). This law is the foundation for non-linear pricing (Tacke 1989).

Aristotle also mentions that the value of a product can depend on the use of another product. This insight provides a rationale for multi-product pricing and for the so-called price bundling. He also observed that the value-in-use will increase if the good can be consumed conspicuously, which leads us to the so-called Snob Effect: demand can actually increase as prices rise because higher prices signal more prestige.

---

[10] Socrates, *Euthydemos*.

[11] Aristotle (384-322 BC) is often cited as the father of the sharing economy. But actually the pioneer was Socrates. The lives of these two philosophers did not overlap. Plato, the mentor of Aristotle, who lived from 427 to 348 BC, overlapped with both Socrates and Aristotle.

[12] Aristotle, *Politics, Book I*; see also Younkins (2018).

Thomas Aquinas on Price

The concept of "just price" dates back to Thomas Aquinas (1225–1274) (Tawney 1948). Today, we use the term "fair price" in a similar sense. Aquinas looked at pricing from an economic and an ethical perspective. His ideas were strongly influenced by the Christian tradition against usury and against interest in general. To raise prices in response to increasing demand was theft in his view. Aquinas also explicitly stated that charging higher prices in the wake of natural disasters is unethical.

This latter topic is highly relevant today, as illustrated by the report "Price Gouging After Hurricane Sandy: Immoral or Law of Supply and Demand."[13] It concerns the pricing for power generators during and after a 2012 hurricane in the United States. Should the seller raise the price after a disaster? If the price is kept constant, the first buyers will buy several generators and resell them at a higher price. Is this just?

We can also look at the case of Uber after a terrorist attack in Australia in 2014. The demand for cars surged, and the Uber program automatically increased the surcharge.[14] This makes economic sense because the higher fees attract more cars to the site from which people want to flee. But that action drew a very negative response in the media. Uber now applies manual intervention if demand rises suddenly and sharply.[15] In the case of a London terror attack in 2017, Uber refunded the passengers who had paid the surcharge.[16]

Very innovative life-saving drugs are another example. Kymriah, a gene-based therapy offered by Novartis, heals a certain type of leukemia with one injection. What is a just price for this product? In the United States, an application of this drug costs up to $475,000. In the United Kingdom, the National Health Service covers a price of 220,000 British pounds, but only for children. In Germany, the price is €320,000.

Would a different price system be more just? One idea brought into the discussion is a refund if the treatment does not yield the promised effect. An alternative could be a price scheme where patients pay 50% of their annual income? A patient who earns $100,000 per year would pay $50,000. A patient who makes $2 million a year would pay $1 million. While such a system

---

[13] "Post-Sandy Price Gouging: Economically Sound, Ethically Dubious," Time, November 2, 2012.

[14] "Uber's Prices Surged in Sydney During the Hostage Crisis, and Everyone Is Furious," New Republic, December 14, 2014.

[15] "London terror attack: Uber slammed for being slow to turn off 'surge pricing' after rampage," Independent, June 4, 2017

[16] "Uber is refunding passengers who used the service after the London terror attack," Mashable, June 5, 2017.

seems unrealistic at first glance, it is actually the basis for income taxes, which one can consider to be the price for government services.

Karl Marx on Price

Are you a Marxist? You are likely to answer "no." So my next question is: "OK, if you are not a Marxist, why is your pricing Marxian?" While Marx's labor theory is totally rejected today, it has survived in pricing. What a strange phenomenon! Let me explain why that is the case.

The most important contribution of Karl Marx (1818–1883) was his labor theory of value, according to which only labor creates value. He writes that the "prices of goods are determined by wages" (Marx 1951). Marx allows for differences in productivity and qualifications of workers, and thus for different values per unit of time. But the core of his theory is that only labor creates value. Consequently, labor costs are the sole base for price calculations.

In modern terminology, we call this method "cost-plus pricing." Based on my decades of observations around the world, I would claim that 80% of all prices in today's markets are primarily determined on the basis of costs. And all costs are labor costs. Lawyers, consultants, and most other service providers charge prices for their time (hourly, daily, monthly rates). If an automotive company buys parts from a supplier, these parts carry labor costs up the value chain.

On Subjective Value

The so-called subjective value theory, which is generally but not universally accepted today, could be expressed as "value is in the eye of the beholder" (Mazzucato 2018). This is also not new. Publilius Syrus, who lived in the first century BC, said: "Everything is worth what a buyer will pay for it." What is this theory's implication for pricing? It is "value extraction" or, in the modern internet vernacular, "monetization" (Ramanujam and Tacke 2016). These terms encompass all variants of price differentiation or price discrimination, across customers, across product variants, across space and time.[17] The internet has radically improved the opportunities for price differentiation due to much better data and much lower costs of implementation.

---

[17] For an in-depth treatment of price differentiation and quantification of subjective value, see Simon and Fassnacht (2019).

However, there is a strong and increasing opposition against "value extraction." Professor Mariana Mazzucato from the London School of Economics is one of the outspoken critics. "Things are only getting worse," she writes. "'Rent seeking' refers to the attempt to generate income, not by producing anything, but by overcharging above the 'competitive price,' and undercutting competition by exploiting particular advantages, or blocking other companies from entering an industry, thereby retaining a monopoly advantage" (Mazzucato 2018). Her views are seconded by Nobel laureate Joseph Stiglitz, who blames weak regulation and monopolistic practices for "rent extraction."

A related key question is whether there is a level playing field between consumers and increasingly sophisticated sellers. I think there is. The reason lies in the much higher price and value transparency the internet provides. Today's consumers have all kinds of price comparisons at their fingertips. The same increasingly applies to value transparency, thanks to widely used customer feedback mechanisms. Marshall McLuhan's "global village," first described in 1962, has become reality. Understanding value creation and delivery on the one side and value extraction (or monetization) on the other side becomes critical for buyers and sellers.

Prices and God

Who makes prices? According to the book, *The Mantle of the Prophet,* the following applies: "Information about prices is the quickening breath that sustains the life of the bazaar, and the mechanism by which these prices adjust to new information on supply and demand is so refined as to seem almost divine. 'God sets prices,' according to a saying ascribed to the Prophet Mohammed, and most Islamic jurists agreed that an unseen hand that operated with such efficiency must be the hand of God" (Mottahedeh 2000). This statement recalls Adam Smith's invisible hand.

Philosophy helps both buyers and sellers to understand pricing challenges better. Many concepts which seem current and modern actually have ancient philosophical roots. But their implementation has only become possible, thanks to modern information technology and Big Data analysis.

My Path to Pricing ... at a Glance

My focus on pricing began with graduate studies and my doctoral dissertation in the early 1970s. At that time, there is no way I could have mapped out where my future in pricing would lead. But pricing became a lifelong, increasing intensive pre-occupation. One can say without any exaggeration that Simon-Kucher has created and continually developed the market for price consulting. The following table provides an overview of the milestones along my personal path through the world of pricing. It took many small steps.

Period/Year	Milestones and experience	Key influencers
1960–1966	Experience in pricing for agricultural goods on my parents' farm	Father
1969–1973	College, especially lectures and the textbook *Preistheorie (Price Theory)*	Prof. Wilhelm Krelle
1972	Price negotiation experiment with a future Nobel Prize winner	Prof. Reinhard Selten
1973–1976	Dissertation "Price Strategies for New Products."	Prof. Horst Albach
1977	Expert analyses on price competition	Prof. Horst Albach
1978–1979	Research at the Massachusetts Institute of Technology; diverse articles on pricing topics	Prof. Alvin J. Silk
1979	Meeting with Philip Kotler, who told me about the "price consultant" Dan Nimer	Prof. Philip Kotler Dan Nimer
1981	Course on price management at INSEAD, Fontainebleau	
1982	Coining the term *Price Management* and publication of the first edition of a textbook with that title	
1983	First consulting projects and talks on pricing topics (BASF, pharmaceutical industry)	
1985	Founded the consulting firm UNIC Institut für Marketing und Management GmbH, which would later become Simon-Kucher & Partners	Dr. Eckhard Kucher Dr. Karl-Heinz Sebastian
1988–1989	Marvin Bower Fellow at Harvard Business School; publication of the English-language book *Price Management*	Prof. Ted Levitt Prof. Robert Dolan
1992	Completely revised second edition of *Price Management* (Germany)	
1993	Development of the BahnCard concept	Hemjö Klein Dr. Georg Tacke
1995	Assumed the CEO role at Simon-Kucher; ended my academic career	
1996	Publication of *Power Pricing* with Robert J. Dolan, Harvard Business School	Prof. Robert Dolan

Period/Year	Milestones and experience	Key influencers
2002	*Business Week* magazine refers to Simon-Kucher as the world market leader in price consulting	
2008	Third edition of *Price Management* (German version) with Martin Fassnacht (WHU) as co-author	Prof. Martin Fassnacht
2009	Retired as CEO of Simon-Kucher	
2012	Publication of *Preisheiten*, a sort of biography about pricing. The English version *Confessions of the Pricing Man* came out in 2015	
2016	Fourth edition of *Price Management* (German version) with Martin Fassnacht (WHU Koblenz) as co-author	Prof. Martin Fassnacht
2019	English-language edition of *Price Management* published	Prof. Martin Fassnacht
2020	*The Philosophy of Price*, an expanded view of price	Classic philosophers

References

Peter Cramton, R. Richard Geddes, and Axel Ockenfels, "Markets for Road Use—Eliminating Congestion through Scheduling, Routing, and Real-Time Road Pricing," Working Paper, Cologne University 2018.

Robert J. Dolan and Hermann Simon, *Power Pricing—How Managing Price Transforms the Bottom Line*, New York: Free Press 1996.

James Glanz, "Contractors Outnumber U.S. Troops in Afghanistan," *New York Times*, September 1, 2009.

Hermann Heinrich Gossen, *Entwicklung der Gesetze des menschlichen Verkehrs und der daraus fließenden Regeln für menschliches Handeln.* Braunschweig: F. Vieweg 1854.

Baltasar Gracian, *Handorakel und Kunst der Weltklugheit*, Berlin: Insel Verlag 2009.

John Kay, "Low-Cost Flights and the Limits of what Money Can Buy," *Financial Times*, January 23, 2013, p. 9.

Karl Marx, *Wages, Prices, and Profits*, Moscow: Foreign Languages Publishing House 1951, p. 28.

Mariana Mazzucato, *The Value of Everything*, London: Penguin Books 2018, p. 57.

T. Christian Miller, "Contractors Outnumber Troops in Iraq," *Los Angeles Times*, July 4, 2007.

Roy Mottahedeh, *The Mantle of the Prophet*, London: Oneworld Publications 2000, p. 34.

Lucas Pfisterer and Stefan Roth, "Value Creation in Usage Processes—Investigating the Micro-foundations of Value-in-Use," *Marketing Journal of Research and Management*, 3/2018.

Madhavan Ramanujam and Georg Tacke, *Monetizing Innovation, How Smart Companies Design the Product around the Price*, Hoboken, N.J.: Wiley 2016.

Michael J. Sandel, *What Money Can't Buy: The Moral Limits of Markets*, New York: Farrar, Straus and Giroux 2012.

Hermann Simon, *Preisstrategien für neue Produkte*, Opladen: Westdeutscher Verlag 1976.

Hermann Simon, *Preismanagement*, Wiesbaden: Gabler 1982.

Hermann Simon and Martin Fassnacht, *Price Management—Strategy, Analysis, Decision, Implementation*, New York: Springer Nature 2019.

Gerald E. Smith (editor), *Visionary Pricing: Reflections and Advances in Honor of Dan Nimer*, London: Emerald Publishing 2012.

Gerald Smith, "Remembering Dan Nimer—A Tribute to a Pricing Pioneer," *The Pricing Advisor*, January 2015, p. 9.

Georg Tacke, *Nichtlineare Preisbildung: Höhere Gewinne durch Differenzierung*, Wiesbaden: Gabler 1989.

Gabriel Tarde, *Psychologie économique, 2 volumes*, Paris: Alcan 1902.

Richard Henry Tawney, *Religion and the Rise of Capitalism—On Aquinas and just price*, New York: Penguin 1948, p. 40.

Neal Thompson, *Light This Candle: The Life And Times of Alan Shepard*, New York: Three Rivers Press (paperback reprinted edition) 2005: p. 388.

Edward W. Younkins, *Aristotle and Economics*, www. quebecoislibre.org/050/050915-11.htm, accessed on September 27, 2018.

10

The Secrets of the Hidden Champions

In 1987, the renowned Harvard Professor Theodore "Ted" Levitt came to Germany and invited me for a one-to-one talk. Levitt had popularized the term "globalization" in a seminal article in the *Harvard Business Review* (Levitt 1983). He was interested in the topic of international competitiveness, and he asked me a seemingly simple question: "Why are the Germans so successful at exports?"

In 1986, Germany had become the world's export leader for the first time. It was amazing that Germany, a relatively small country compared to the United States or Japan, could become the world's largest exporter. But at the same time, it had taken 40 years after the end of World War II for Germany's export strength to reach its full potential.

My encounter with Prof. Levitt left a lasting impression on me, as I will elaborate on in Chap. 13. His question stayed with me. Why *is* Germany so successful in exporting? When trying to unpack this question, one would naturally think first about large companies. And it was true that very large companies such as Bayer, Siemens, Bosch, BMW, and Daimler were very large exporters at that time, and remain so today. They had been building up their international sales networks since the nineteenth century. Bayer originally entered the US market in 1864. Before World War I broke out, Bosch was already earning more than half of its revenues outside of Germany. Siemens began its internationalization even earlier, and by 1890 it had entered the Chinese market. The German *Mittelstand*, however, was at the dawn of its internationalization in the 1980s. Even today, not every *Mittelstand* company is an exporter.

The journalist Peter Hanser from Germany's leading marketing magazine *Absatzwirtschaft* interviewed Levitt and me at our meeting (see photo). One of his questions was: "A problem in German industry is the large number of *Mittelstand* companies with a high share of exports. Is 'global marketing' also a strategy for these companies?" (Hanser 1987). Levitt stressed that all companies start small, but it is primarily the large ones that survive. Family-owned companies, in contrast, need to fight for survival. I argued that young people are going to the *Mittelstand* companies in increasing numbers. Levitt disagreed. At the time, neither of us had given a thought to the phenomenon of the companies I would later refer to as Hidden Champions.

Interview with Professor Theodore Levitt (middle) and reporter Peter Hanser (right)

Around 80% of German companies belong to the *Mittelstand*. That includes the baker on the corner and the tradesman who comes to fix your plumbing. Most of them have no exports whatsoever. But as I wrestled more and more with Levitt's question, I discovered that within the *Mittelstand* there was a considerable number of companies that were either world market leaders or growing very rapidly. They were making an increasing contribution to Germany's export success. Then it suddenly dawned on me: is it possible that these world market leaders from the *Mittelstand* are the true engines behind the extraordinary export success of the German economy?

Of course, I already knew several of these firms. Remember Berthold Leibinger, the one whose helicopter tore off part of the roof when he visited Castle Gracht? He introduced his company, Trumpf, which at that time was making the transition from mechanical sheet-metal-cutting machines to precision laser machines. I was familiar with Hauni, which had a world market share of over 90% in cigarette machines. While in Bielefeld, I had encountered companies such as Union Knopf (world market leader in buttons), Dürkopp-Adler (world market leader in industrial sewing machines,) and Weidmüller, one of the leading companies in industrial connectivity technology. Kannegiesser, the global number one in laundry technology, and Sennheiser, a specialist in high-performance microphones, were also familiar names. Claas, one of the biggest manufacturers of harvesting equipment, was a name I knew from my childhood on the farm. But how many such world market leaders existed in Germany? Were these familiar names the exception or more like the rule? And if it were a large number, were they collectively responsible for a large part of the country's export leadership?

These questions compelled me to dig for better answers. In 1988, I assigned a master's thesis to Daniel Klapper, who today is a professor at Humboldt University in Berlin. He was charged with finding more world market leaders in the *Mittelstand* and collecting basic data on them. Klapper identified 39 of them. I found what we discovered to be so extremely interesting that I decided to conduct additional research. These firms were rapidly growing, had a large number of wholly owned foreign subsidiaries, and were successful even in difficult markets such as Japan. Trumpf had entered Japan in 1964. Lenze, a manufacturer of small mechanical and electrical drives, had cooperated closely with a Japanese company for many years. These companies were true champions, but except for a handful of specialists in their respective fields, nobody knew them.

What should these globally successful *Mittelstand* companies be called? After a lot of thought, I came up with the phrase "Hidden Champions." What exactly does this expression mean? According to my current criteria, a Hidden Champion is a company that:

– Is in the top three in its world market, or number one on its own continent
– Has less than US$5 billion in annual revenue
– Is not very well known to the general public

In other words, it is a world champion that hardly anyone is aware of.

"Hidden Champions" turned out to be a clever and fortuitous choice. Part of the appeal is the implied contradiction. The two words do not fit together at first glance. Champions are normally well known. So how could they be hidden? I used the term publicly for the first time in an article in September 1990. The title was "Hidden Champions—the spearhead of the German economy" (Simon 1990). I could freely speak of a "spearhead" although I still did not know the full extent of their contribution to Germany's exports. A few years later, the doctoral dissertation of Eckart Schmitt at the University of Mainz took us a major step closer to understanding the phenomenon. He identified 457 Hidden Champions (Schmitt 1996).

In the early 1990s, I had no idea what the Hidden Champions concept would evolve into. On January 25, 1993 I met with Nicholas Philipson of the Harvard Business School Press in Boston. We discussed some rather nebulous plans for a book about Germany's *Mittelstand*. That brainstorming session eventually led to the book *Hidden Champions. Lessons from 500 of the World's Best Unknown Companies*, which Harvard Business School Press published in 1996 (Simon 1996). The book demonstrated once again that ideas and plans can come about far in advance of their actual realization. Putting one's ideas and goals into writing appears to be an important part of that process. I started that habit way back in my days as an assistant, and I am astonished by how many of those ideas became reality. Nick Philipson eventually moved to Springer Nature in New York, and he remains my publisher to this day. I prize continuity.

By 2007, our constant vigilance and research had led to the discovery of 1167 Hidden Champions in Germany alone. That number had swollen to around 1300 by the time the third German edition of the book was published in 2012 (Simon 2012). I broadened the research to include the entire world, and to date we have found around 3400 small- and medium-sized business that meet the Hidden Champions criteria. Switzerland and Austria have roughly the same number as Germany on a per-capita basis. But outside the German-speaking countries, the presence of Hidden Champions is very sporadic. The Hidden Champions are something that distinguishes Germany most prominently from the rest of the world. The table below is a bit tongue-in-cheek, but it shows that Germany's share of world market leaders is greater in Hidden Champions than in any other category:

Field	Criterion	Germany's global "market share" (%)
Mittelstand	Number of Hidden Champions	46.2
Contemporary artists	Power 100	29.0
Formula 1	World champions	16.1
Soccer	World champions	15.8
Science	Nobel Prizes	12.5
Universities	Times University Ranking 2018 (Top 100)	10.0
Sports	Olympic gold medals 1896–2016	9.3
Large companies	Number in the Global Fortune 500 in 2017	5.4
Tennis	World rankings, men	5.5

Field	Criterion	Germany's global "market share" (%)
Wikipedia	Entries (2.15 mill. out of 53.9 mill.)	4.6
Society	Time: The 100 most influential personalities, 2009–2011	3.3
Population	Residents	1.2
Land area	Square miles	0.2

In July 2019—32 years later after that meeting with Prof. Levitt—the German historian and sociologist Rainer Zitelmann wrote in *Forbes* that: "Many extremely successful companies escape the attention of those whose business it is to know everything (media), understand everything (scientists), or improve everything (consultants). This is the sphere of the world's best midsize companies, the world of the "Hidden Champions." Deeply hidden under the headlines of sensational business successes lies a completely unnoticed source of leadership wisdom. Hermann Simon coined the term 'Hidden Champions'" (Zitelmann 2019).

Successful Strategy and Leadership—from a Contrarian Perspective

What has the discovery of the Hidden Champions meant to my life? It was more a result of coincidence than intent that this topic burrowed itself deeper and deeper into my mind. The more I explored, the more fascinated I became. Prior to the discovery, I was well aware of the world of large companies, thanks in large part through the exposure at Castle Gracht. But the encounters with the Hidden Champions opened up a completely new perspective on strategy and leadership. Instead of distilling the content from my various books, though, I will highlight these differences with some stories about the people who lead these companies.

From a quantitative standpoint, one of the most striking characteristics of the Hidden Champions is how long the CEO stays at the helm. The average tenure for a CEO at a large company is around six years, but at a Hidden Champion it is 20 years on average. Better than words ever could, this statistic alone attests to the Hidden Champions' commitment to continuity and their long-term orientation. The CEOs of the Hidden Champions also defy easy categorization. They are distinct individuals and many have their share of quirks. What they do have in common is shown in this image:

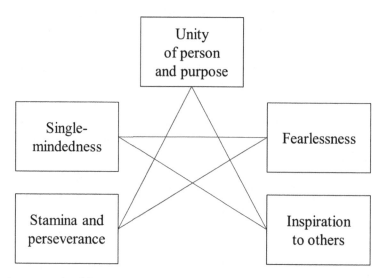

What the CEOs of Hidden Champions have in common

Unity of Person and Purpose

Leaders such as Hans Riegel, Reinhold Würth, Martin Herrenknecht, Heinz-Horst Deichmann, and Günther Fielmann form such a tight bond with their companies that goes beyond merely being synonymous with the company. The person and the company are inseparable. One salient comment about Hans Riegel of the gummi bear maker Haribo was: "His person and his company have always been one entity." Heinz-Horst Deichmann, whose father ran a cobbler's shop that evolved in the European market leader for shoes, said: "I savored the smell of leather from my infancy. I love people, and I love shoes."

Those kinds of bonds resemble the relationship that artists have with their work: "For many creative people the life is the work. They integrate rather than separate their personal life and their work" (Wallace and Gruber 1989). One could say the same about many leaders of Hidden Champions. The total identification with their companies lends them an enviable charisma and power of persuasion. In contrast to some of the outsiders hired as managers, especially within large companies, the leaders of the Hidden Champions are not playing a role. They live out both what they are and what they want to be.

Their attitude toward their work means that this special brand of leader does not view money as the primary motivation. Instead, their primary motivation is derived from the identification with their company and the satisfaction they gain from their work. Financial success plays a subordinate role. Robert Bosch once said that he would "rather lose money than lose trust. It was always an unbearable thought for me that someone would use my products and say that I am delivering poor quality." Henry Ford followed the same line of thinking: "When one of my cars doesn't work, it's my fault." Their absolute commitment and responsibility give such leaders tremendous credibility. They have no reservations about their work and assume full responsibility. True leadership can never be play-acted; it must reside in the leader's core.

Single-Mindedness

Peter Drucker wrote about two scientists he knew personally and who made history, physicist Buckminster Fuller and communication expert Marshall McLuhan: "They exemplify to me the importance of being single-minded. The single-minded ones, the monomaniacs, are the only true achievers. The rest, the ones like me, may have more fun, but they fritter themselves away. The Fullers and the McLuhans carry out a 'mission'; the rest of us have interests. Whenever anything is being accomplished, it is being done by a monomaniac with a mission" (Drucker 1978).

These remarks definitely hold true for the leaders of the Hidden Champions. They are often "monomaniacs" consumed by their missions. But I prefer a more moderate term and refer to this trait as "single-mindedness." Beware of these single-minded competitors! In my research of the Hidden Champions and in my consulting activities, I have met more of them than I can count. If you wake them up at 2 a.m. and ask them what they are thinking about, they will have one answer: their product. How can they make it better and get it to customers more effectively? As Drucker said, behind every major success is a single-minded person with a mission.

Fearlessness

Courage is a trait often ascribed to entrepreneurs. Trumpf's Leibinger regards "courage to take a risk" as the most important entrepreneurial quality. However, I would prefer to call the Hidden Champions' entrepreneurs fearless rather than courageous. They appear to have understood and embraced the Chinese philosophy that "ignorance of your freedom is your captivity."

The leaders of the Hidden Champions do not have the same inhibitions and fears as other people, so they can deploy their skills more effectively. It is really impressive to see how many of these leaders have conquered the world's markets without higher education, foreign experience, or language skills. But they are not reckless gamblers who have bet too much on one card.

Hermann Kronseder founded Krones, today the world market leader in bottling systems.[1] He describes his entry into the American market: "In 1966, an American businessman called me. Four weeks later I flew to the USA, accompanied by my nephew who spoke English and acted as an interpreter. It was my first visit to the USA and I was overwhelmed. We visited New York, Chicago, Detroit, and finally Milwaukee. I came to the conclusion that we needed our own subsidiary in the US. Two days later, we founded Krones Inc. in a room at the Knickerbocker Hotel in Milwaukee. Another two days later we had our first order from a Milwaukee brewery."

The entry of Brita water filters into the US market is another example of this fearless approach. Founder Heinz Hankammer recounts: "Somebody in Salt Lake City expressed interest in our products. I flew over to see whether Brita water filters could be sold in the USA. I went to a drugstore and asked whether I could install a table. I started to make tea with Brita-filtered water and talked to passing customers, and I sold my filters. After three days, I knew what works in America, and what does not. That was ten years ago. Today, our revenues in the US are more than $150 million. Four weeks ago, I was in Shanghai and did exactly the same. Last week, I was in Tirana, the capital of Albania. I want first-hand experience of new markets."

The decisive will to internationalize the company creates a climate of readiness that allows the company to seize even coincidental opportunities without much hesitation. Hankammer describes another experience to me: "I sponsor a soccer club that was visited by a Russian team. I met the mother of one of the Russian players. She spoke English and seemed to think like an entrepreneur. She started our business in Russia, and only one year later, the company had 25 employees and revenues exceeded $1 million. Not a bad start!" Brita is the global market leaders in point-of-use water filters and had a revenue of 474 million Euros in 2018.

Manfred Utsch is the global "king of license plates" which he sells in more than 120 countries. Like an adventurer he has toured the whole world peddling his plates. His adventures in Libya, Kuwait, Belarus, Turkmenistan, and other distant places are legendary. Fear is indeed alien to many of the Hidden Champions leaders.

---

[1] Krones had revenue of 3.7 billion Euros in 2018.

Stamina and Perseverance

The leaders of the Hidden Champions appear to have inexhaustible energy, stamina, and perseverance. Is this energy fed by their identification with their missions? Probably! One expert expressed it this way: "Nothing energizes a person or a company more than clear goals and a grand purpose" (Smith 1994). The fire continues to burn in them, even to retirement age. Some never retire, which could become a problem unto itself. Nonetheless, many of the leaders remain active in their companies well into the 70s. When I meet with them, I truly believe that the energy they exude is palpable. It is as if there is an unknown force or form of energy they have that defies explanation.

Inspiration to Others

Artists may acquire world fame as individuals, but in an economic enterprise nobody can single-handedly create a world market leader. He or she always needs cooperation and support from others. It is not enough if their fire only burns within themselves. They need to ignite that flame in many others. According to leadership expert Warren Bennis, we still do not know why people follow certain leaders and do not follow others (Bennis 1989).

A key capacity among the leaders of the Hidden Champions is to inspire others with enthusiasm for the company's mission and encourage them to deliver the best performance they can. Their 100-percent commitment and enthusiasm not only inspire followers, but is a prerequisite for success. As Steve Jobs once expressed: "Unless you've got a lot of passion for this, you're not going to survive."[2]

I can say that the leaders of the Hidden Champions are very effective and successful in inspiring others. But that is not necessarily because of their outward appearance or the way they communicate. Many of them are not born communicators, at least according to superficial criteria. Personally, I believe that the character traits cited above—the unity of person and purpose, the single-mindedness, the stamina, and the energy—are the key determinants of the ability to inspire others. Ultimately, the leaders are the foundation for the outstanding success of the Hidden Champions. To cite the *Forbes* article on the Hidden Champions by Rainer Zitelmann again: "Not many people combine these personality traits. Leaders are a rare breed" (Zitelmann 2019).

---

[2] https://genius.com/Steve-jobs-1995-interview-with-computerworlds-oral-history-project-annotated.

Over the last few decades, I had the honor and pleasure to meet hundreds of this rare breed of leaders. Each and every one of them left a powerful, lasting impression. People like Berthold Leibinger and Reinhold Würth push relentlessly for growth. When his eponymous company reached annual sales of 300 million DM, Würth reset the goal for 1 billion DM. But that threshold was only the starting point for the next goal: 3 billion DM. That process continues, and in 2018 Würth achieved annual revenue of 13.6 billion euros (26.6 billion DM) and employed 77,000 people. But leadership and globalization are not a matter of size, as the company Flexi demonstrates. Led by Manfred Bogdahn, the company built a share of 70% in the global market for retractable dog leashes, yet its annual revenue is only around 70 million euros. I also think of younger entrepreneurs such as Frank Blase. His firm, Igus, is hardly known to anyone. But it is a world market leader in two markets, in plastic bearings and in energy chains. Igus is not exactly small anymore, with 750 million euros in sales, 4200 employees, and a presence in 40 countries. Igus's closeness to customer is exemplary. Their guiding principle is "KNOC," an acronym for the German phrase "No 'no' without the boss." No employee can dismiss a customer's wish without getting clearance from the CEO.

Another "tough cookie" is Klaus Grohmann, the founder of Grohmann Engineering. This company, based in the Eifel town of Prüm, sells among other things the machinery to assemble electronic and automation components. Elon Musk, the CEO of Tesla, was so impressed by the company that he bought it in January 2017. The firm is now known as Tesla Grohmann Automation. Whether the cultures will mesh remains to be seen, but Klaus Grohmann himself parted ways with the new company a few months after the purchase.

The Hidden Champions are not exclusive to Germany. I have gotten to know many of them around the world, in countries ranging from China to New Zealand and from South Africa to Eastern European countries. Of course, they exist in the United States too. What I have noticed is that the leaders of these small and medium-sized companies—independent of where they are—show similar personality traits. In Chap. 13, I will go into greater detail on two of them, China's Yang Shuren and Japan's Tomohiro Nakada.

Most of these CEOs lead family-owned companies that are not publicly listed. They think in terms of generations, not quarters. Many of them, however, share a common problem, namely how to handle succession. Globalization confronts these leaders with considerable challenges, and there is not always someone in the family who can deal with them. As a result, the share of managers from outside the family ranks continues to increase. One can only hope that these changes do not rob the Hidden Champions of the identities they have cultivated.

Harvard's publication of the first Hidden Champions book in 1996 brought sudden and global attention to the concept. The different versions of the book have appeared in 25 languages in the meantime. Alone in China there have been five editions. I estimate that Hidden Champions have been the subject of well over 5000 articles and interviews. The magazine *BusinessWeek* devoted a cover to the Hidden Champions and chose Nerio Alessandri (pictured), the founder and CEO of Technogym, to represent them.[3]

Hidden Champions on the cover of *BusinessWeek*

---

[3] Business Week, January 26, 2004.

The concept's growing attention has had other ripple effects. Judging from the number of queries I receive almost daily, there have been several hundred master's and doctoral theses written about the Hidden Champions. On Amazon's German website, there are more than 20 books with "Hidden Champions" in the title that I have not written myself. The television news network n-tv awards an annual Hidden Champions prize, and the German state Hesse honors *Mittelstand* leaders with its own Hidden Champions award. The European School of Management and Technology (ESMT) in Berlin established the world's first Hidden Champions Institute (HCI). Its task is to conduct research into the topic beyond the scope of what I have been able to accomplish. In Korea, Yoonsung Cho founded the Hidden Champions Management Institute which organizes educational activities inspired by the concept. As I will elaborate on in Chap. 12, the "Hermann Simon Business School" in China is dedicated to the dissemination of the Hidden Champions idea. The first fruits of the concept are also emerging in finance. Avesco Financial Services AG in Berlin operates a "Sustainable Hidden Champions" fund. A successful Hidden Champions fund exists in Singapore as well. In Taiwan, there are several Hidden Champions competitions. Interest in the secrets of Germany's *Mittelstand* has grown enormously. That is particularly true in China. But interest continues to grow even in Korea and Japan, whose sectors of small- and medium-sized business are historically weak.

France is a special case with respect to Hidden Champions. The French took a very close look at the German model in the wake of the Great Recession of 2008–2009. Wanting to understand the reasons behind Germany's success and learn from them, they homed in on the *Mittelstand.* That led to my being invited to give numerous talks on Hidden Champions, including one to the French Senate.[4] I introduced the Hidden Champions concept and posited two provocative theses. First, a highly centralized country will not create a *Mittelstand.* Second, if a country places extremely high value on elite education, it can hinder the development of a *Mittelstand.*

In my opinion, both of these hypotheses apply to France. The country's high level of centralization means that Paris attracts all the talent. The recipe for the dream career in France is a degree from an elite school, followed by a job in a large company or a ministry. Hardly anyone is interested in working

---

[4] The French senate (Sénat) is the upper chamber (chamber haute) of the French parliament. There is also a lower chamber (chambre basse), the national assembly.

in a rural area or for a small- or medium-sized business, which by definition has little name recognition and status in a centralized society.

I have the impression that the constant comparisons to Germany are a point of frustration for many French. They have learned that it is extremely difficult, if not impossible, to replicate the German *Mittelstand*. This paralyzing realization, in my view, has caused interest in the German economy to ebb in France. Nonetheless, Emmanuel Macron, who was elected president in 2017, called for a new *Mittelstand* initiative. In this context, a "Club des Champions Cachés" was established. Stephan Guinchard, who translated my book into French, tells me that all such initiatives struggle to make progress.[5]

Korea struggles in a similar way, despite considerable effort and many initiatives. To this day, the handful of large corporations, the chaebols, are the centers of economic power. China is a much different case. With few exceptions, the large Chinese companies—China Mobile, the electric utilities, the banks—focus on the domestic market. Roughly, two thirds of China's enormous exports come from small- and medium-sized companies. Many of these companies are eagerly embracing the Hidden Champions concept. In my view, these Chinese companies will become the most dangerous competitors to the German *Mittelstand*. Among other areas, one sees this in mergers and acquisitions activity. The cement pump maker Putzmeister was taken over by the construction machine manufacturer Sany, and the Chinese company Midea has bought the robotics Hidden Champion KUKA. My estimate is that Chinese companies acquired about 25 German Hidden Champions from 2011 to 2019. The Chinese show a keen interest in the Hidden Champions concept. When I give a speech there and ask who wants to become a Hidden Champion, often more than half of the listeners raise their hands.

Hidden Champions became the second professional theme in my life. Together with my contributions to price management, it is an important reason for my induction to the Thinkers50 Hall of Fame. The term has made inroads into the global management language. Googling "Hidden Champions" yields more than 1700,000 hits.[6] Interest remains strong and growing even 25 years after the publication of the first Hidden Champions book. In my lectures, I am often asked whether "Hidden Champions" is an outdated model, as Ted Levitt suspected in our conversation back in 1987. My answer is an emphatic "no." I see the Hidden Champions as models for strategy and leadership in the twenty-first century. If they remain true to their

---

[5] Stephan Guinchard writes: "Regarding the topic of Mittelstand in France, there is a lot of buzz being made around it, but actions are slow to follow," e-mail from September 5, 2017.

[6] Accessed on February 16, 2021.

principles—such as focus, globalization, innovation, and the ambition to be the best in the world—I am not concerned about their future.

Another consequence—and one more important for me personally—is that I resolutely followed the Hidden Champions strategy as founder and CEO of Simon-Kucher & Partners. That firm's development is the theme of the next chapter.

References

Warren Bennis, *Why Leaders Can't Lead*, San Francisco: Jossey-Bass 1989.

Peter F. Drucker, *Adventures of a Bystander*, New York: Harper & Row 1978, p. 255.

Peter Hanser, "asw-Fachgespräch mit Theodore Levitt und Hermann Simon," *Absatzwirtschaft* 8/1987, pp. 20–20.

Theodore Levitt, "The Globalization of Markets," *Harvard Business Review*, May/June 1983, pp. 92–102.

Eckart Schmitt: *Strategien mittelständischer Welt- und Europamarktführer*, Wiesbaden: Gabler Verlag 1996.

Hermann Simon, "Hidden Champions—Speerspitze der deutschen Wirtschaft," *Zeitschrift für Betriebswirtschaft* 60 (9/1990), pp. 875–890.

Hermann Simon, *Hidden Champions—Lessons from 500 of the World's Best Unknown Companies*, Cambridge, MA: Harvard Business School Press 1996.

Hermann Simon, *Hidden Champions—Aufbruch nach Globalia*, Frankfurt: Campus 2012.

Lee Smith, "Stamina: Who has it. Why you need it. How to get it," *Fortune*, November 28, 1994, p. 71.

Doris Wallace und Howard Gruber (eds.), *Creative People at Work, Twelve Cognitive Case Studies*, New York-Oxford: Oxford University Press 1989, p. 35.

Rainer Zitelmann, "The Leadership Secrets of the Hidden Champions," *Forbes*, July 15, 2019

11

On Wings of Eagles

Every Beginning is Hard

In addition to my academic research, I was always committed to establishing contacts in the business world. The reputation and the network of Professor Albach proved to be very helpful in this regard because he allowed me to take part in executive seminars and expert-witness analyses and preparation.

When I was appointed professor at the University of Bielefeld, I invested my own efforts into practice-oriented research and teaching. Companies would approach us with requests to help them solve specific marketing problems, and those requests sometimes turned into small consulting projects. But one project turned out to be decisive in shaping my future plans. It was for the industrial paints division of BASF, the largest chemical company in the world. The fee—125,000 DM (around 62,500 euros)—was a very high sum relative to my circumstances at that time.

We visited more than 100 companies that use industrial paints, and we conducted extensive interviews. Then using modern statistical methods such as multidimensional scaling and discriminant analysis, we developed a customer segmentation based on differences in customer behavior and purchasing volumes. While the analyses were complex, the results were simple enough for the BASF teams to apply and manage. The consequences for product and price differentiation as well as for the sales organization were significant. Under the new segmentation, customers that fulfilled certain criteria regarding their technical requirements and their purchase volumes were served by a central organization with a correspondingly high level of technical competence. Customers with more basic technical requirements, greater price

© The Author(s), under exclusive license to Springer Nature Switzerland AG 2021
H. Simon, *Many Worlds, One Life*, https://doi.org/10.1007/978-3-030-60758-6_11

sensitivity, and relatively lower purchase volumes remained in the purview of regional sales units.

My first graduate assistant, Eckhard Kucher, supervised the project day to day. Kucher, who had yet to complete his doctorate, executed the project with absolute confidence, demonstrating a high degree of methodological rigor and subject matter expertise. The client's acceptance of our work—and the knowledge that we could handle such a project—were huge confidence builders for us. At the same time, the success taught me that one cannot conduct such projects with a consistent level of professionalism and confidentiality while working within a university. The team that worked on the project was paid well, and with the exception of a small amount of computer time, we did not draw on any university resources. But I was uncomfortable handling highly confidential data and impactful recommendations within the university. If we wanted to pursue the idea of management consulting seriously, it seemed wise to set up an organization independent of the university. At the time, though, I was a young professor occupied with building up my academic chair. Research had a high priority. Nonetheless, the seed of the consulting idea had been planted, and it would continue to develop and germinate.

During my sabbatical in Japan in 1983, I received a letter from Kucher and my second graduate assistant, Karl-Heinz Sebastian. They were reflecting on their impressions from our consulting projects and from the Marketing Services trade fair in Frankfurt several months earlier. Our booth at the fair, under the motto "Decision Support for Marketing," had resonated well with the attendees. Many of them asked if we provided consulting. These experiences and impressions inspired Eckhard and Karl-Heinz to suggest a very forward-looking initiative. In their letter of November 21, 1983, they wrote:

> "At this point we want to thoroughly address potential ideas, thoughts, and suggestions regarding how we could work together professionally in the future. The marketing services trade fair demonstrated that there is demand for the analyses we do. For you that is certainly nothing new. It is our opinion that we should take a closer look at this aspect as an opportunity for the time after we have completed our doctoral dissertations. Serving existing demand and stimulating new demand is something we could manage best as a team. For many reasons we see the current team of Simon-Kucher-Sebastian as qualified to successfully capitalize on these opportunities. As a team, we would distinguish ourselves in the following ways
>
> 1. Deep, fundamental qualification in the areas of quantitative market research and decision support.
> 2. Excellent contacts in the business world
> 3. Synergy effects in terms of both competencies and personalities.

Taking all this into account, we see ourselves offering analytical services in an area where we would have no significant competition. We see the formation of a team to work together in the future as an opportunity for all of us.[1]

These ideas landed on fertile ground in my mind. I spent a week thinking about the topic and wrote back on December 1st to say that I welcomed their vision and that we ought to develop a concrete concept after my return from Japan and Stanford in the spring of 1984. I was indeed very happy that my two assistants reached out to me on their own initiative. But there were barriers between having the idea to start a consulting organization and actually implementing it. Overcoming them would require team members who not only have the ability and qualifications to be consultants, but also have the courage to join a start-up and begin at square one. A start-up would mean that my two assistants would need to take on a big risk, while I would at least have my professorship to fall back on. Of course such a venture could damage my reputation as well, but at least my financial risks would be rather limited.

After Japan I spent three months at Stanford, as I described in Chap. 6. When I returned to Germany, the three of us got together and fleshed out the concept. Most of our meetings took place at a hotel in the Ahr river valley, a tranquil location we knew from executive seminars. The peace and seclusion allowed us to brainstorm without disruptions and to formulate concrete plans. Because I had a professor's chair, I did not want to lend my name to the venture. So we settled on the name UNIC, which is short for University Connection. The name was meant to represent our use of academic research tools to solve hands-on, real-world problems. Our "sub-title" was Institute for Marketing and Management.

We launched the venture formally at the beginning of 1985. We created a limited liability company (GmbH in German) with Eckhard, Karl-Heinz, my wife, and I each holding equal shares. Our start-up capital was 100,000 DM (ca. $55,000.) We rented a small, affordable office on the outskirts on Bonn, a city we chose primarily for one simple reason: that is where I lived. That decision is also in line with my general experience with decisions on where to locate a business. One need only look at who makes the location decision and what his or her preferences are. That is usually all it takes. We worked very modestly and cost-consciously. The cost-consciousness I enforced has remained at the forefront of our thinking, so much so that a speech on the occasion of my 70th birthday cited my obsession with it.

---

[1] Letter from Eckhard Kucher and Karl-Heinz Sebastian to Hermann Simon in Tokyo, November 21, 1983.

Eckhard Kucher was UNIC's first employee. He started shortly after completing his dissertation. A few months later, Karl-Heinz Sebastian joined after completing his. We hired 23-year-old Christiane Nelles as our secretary. Today, she is still with the firm (now Simon-Kucher & Partners) and serves as head of administration.

The biggest challenge—as it is with any start-up of this kind—is acquiring projects. Where will the projects come from? Getting initial projects was hard work, even though we had a considerable network to tap into. Projects of $10,000 or even $50,000 were celebrated as huge successes. The saying that every beginning is hard definitely applied to UNIC. In the first year, with three employees, we generated revenue just under $400,000. We considered that to be a success and were proud of our achievements. The first year is considered to be the most precarious one for any start-up, and we had cleared that hurdle.

Four years later, we achieved revenues of $2.5 million with a team of 13, and by 1994 revenues had increased to $6.5 million with a team of 35 associates. That is when I ended my university career and took the reins at Simon-Kucher & Partners on a full-time basis. I served as CEO from 1995 to 2009, then became chairman until my 70th birthday in February 2017, when I assumed the title of honorary chairman.

My secret wish was that the firm would have over 1000 employees by the time I turned 70. At my birthday party on February 11, 2017, CEO Georg Tacke announced that the firm had 1003 employees. The wish had come true! Simon-Kucher & Partners remains the world market leader for price consulting. In 2020, the firm's global revenues reached $412 million, and the number of employees had grown to 1600 working in 41 offices and 25 countries on six continents.

One expectation when we founded the firm, however, went unfulfilled. Our original objective was to use econometric methods to support business decisions. Econometrics uses historical data to measure the effects of price, advertising, and sales activities. Our particular focus was price, the topic of my dissertation as well as Kucher's. He relied on scanner data, a very novel source of data at that time. Sebastian's dissertation analyzed the effects of advertising on the spread of fixed-line telephones. From a research and competency standpoint, we were all highly qualified to apply econometric methods to improve marketing decisions.

But we were not aware of the practical limitations of these techniques in real life. Lester G. Telser, a professor at the University of Chicago, had already foreseen the limitations back in 1962 (Telser 1962). The amount of variation observed is the most important and most common differentiator. In a market with a high price elasticity, one will probably observe little change in the differences of competitors' prices. From an econometrics perspective, the independent variable (price) stays within too tight a range to permit valid estimates of what the demand curve looks like. In a market with low price elasticity, one may indeed observe significant variation in prices and price differences, but they yield only very slight shifts in sales volumes or market shares. In the language of econometrics, that means that the dependent variables (sales or market share) move in too narrow a range to allow for valid estimates of what the underlying price elasticity truly is.

The result: Simon-Kucher & Partners has conducted more than 9000 pricing projects around the world, but no more than 100 of those relied primarily on the application of econometric methods. In addition to Telser's arguments, we learned two other lessons over the years. First, historical data has little value for the pricing of new products or new situations. In some cases, it is completely useless. Second, the need for complex price analyses with the help of a consultant is most acute when there is a "structural break" in the market. Examples include the entry of a new competitor, the launch of generics when a pharmaceutical patent expires, the emergence of new distribution channels (such as online), and radical changes to business models (such as the sharing economy). In all of those cases, historical data offers few clues about how customers will respond to prices in the future. In the era of Big Data, however, econometrics may become more useful. The internet makes it possible to conduct price tests at low cost and design them so that one can observe and measure how the desired spread of prices affects sales.

Instead of econometrics, we used a new method called conjoint measurement in many projects. I first encountered the method during my stay at MIT, but in a rudimentary form under the name "tradeoff analysis." The objective is to understand the tradeoffs someone makes between utility and price. Survey respondents see different alternatives for the same product or service (a car, a trip, a software package) and need to indicate which of the alternatives they prefer, and in some cases to what degree they prefer that option over the others. The alternatives present a mix of product characteristics such as quality, brand, technical performance, and also price. Each alternative has some stronger and some weaker features, which means the respondents need to make tradeoffs. The data from all these answers allows us to quantify the utility of individual product features and to estimate customers' willingness to pay for them.

Conjoint measurement methods have continuously improved. A breakthrough came with the advent of the personal computer. Unlike a paper questionnaire, a PC-based survey can be customized to the individual respondent.

One of our first projects using this method was designed to measure the value of the fashion brand Jil Sander for eyewear. To make the survey very realistic, we actually had glasses made with different designs and brands. Advanced versions of conjoint measurement are still an important tool in our work, but we long ago delegated the conducting of the surveys to market research firms. The analyses and interpretation of the data, however, remain one of our core competencies. We do all of that work in-house.

In 1988, two freshly minted PhDs—Georg Tacke and Klaus Hilleke—joined the firm and would strengthen its core for decades to come. Georg wrote his dissertation on nonlinear pricing. His work laid the groundwork for the BahnCard 50, which we would develop years later with the German federal railroad (Deutsche Bahn). Klaus, who wrote his dissertation on competitive strategies in the pharmaceutical market, added his expertise to our growing business in the pharma industry. Such high-caliber talent obviously had competing offers to consider. In order to secure their services for Simon-Kucher, we offered them the opportunity to become partners quickly. I am proud that these core team members—Kucher, Sebastian, Tacke, and Hilleke—have remained with the firm for their entire professional careers.

The two photos below show this core team in 1988 and in the same pose in 2015. The intervening 27 years may have left their marks on the way we look, but could do nothing to erode the bond between us.[2]

Core team of Simon-Kucher in 1988 and in 2015. Left to right: Karl-Heinz Sebastian, Hermann Simon, Georg Tacke, Eckhard Kucher, Klaus Hilleke

---

[2] The older photo was taken by *Manager Magazin* for an article about professors as consultants; see *Manager Magazin* 6/1988, p. 188. The second photo, imitating the first one, was taken in Bonn in 2015 to mark the occasion of the 30th anniversary of Simon-Kucher & Partners.

Price and Beyond

I have encountered prices in thousands of forms. This challenging topic has been immense fun at times. There have been "Eureka" moments when I unlocked another secret about price. The triumphs included the original introduction of the BahnCard 50 in 1993, and its resurrection in 2003. Another victory came when Daimler launched the revolutionary Mercedes A-Class with a higher price than they originally planned. Our teams have helped Porsche launch several new models, with the direct and intensive personal involvement of CEO Wendelin Wiedeking. Our competencies are increasingly in demand by internet companies. In the Silicon Valley alone, we have more than 40 "unicorn" clients, among them Uber and similar heavyweights.[3]

But price has also pushed me to frustration, confusion, and occasionally to the brink of helplessness. In some cases, an attempt to implement higher prices did not succeed, while in other cases, attempts to cut prices resulted in lower margins instead of the expected boost in sales. There have also been outright flops. But fortunately, these missteps have been rare. Of course, I also had battles with consulting clients who rejected our recommendations. In some of those cases, even hindsight does not reveal which party was right because in reality a company can only implement one alternative. It is difficult, if not impossible, to determine whether another choice would have brought better or worse results.

The world can also change very abruptly. We had developed a new pricing scheme for TUI, the world's largest tour operator, and were on track to launch the system on October 1, 2001. But the devastating terrorist attacks of September 11 and the subsequent collapse of international travel challenged the assumptions and analyses on which our recommendations regarding the new system were based. It was comforting to hear from TUI's top management a year later that the company would have been much worse off if they had kept the old system in place.

Sometimes, the poor outcomes were self-inflicted. I will illustrate this with two examples. After German reunification, we conducted a project for a company in the former East Germany. A company from the West had taken control and planned to restructure it. Toward the end of the project, the East German firm filed for bankruptcy. What was our mistake? We had signed the contract with the East German firm rather than with the West German company that had acquired it and commissioned our project. Our attempts to

---

[3] A unicorn is a young company with a valuation of at least $1 billion.

collect from the new parent company were in vain, and we had to write off the project fee. That was the price we paid for our naiveté.

The second example involves the German electricity market, which was deregulated at the end of the 1990s. The mood in the market was swinging back and forth between euphoria and fear. One competitor wanted to capitalize on the newfound market freedom by launching an across-the-board attack. It signed up for a very large project with us. But acquiring that project was a double-edged sword. It was a huge success thanks to the project fee, but also a potential risk because it meant we could not work with any other companies in the sector.

In the course of the project, there was friction within the company's own management as well as between their management and us. We were working with an increasingly unpleasant CEO on the other side, whom I will call Mr. Rupture.[4] He was under massive pressure, and the relationship between him and our lead partner on the project was starting to deteriorate. In the fall of 1999, we met on "neutral territory" at a conference room at an airport.

"Are you nervous?" the lead partner asked me prior to the meeting. He had invited me to join this sensitive negotiation.

"I'm OK," I responded. But I was in fact nervous. Several million euros and additional conditions were at stake, and we needed to find a resolution that evening. This would only be the second time I had met Mr. Rupture. I hardly knew him, but had reason to distrust him.

True to his style, he kept us waiting. When he finally arrived, the mood was cold. As the arguments flew back and forth, Mr. Rupture and I stared at each other without saying a word. Both sides dug in, and we drifted further and further away from a compromise. The current dynamic was not working, so I left our partner and Mr. Rupture—who had known each other much longer—alone in the room. After quite a while, our partner came out of the room and shared a suggested compromise with me. I found the proposal unacceptable. We contacted our attorney (who was on vacation at the time) and he was certain that we could achieve a much better outcome in court.

The idea of suing another company and seeking relief in court goes against my grain. We have never sued a client, and that will never change.[5] Mr. Rupture was ready to call things off, but I tried hard to move him in our direction. Ultimately we reached an agreement. I was not satisfied with the monetary sum, but at the same time we had regained our freedom to work with other companies in the sector. That freedom was worth a financial sacrifice. I

---

[4] The meaning of the real name in German is very similar to rupture.
[5] See also the section in Chap. 14, "Avoid lawyers."

was relieved to put the whole episode behind me rather than having to stand up for our rights in court. We have better places to channel our energies than the courtroom. In this case, however, engaging an attorney was worthwhile. He reminded us to make sure that the agreed amount due to us and the written agreement contained a "plus value-added tax" clause. We would have sacrificed an additional six-figure sum if we had neglected to include that clause. I never saw Mr. Rupture again.

Vision and Leadership

When I took over as CEO of Simon-Kucher & Partners, a new phase in my life began, a second career after 16 years in academia. Consulting was nothing new for me, but I needed to adjust to running a consulting firm as a full-time job: the laborious aspects of managing day-to-day operations, the necessity to acquire projects, and the obligation to complete those projects reliably and professionally. The questions "Where do we stand at the moment?" and "Where do we go from here?" became my companions 24/7.

The core element of our strategy was that we were hell-bent on doubling our revenues every three years. And thus far we had done exactly that. Our average annual growth rate from 1985 to 1994 was 34%. We had grown steadily except for a slight headwind in 1991 due to the effects of the first Gulf War. It was as if we were being carried on the wings of eagles.

But we had only one office. With few exceptions, all of our associates were German, and more than 90% of our projects came from German-speaking countries. The reality was that we were a small "boutique" German consulting firm. But our ambitions were grander than that. We wanted to become a global consulting firm, and we worked out at Vision & Values Statement that defined our firm as follows: "We are a global consulting company in strategy and marketing. Our standard is the world class." We expressed our core value in these four principles:

- Honesty
- Quality
- Creativity
- Speed

These principles applied externally to our client relationships as well internally to our relationships with each other. Honesty is the only way one can develop trust. Sometimes clients will approach a consultant with a set opinion that they want the consultant to confirm. In other cases, one uncovers mistakes or weaknesses that the client does not want to hear about. Sometimes, one must also tell employees an uncomfortable truth. I cannot claim that we always fully upheld that principle. But we never lowered the bar, and even if it occasionally took some time, we were true to the maxim that "if you lie, you're out."

"Quality" in our context means that we work with the most modern quantitative methods in order to achieve results with the highest validity and reliability. The basis for this is our highly qualified team members with their commitment to lifelong learning. A project early in our history taught us first-hand how important quality is in even the smallest details. An error occurred during data collection. A decimal point was off by one place. Instead of 1000 tons, a volume of 10,000 tons was entered into the database. That meant that our estimates of market potential were off by a massive amount. Fortunately, we caught the error before the final presentation; otherwise, we would have looked ridiculous in front of the client.

But quality means much more than avoiding mistakes. The roots of quality in a consulting firm rest in the competencies and commitment of the team, which is comprised almost entirely of "knowledge workers." In contrast to a line worker in a factory, one cannot control the process through which a knowledge worker creates value. In consulting, it is also hard to validate the outputs of those processes. The person overseeing the process would have to go through each individual step of how the results were derived, such as discussions with the client's management or customers. Ultimately, the only way to ensure high quality is to carefully select, evaluate, and continually develop the team.

The principle "creativity" has many facets for us, both external and internal. Externally, creativity require us to find specific customized solutions to each situation. While we have a toolbox of methods, we do not have a cookbook for strategy and marketing. This distinguishes us sharply from market research agencies, which often use standardized approaches. Internally, it means that our colleagues must have the ability and the desire to think for themselves while keeping the consequences in mind, especially how what they do can impact their colleagues.

"Speed" is the principle most often violated in practice. The modern buzzword is "agility." Many people struggle with implementing the motto "don't put off to tomorrow what you can do today." This pervasive snail's pace bothers me to no end. At the same time, there is hardly anything that can be a more positive surprise for a client than speed. I know of no other aspect that draws positive feedback more often than a quick response. That is precisely the reason why I work hard to instill the principle of speed in the organization. Unfortunately, some people are immune to those efforts, but most catch on.

Implicit in the principle of "speed" is the aspect of being on time, both in the sense of showing up at an appointed time and also delivering results by an agreed or promised deadline. Personally, I cannot say that I have always been on time, but I can truly say that I am not far off from that goal. Sometimes one has no influence on the circumstances, such as flight delays or unexpectedly long traffic jams. But one can influence one's departure time. As the French fabulist and poet Jean de La Fontaine once said: "Hurrying doesn't help. The important thing is to start on time." How true!

Within Simon-Kucher I have continually hammered home these four principles. But sometimes situations arise when one can no longer hear oneself talk because everything is repetition. The former European CEO of the Swiss conglomerate ABB, Eberhard von Koerber (1938–2017), once told me "I can't listen to myself talk anymore, because I've said everything 100 times already."

My answer to him: "You are the only one who has heard you say something 100 times. Each and every employee in such a large organization as ABB has probably only heard your statements once or twice. You can comfortably repeat yourself 100 times, because then there is a good chance that every employee will have then heard you a third time."

Our value system of Simon-Kucher continues to evolve under my successors. As of 2018, it comprised six elements: Integrity, Respect, Entrepreneurship, Meritocracy, Impact, and Team.[6] Values and their codification are living systems. But more important than the words are the deeds. In other words, the most important point is that people live out the values day to day, or, in management speak, "they walk the talk."

I often concluded my speeches and written statements with a quote borrowed from the Roman philosopher Seneca: "*per aspera ad astra*" (on rough roads to the stars). My goal was to express that one must set ambitious goals, but also recognize that the path to achieving them is rarely easy and smooth. It may sound trivial to say it, but people should not let the potholes and rough patches on the way to the stars discourage them. At Simon-Kucher, we have faced our share of potholes. The opening of new offices is a good example. In some cases, we needed to replace the local leadership, in other cases it took an unexpectedly long time to reach the break-even point, and in two cases we even closed offices.

---

[6] Georg Tacke, "Core Values—Key Ingredients to Our Long-Term Success," Simon-Kucher & Partners: *Our Voice*, December 2017.

One of my biggest disappointments was the loss of partners. Some were let go because they did not achieve the expected level of performance. Others departed on their own because they could not mesh with our entrepreneurial model or our culture. In the first 30 years of the firm, we lost 25 partners, or around 0.8 partners per year. Considering that we have over 130 partners now, that is a very low churn rate at the partner level.

Globalization

When I joined Simon-Kucher full-time in 1995, we wrote in our vision "we are a global consulting company" and "our standard is the world class." Those statements are open to different interpretations for a consulting firm with one office in one country. One interpretation is that we have expressed our very aspirational ambitions but have yet to realize them. Less positive is the view that we are cocky and pretentious. For us, the first interpretation applies. We meant those two vision statements literally. We had a goal to reach, and we knew what we wanted.

But admittedly, we had not completely thought through the entire path to achieving that goal. In what country should we begin our internationalization? How should we go about it? And who would do it? When globalization is the goal, opening a second office in a German-speaking location, such as in Zurich or Vienna, does not contribute much. The idea to open an office in the United States came up for the first time in 1993 after a visit to a biotechnology firm in Colorado. Our presentation went very well. On the return flight, I gave a lot of thought to my impressions. I doubted that we would win the project. Would a company in the Rocky Mountains let a small consulting firm from Bonn, Germany take on a vitally important study on the introduction of a breakthrough innovation? Could a consultancy do that project without its own US presence? Most probably not.

A global consulting firm with a claim to world-class standards must be able to hold its own in the lion's den of the consulting market: the United States. That is particularly true when the firm wants to acquire projects from US companies. Our group of partners, which numbered seven in 1995, agreed unanimously with that idea. The decision was taken. We would open our second office—and first office outside of Germany—in the United States. But we still had to figure out the answers to the "how?" and the "who?" questions.

Our first idea was to acquire a smaller US consulting firm whose founder I had known for a long time. But in our talks it became clear that this firm fell short of our quality and competency standards. Then the idea arose to open a US office together with a Harvard professor. We negotiated for a long time. The professor had a keen interest in the joint effort and would have certainly opened a lot of doors. But on March 14, 1996, the negotiations broke down. That left both of us very frustrated. The Harvard professor indicated that he would open his own firm, but he never did take that step. He and I have remained good friends. The frustration and the hard feelings soon faded away.

We now knew that we would have to take the plunge on our own. When I asked at our next partner meeting who would make the move to the United States and open the office, no one made eye contact. So we took a break to think about it. We were relieved when Klaus Hilleke finally declared that he would move to the United States for three years to open the new office. His family would accompany him.

This situation would recur often. The plan for a new office is not worth the paper it is printed on as long as no one takes on the direct responsibility to actually do it. Hilleke was accompanied by a young consultant named Stephan Butscher, who had studied under me at Johannes Gutenberg University in Mainz. Born in Casablanca as the son of a diplomat, Butscher already had considerable overseas experience despite his young age.

We did not choose New York as our location, however, as one might expect a consulting firm to do. Instead, we chose Boston for two primary reasons. First, I knew the Boston area rather well. I had lived there for two years and still maintained many contacts at Harvard and MIT. Second, Hilleke preferred to relocate his family to a more manageable area than the Big Apple. Beyond that, though, was the Boston area's long tradition as a home for consulting firms. That is where the world's first consulting firm, Arthur D. Little, was founded in 1864. The Boston Consulting Group also had its origins there, as the name implies.

Now we needed to get an office up and running. We established a Limited Liability Company (LLC), rented office space, and hired the first American employees. We chose Kendall Square in Cambridge as the office location, literally just a few steps away from my own first office in the United States at MIT's Sloan School of Management. I gladly return to the places where I used to work. They evoke pleasant memories.

I recall my first interviews with two candidates in Boston who had just graduated as MBAs: Juan Rivera und Steve Rosen. Both accepted our offers. As part of their initiation, each spent one year in the Bonn office. We are convinced that the best way to transfer our corporate culture from one office to the next is through our people, not through declamations or pieces of paper. With Juan and Steve, it definitely worked out very well. Juan only recently retired as managing director of Simon-Kucher & Partners LLC. Steve Rosen is still active as a senior partner in the Life Sciences division.

In the start-up phase, I flew to Boston about once a month. During this time, I kept a small wardrobe at the Charles Hotel in Harvard Square in Cambridge, so that I would not need to transport clothes back and forth across the Atlantic every trip. I quickly recognized that I was not able to accomplish much with American clients. Consulting is a people business. I had business cards with a US address, but I made no secret of the fact that I was only sporadically in the United States. A client is not impressed when the CEO of a small consulting firm appears at a pitch meeting, but otherwise rarely shows up.

Our original plan to support German companies in the US market did not pan out. Many German consulting firms had tried a similar approach in foreign countries, but did not succeed. After a short time, it was clear that we needed to acquire projects with US companies and staff them locally. Had we underestimated the challenges or overestimated our abilities? Our experience from the start-up years in Germany "every beginning is hard" repeated itself in the United States. American clients were surprisingly open and we received invitations to pitch. But the path from first meeting to a commissioned project was rocky. One factor was the pervasive presence of competitors. If there is one thing the United States does not lack, it is consulting firms! But none of those firms was as focused on pricing as we were. Klaus and his team coped with a lot of frustration and showed exemplary perseverance. Then the dam broke, and the US business started its path of continuous growth. Today, we employ around 250 people in our US offices in Boston, New York, Atlanta, Chicago, Houston, San Francisco, and Silicon Valley.

The success in the United States whet our appetite for more. Four years later, we opened an office in Zurich, and shortly before that we established a second domestic office in Munich. Opening those offices was relatively easy compared to the office we opened at roughly the same time: Paris. We did not have a partner or associate that we felt comfortable entrusting with that task. So I contacted an executive search firm and interviewed several candidates at their offices on the Champs Elysées. In that process I learned once again how small the world is. The person who managed our project was Cathérine

Dunand, whom I knew from her time as an assistant to the global head of sales at Hoechst Pharma. Among the candidates I interviewed was Kai Bandilla, at the time a young partner at Roland Berger in Paris. But we did not come to an agreement.

Instead, I hired a French consultant to open the office. He was later joined by Florent Jacquet and Franck Brault, two graduates of the Grande École HEC, whom we had hired earlier. Both of them returned to Paris after spending a year at our headquarters in Bonn. Similar to Juan Rivera and Steve Rosen in Boston, both of these young consultants eventually became partners and remain with Simon-Kucher to this day.

But it did not work out in Paris with the external hire. We replaced him with a German partner, but he was also unable to achieve the necessary breakthrough. After three years, we still had not reached break-even, so we could not keep going down the same path. Then I remembered Kai Bandilla from that first round of interviews at the headhunter's office. I called him up, and a few days later we came to terms. Today, Kai not only manages our Paris office, but is also responsible for a division and a member of our corporate board.

We also had setbacks. In November 2008—probably the worst conceivable point in time—we opened an office in Moscow. The costs of this office were very high, however, and order inflow was negligible. After one year, we pulled the plug. But our globalization continued unabated. The figure shows the story of our expansion around the world from 1985 to 2019:[7]

---

[7] For further information about the development of Simon-Kucher & Partners, see Simon and Krütten (2008).

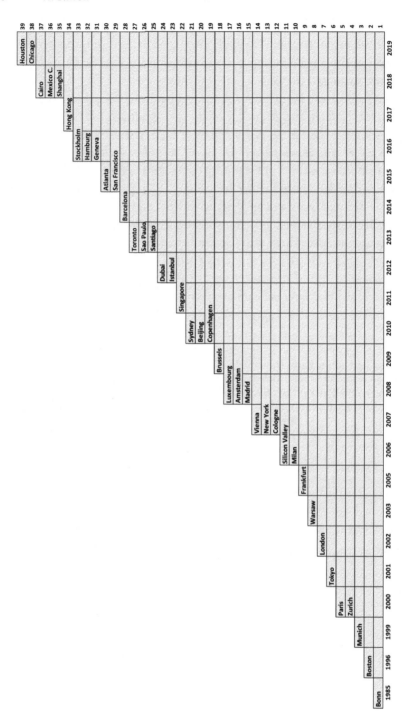

The challenges remain the same as always. The hardest task is finding the person to lead the office. If one has a capable solution, i.e., an appropriate partner or consultant, then the challenge is much more manageable. But without such a person, an office can be a problem child for years. No less important is the acquisition and development of local talent to ensure the team knows the country or region and masters the local language. A consulting firm cannot expand internationally solely by sending its own people abroad. Experienced people from existing offices are important for transferring the culture and competencies to the new offices, but strong local talent is essential to build and sustain the business.

Over the years, we have sent many capable partners and associates to offices around the world. Many of these expatriates stayed in their adopted countries for several years, while others stayed permanently. But altogether, we have fewer than ten partners of German origin in our foreign offices.

Once we began our globalization, we declared English to be our corporate language. Every employee must have a command of English, and all corporate documents are formulated only in English. This transition proved challenging for some employees at the outset, but after a few years, everyone took for granted that English is the corporate language. I can only advise any company that wants to internationalize to follow that same path without compromise. Using English as the corporate language simplifies communication, saves duplicate work for translations, and makes the firm more attractive to foreign nationals. A company that operates around the world needs one common, standard language.

A difficult challenge in a firm built on human capital is to cultivate and maintain a uniform set of values and a uniform corporate culture that transcends borders and local habits. Only when that effort succeeds can clients expect consistent quality from the firm. We have the goal of offering our clients a comparable level of service no matter where they are located. At the same time, such a system must be flexible enough to integrate peculiar aspects of local cultures, and also not stand in the way of the change and innovation that drives a continually growing international consulting firm. Globality is a core element of our identity. For us, being global means that we have clients, staff, and offices in all relevant markets. We also see that a global network like this helps us attract and keep talent.

Today, the firm has 41 offices in 25 countries, but there are still many white spaces on our world map. Our commitment to one day being present everywhere in the world has not waned. The foundation we are building to achieve this goal is broader and more solid than ever. That means that our globalization should actually accelerate in the coming years.

Human Capital vs. Financial Capital

In 1968, Peter Drucker coined the term "knowledge worker" to describe employees whose work is primarily mental, not physical. They work with their brain and their intellect rather than with their bodies. Companies who predominantly employ knowledge workers depend more on human capital than on financial capital. Such firms play an important role in today's modern economies. They include consultancies, law firms, medical practices, and inspection companies. Schools and universities, of course, also fall into that category, as does Simon-Kucher & Partners. More than 80% of our colleagues hold an advanced academic degree, and more than 10% have a doctorate. We produce no tangible goods. Our project reports, whether in digital or paper form, contain only information and knowledge.

A firm cannot control the value creation process for knowledge workers. If a knowledge worker stares out a window, one cannot tell whether the person is doing nothing, daydreaming, or cooking up an ingenious solution to a client's problem. Someone who comes up with a terrific solution to a problem in one hour has accomplished more than someone who has chewed on a problem for an entire day without finding a compelling answer. Karl Marx's labor theory of value—that value is defined by the human labor time invested—is even more off base in a knowledge-based company than it is in a manufacturing firm.

Another special aspect of knowledge-based companies is that their most important resources walk out the office door every evening. One can only hope that they show up again the next morning. The critical resources are what is between the ears of the employees. This is especially true for the highly qualified employees and even more so for the partners. Keeping them onboard is both a necessity and a major challenge.

A knowledge-based company does not require much financial capital. They normally rent their offices rather than own the buildings. Working capital is also limited. They do not need to store raw materials or finished goods. Financing is therefore rarely a bottleneck. Nonetheless, many newly established knowledge-based companies lose their identity because of financial maneuvers.

One often hears that everything depends on the boss. That might be true for an industrial company with a strict hierarchical structure. But that statement is much less true for a knowledge-based company. When such a company reaches a certain size, success depends more on the partners than on the boss. The partners lead groups that behave like small companies. That is one of the main reasons why partners should be true entrepreneurs. Charles O'Reilly, a professor at Stanford, postulates that the shares of a knowledge-based company should be held by the partners and not by outside investors. His rationale is that the scarce resource in such firms is human capital and not financial capital.

But it is not that easy to transfer ownership from older to younger partners as a firm expands and ages. The founders are by definition the only shareholders when the company is launched. Many founders have a tendency to retain the highest possible equity share for the longest possible period. Time flies by, and suddenly these founding partners are in their 50s. If a company has been successful up to that point, the shares will be too expensive for the younger partners. The consequence? The firm is sold to a larger consulting firm and loses its identity. That happened to one of our early competitors, the Strategic Pricing Group, which was founded by Thomas Nagle. The firm was sold to Monitor, the firm founded by Harvard Professor Michael Porter. Monitor itself soon landed in the hands of Deloitte. Roland Berger sold his eponymous firm to Deutsche Bank, and the partners had to buy it back later. A.T. Kearney was sold to EDS, the information technology giant founded by Ross Perot, and EDS was eventually absorbed by Hewlett-Packard. Similar to Roland Berger, the A.T. Kearney partners later bought their firm back. There are countless examples of consultancies that are sold by their founders. I estimate that 90% of all consulting firms are sold off after the first generation. Only a small number manage to continue the firm into a second generation of leaders. If the shares are not sold to younger partners right from the start, the firm has only one alternative to remain independent, namely that the founders give the shares to younger partners. That can happen without compensation or at a nominal price. The fact that McKinsey, Boston Consulting Group, and Bain still exist can be traced to that concept. Marvin Bower, the founder of McKinsey, gave his shares to the firm's partners in 1964. Bruce Henderson, the founder of Boston Consulting Group, and Bill Bain, the founder of Bain, did likewise in their respective firms.

One result of this "give away" is that the shareholder model for the following generations is not truly entrepreneurial. By "truly entrepreneurial" I mean that new partners purchase their shares at a market price and sell them at the prevailing market value when they leave the firm. If one receives shares for free or at a nominal price, it is hard for those partners to sell the shares to the next partner generation at a market price. The partners in such firms are more like trustees than true owners, and the firm's true enterprise value is never realized unless the firm is sold to another party or goes public, as Goldman Sachs did.

At Simon-Kucher & Partners, we have purposely followed a different model from Day One. The founding partners were determined to keep the firm on independent footing. There was no way we were going to reach 55 or 60 years old and then wipe out the identity of our "baby" by selling it to some large firm. For that reason, in our fifth year we already started transferring shares to the next generation of partners. The amount and price were subject to negotiation. Of course that inevitably led to some "chess playing" by both parties. That bothered me to such an extent that I dreamed of having another model, something similar to what a stock exchange does.

In 1998, we decided to implement such a model, which to my knowledge is still unique to this day among consulting and advisory firms. The three founding partners (Kucher, Sebastian, and I) agreed to part with all of our shareholdings except for a total of 7.5%, which the three of us could hold lifelong, without any further obligation to sell. Every year, there would be a price interval established for shares. Senior partners (those who have been partners for at least ten years) could sell, and all other partners, including newly anointed partners, could buy shares. Within this framework, the process proceeds similar to that of a stock exchange. The potential sellers state how many shares they would be willing to sell at a given price, and the potential buyers state the number of shares they are willing to buy at a given price. Both the statements of the potential sellers and buyers are binding. The aggregated result of these "bids" and "asks" is a supply curve and a demand curve whose intersection indicates how many shares will be transferred and at what price. The illustration shows this model and its results for the buying/selling window in one specific year.

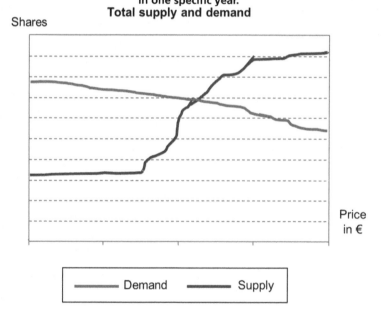

The system has run smoothly for years. Only on two occasions did we hit a wall, so to speak, because the price interval was defined too narrowly. We closed the gap between supply and demand through an apportionment of the transferable shares. Those experiences led us to fine-tune the model, but by and large it operates the same way as originally conceived. Currently, the firm's shares are spread across more than 130 partners.

This system of true entrepreneurship creates many advantages. It is an attractive model for entrepreneurial types, and we are especially proud of our entrepreneurial culture. New partners decide, on their own, what their initial investment will be (subject to a minimum level, which is significant). This culture may discourage people who are happier as rank-and-file employees as much as it inspires and energizes people willing both to take on risks and to invest their own energy and effort to make sure those risks pay off. Such people are the drivers of our growth, and growth is what creates enterprise value.

We do not know what our future growth will look like. That makes the investment risky. But if the past is any indication, investment in shares of Simon-Kucher & Partners has been extremely attractive for young partners. In its first ten years (1985–1994), the firm grew at an average annual rate of 34%. Admittedly, high growth rates are easier to achieve when one starts from zero than when the firm gets increasingly larger in later years. From 1995 to 2008, we increased our revenue by a factor of seven, which translates to an annual growth rate of 24%. From 2009 to 2019, we achieved an annual revenue growth rate of 15%, despite the effects of the Great Recession at the beginning of that period. We are determined to keep growing, but no one can say what the future will bring.

Given those growth rates, it is no wonder that we have received a large number of takeover offers over the years. The first came at the beginning of 1989 during my stay at Harvard. We had caught the attention of Carl Sloane, the founder of the firm Temple, Barker & Sloane (TBS) in Lexington, Massachusetts. TBS would later be taken over by the firm United Research, which in turn was sold to Cap Gemini. Sloane knew Germany well and had observed us there.

Large consulting firms and the leading accounting groups have also contacted us. But selling the firm was never a serious consideration, neither for the founders nor for the new partners. We could have achieved higher prices than those from our internal stock exchange, but the preservation of our independence was more important than a short-term financial windfall. I also believe that most of our partners would not want to work in a larger corporate group with its associated bureaucracy. Our partners highly prize the entrepreneurial freedom they enjoy at Simon-Kucher. That remains the basis from which we will take on the challenges of the future with undiminished ambition.

Beyond the Captain's Bridge

I turned 60 in February 2007. At a celebration with the partners of Simon-Kucher, I announced that I would resign as CEO by age 65 at the latest, and probably earlier. My secret plan was to resign roughly midway through that five-year period. In order to avoid an extended lame-duck period, I wanted to give short notice on the exact date.

My years as CEO had flown by. After a slow start, due in part to illness, I felt up to the job. But I also needed to respect the aging process. We had opened 16 new offices in 11 countries. I was traveling constantly, and the stress of some of those trips had become unreasonable. One week in October 2000 exemplifies this. In the span of seven days, I traveled the following route: Bonn-Frankfurt-Atlanta-Boston-Atlanta-Frankfurt-Cologne-Bonn-Vienna-Frankfurt-Koblenz-Bonn-Berlin-Frankfurt-Bonn. That week is not representative, but overall the travel was rough.

I recall one evening when the phone rang after I had crashed in my hotel bed, totally exhausted. I absent-mindedly picked up the receiver. Bill, a client from the United States, was on the other end of the line.

"Hi, Bill. Where are you?" I asked.

"I'm in New York," he responded.

As if I were sleepwalking, my mind went blank for a moment.

"And where am I?" I asked him.

"Oh, you're in Boston," he said.

That episode recalled a statement that a colleague made while imitating me in a satirical skit at a company event: "Ms. Rodewald, please determine where I am at the moment, what I'm doing there, and how long whatever-it-is will take." Ingrun Rodewald was my secretary at that time. The moral: One can only be in one place at any given time ... and should know where that place is.

The firm was a well-oiled machine in 2007, as revenue rose by 26% from roughly $70 million to around $90 million. In 2008, we grew strongly again to $144 million. The plan I crafted in 2007—to hand off a flourishing firm to my successors at age 62 or 63—seemed to have succeeded without a hitch. Then the fourth quarter of 2008 arrived. We could not escape the economic crisis which began then and which gained intensity throughout 2009. That thoroughly disrupted my succession plan. Could I leave the bridge during these rough waters? Would that look like I was throwing in the towel? What would my partner colleagues and my CEO successor think about needing to guide the firm through the crisis? At the same time, I asked myself if I could handle the greater challenges that a major crisis period would no doubt bring. Was I not already too old for this potentially Herculean task? Would it not be better to have a younger, fresher leader at the helm?

After an in-depth consultation with my eternally dependable advisor Cecilia, I announced on my 62nd birthday in February 2009 that I would step back from the CEO role, effective April 30th. On April 23rd, a regularly scheduled partners' meeting took place in Luxembourg. The partners elected Klaus Hilleke and Georg Tacke as co-CEOs for a five-year term. They took office on May 1, 2009. Both were optimally prepared for that responsibility. They had known each other since their graduate studies and in the meantime had accumulated more than 20 years' experience apiece as consultants. They also formed a smoothly functioning team. After their five-year term, they were re-elected jointly for an additional three years.[8] After a total of eight years as co-CEO, Klaus did not run for election again. Georg continued as sole CEO for another three-year term, up to the maximum of 11 years allowed by our statutes.

Klaus and Georg can look back on stellar achievements during their tenures as a CEO team and sole CEO, respectively. Revenue over that time more than tripled to $400 million in 2019. Even more importantly, they brought true rigor and professionalism to the leadership and the organization. During my CEO tenure, everything was rather "hand-crafted," which is typical for a founder. But that kind of approach cannot tame the immense complexity of 41 offices in 25 countries, multiple profit centers, and a large array of industry practices and divisions. Simon-Kucher now uses tools such as SAP and evaluation systems that enable precise and virtually real-time management of projects and associates.

In January 2020, a new CEO team took over. Andreas von der Gathen, who had successfully led the consumer and retail division for many years, and Mark Billige, who had built a fast-growing office in London, were elected as co-CEOs. I trust that they will lead Simon-Kucher to new heights.

---

[8] At Simon-Kucher, the CEO or CEOs are elected for a first term of five years, and then may be re-elected to no more than two subsequent three-year terms. The maximum tenure is therefore 11 years.

On Alien Territory

Entering life's third phase brings a drastic change for most people, especially for leaders. Their management tasks often meant that they were working at 150 or 200% capacity. They wielded power and influence. All of that vanishes when they have to give up their leadership position.

How did I deal with this situation? My transition was much less abrupt than what many CEOs experience when they retire. I remained a partner in the firm and could retain my office. Some informal influence still existed, thanks to my status as the oldest partner and as one of the founders, and I still offered my opinions freely at partner meetings. But my formal power within the firm was gone. Of course, my influence decreases as my age increases, and rightfully so. I hope I am not affected by the stubbornness of old age and therefore clever enough to hold back and not impede the decisions and actions of my younger partners. Now, in my mid-70s, I am committed as ever to our firm and can perhaps make a small contribution to its further growth.

The upside of retiring as CEO was that I had more time for speeches, publications, and new activities. The pressure of the day-to-day business ebbed away and the newly acquired freedom allowed me to break new ground.

One field that strongly interested me was investments and capital markets. Up until my retirement as CEO, I had mostly followed the advice of investment advisers, with modest results. But now I started to take a more active role in my investment and asset management activities. Through a high-tech founders' fund, I was able to invest in several start-ups with mixed success.

Another project was the so-called Search Fund, the first fund of its kind in Germany. Under this concept, a young entrepreneur recruits several investors, each of whom puts up a relatively small sum. Then the entrepreneur seeks out a company to acquire. Alexander Kirn, a Harvard MBA, introduced me to the concept (Müller 2017). He found 12 investors who each committed 25,000 euros. The search process forced Kirn to muster a large amount of patience and perseverance. But after around two years, he succeeded in purchasing the company Invers, located in the German city of Siegen.

Invers, a true Hidden Champion, is the global market leader in car sharing systems, which have both hardware and software components. The company was founded in 1993 by the engineer Uwe Latsch, who wanted to step back from active involvement in the business. Kirn and I worked together to convince Latsch to sell. The decision was based on more than financial considerations. Personal chemistry played an important role. The 12 investors in the Search Fund now had the option to participate in the acquisition. All agreed, and Kirn took over as CEO. That project was definitely a success, and I exited the venture several years later with a tidy profit. Kirn is still CEO, and Invers—driven by the growth of shared mobility—is doing very well.

A second project took on a different dimension. That was the Special Purpose Acquisition Company (SPAC), which I launched together with the French investment house Wendel and the investment banker Roland Lienau. Lienau gained his knowledge of capital markets at Deutsche Bank. Because he had studied in France and met his wife there, he joined Wendel, which had its roots in a steel company founded in the Lorraine region in 1704. In 1978—ironically during the conservative administration of President Valéry Giscard d'Estaing—France nationalized its steel industry, and the Wendel family invested the funds it received in numerous ventures.

To launch the SPAC, the three initial investors provided a certain amount of seed capital. Then they sought out co-investors to provide additional funds. We did this through a campaign that opened up an entirely new world to me. We presented our idea to potential investors in all major financial centers on both sides of the Atlantic. The hook for these meetings was the Hidden Champions concept. Our goal was to use the funds we collected to acquire a Hidden Champion. An important aspect of an SPAC is that the acquiring shell company would be listed on a stock exchange in advance of the acquisition. The target company would then be merged into the SPAC and would thus become a publicly listed entity.

Lienau and I started the campaign in mid-2009, and by year's end we had raised the 200 million euros we had planned on. In those six months, we had many exciting encounters. In New York, we met with a 34-year-old Harvard graduate who managed a billion-dollar-fund that only invested in SPACs. When I asked her who made the investment decisions on behalf of the fund, her answer was swift and crystal clear: "I do." Another encounter took place on the 26th floor of a New York office building. When we exited the elevator, a small door opened and led us into what resembled a hunter's trophy room in the Black Forest. We were greeted by the descendants of the founder of a very large investment firm. The founder had come to the United States from Germany in the 1920s. He brought several rare birds with him that he had received as payment from a customer who had declared bankruptcy. In the United States, he founded a pet supply company that grew to become the second largest of its kind in the world. After an even larger company acquired that business, the proceeds were used to establish the investment fund. A prominent US business school is named after the founder.

I also had the opportunity to look into the trading rooms of the major banks. I asked myself who is in control and has the overview of all that complexity. What do the thousands of traders do as they sit in front of their screens? Each of them had three, in some cases five screens in front of them, not just one. I gained a powerful respect for capital markets, which until that time were more of an abstract construct to me.

In February 2010, we launched Helikos S.E.[9] on the Frankfurt Stock Exchange. The company's balance sheet had 200 million euros in cash and 200 million euros in shareholder equity. The search for an acquisition candidate began, and my role came to the forefront due to my relationships with the Hidden Champions. At the time, the economy was showing the full effects of the Great Recession. When I called companies and waved 200 million euros of equity at them, the interest among many was obviously high. But when I said that the transaction would result in the company's being listed on the stock exchange, the interest among more than 80% of the family-owned companies evaporated. The public listing was the core of the SPAC concept. If that were a knock-out criterion for an owner or an owner's family, there was no point in scheduling a follow-up visit or presentation. We did schedule several meetings, but many potential targets dropped out of the discussions after one round.

Lienau and I were on the road for 18 months before we finally acquired Exceet Group S.E, a Luxembourg-based manufacturer of embedded computers. These are custom-built units used in security technology as well as in medical technology applications such as hearing aids, pacemakers, and MRI machines. In July 2011, the acquisition, merger, and the public listing of Exceet took place. The picture shows the three protagonists in this story standing in front of the bull at the Frankfurt Stock Exchange.

---

[9] Wendel, the German name of the main investor, means "helix." Helikos is the Greek word for helix.

On the occasion of the public listing of Exceet Group S.E. on the Frankfurt Stock Exchange (left to right: Me, Exceet-Group CEO Uli Reutner, and Roland Lienau)

How did I feel about these forays into alien territory? The whole experience was rather unsettling. Could I trust the people I met on the capital markets? Would I be able to stand up to them? The answers to those questions have left me skeptical. Perhaps I was already too old when I entered the world of investing and capital markets? In any event, I did not truly feel comfortable there. Today, I tend to leave investment decisions to professional wealth managers.

Traveling Poet

After those adventures, I returned to the two familiar territories of writing and speaking. They are fun for me rather than a burden. They also afford me more freedom than other business activities and give me the opportunity to travel throughout the world. My main topics—pricing and Hidden Champions—draw interest in many countries. The continued success of the German economy, and the *Mittelstand* in particular, plays a central role in driving that interest. Finally, the translations of my publications into many languages have given me some level of international notoriety. On the website Managementdenker.de, I have been ranked as the most influential living management thinker in German-speaking countries since 2005.[10] The magazine *Cicero* listed me as one of the 100 most important intellectuals in Germany. In 2017, I was ranked 25th on Thinkers50 list of the world's most influential management thinkers.[11] A few members of that list are inducted annually to the "Thinkers50 Hall of Fame" because they have "made a lasting and vital impact on how organizations are led and managed."[12] I received that honor in 2019.

There is an enriching side effect of lectures. I have met many notable personalities at the meetings, conferences, and talks I have taken part in. They include heads of state and ministers from around the world. At a German-Russian conference in Bonn, I met Mikhail Gorbachev and gave him a signed and dedicated copy of one of my books. I found him to be personable, pleasant, and approachable, with no trace of arrogance.

On December 16, 2001, at a session attended by 4,000 people in Augsburg, Germany, I was one of the keynote speakers along with former German finance minister Theo Waigel and former US president Bill Clinton. I am somewhat ambivalent in my view toward Mr. Clinton. As a speaker on the grand stage, he struck me as rather weak. "Not a strong personality," was my impression from the listener's perspective. But my perception of him was very different when I experienced him working the room at the reception after the event. Although everyone there—except for Waigel—was totally unknown and anonymous to him, he directed his full attention to each person he spoke with and made each one feel like the most important person in the world. Apparently, he has an unusual talent to win people over to his side. I could not resist the opportunity to speak with someone who was once the most powerful person in the world. Ten years later, I had the chance to hear him speak again. On that occasion, he seemed even more erratic.

---

[10] See http://managementdenker.de.www258.your-server.de/wp/.

[11] See http://thinkers50.com/t50-ranking/.

[12] https://thinkers50.com/hall-of-fame/, accessed on 9 Oct 2019.

In discussions with Mikhail Gorbachev (1992) and Bill Clinton (2001)

Over the years, I have attended all kinds of events. In addition to the serious, reputable management congresses and seminars—which admittedly have an element of showmanship—there have also been events organized by people who are in my opinion the modern equivalents of get-rich-quick hucksters, snake-oil salesman, and other shady types. That latter group of "business" conferences draws large crowds. Not completely knowing what I was getting myself into, I agreed to speak at one such conference. More than 1000 people attended. I tried to maintain a more serious approach—a clear contrast to the rest of the program—and had the impression that my talk was well received. On the way back, I sorted through my impressions. It was indeed an interesting experience although I would not perform at such an event again. I discussed these thoughts with an acquaintance who organizes professional events. Here is his simple and compelling explanation for why attendance is so high at those less serious events: the world's "unsuccessful wannabes" greatly outnumber the "successful wannabes." This creates a nearly limitless market for people who give the impression that they have discovered the secrets or shortcuts to success. I believe this view is spot on.

Despite my relatively advanced age, the intensity of my travel and speaking activities has increased in recent years, and in some cases has become a chore. Here is a list of my trips in the fall of 2016.

September	Oktober	November
1. Bergisch Gladbach)	7. Seoul	3. Warschau
5. Eupen (Belgien)	10. Nakatsugawa (Jap.)	8. Hamburg
9. New York	12. Tokio	9. Wien
10. New York	15. Weifang (China)	16. Wien
13. Shanghai	16. Beijing	17. Wien
14. Shanghai	25. Houston	21. Zürich
21. Wittlich	26. Dallas	28. Moskau
23. Amsterdam	28. Boston	

I can manage such an intense travel program only because these trips are less stressful than the ones during my time as CEO of Simon-Kucher. Back then, my days were crammed full of meetings. Nowadays, the flow of the days is less strenuous. I make my speech and sometimes give interviews.[13] In most cases, I will be invited to a lunch or dinner after the talk or the event. Sometimes, Cecilia accompanies me on these trips, so that we can combine business with leisure. I relish my role as "traveling poet" and will continue to play it as long as my health holds up, with decreasing intensity though.

New Content

The nature and content of my writings also changed after I entered the third phase of my life. With the possible exception of the *Price Management* textbook (Simon and Fassnacht 2016, 2019), I no longer have big academic aspirations with my books and articles. Professor Martin Fassnacht of the WHU Beisheim School of Management now covers the academic side of that textbook, while I mainly contribute practical and experience-based insights. The book *Confessions of the Pricing Man* (Simon 2013/2015; Simon 2015) contains a mix of autobiographical and price-related elements. I took great pleasure in writing and publishing the book *Die Gärten der verlorenen Erinnerung* (Simon 2017) (English: *The Gardens of Lost Recollections*) about my growing up in the Eifel. This book is not primarily autobiographical. Rather, it deals with community, farming, the one-room schoolhouse, the role of the Catholic Church, and many related aspects of village and farm life after World War II. The autobiography you are reading right now falls into that same non-academic category. If I write other management books, I will draw on my experience rather than on academic research or analyses. This certainly applies to my most recent book in German with the freely translated title *True Profit! No Company Ever Went Broke from Turning a Profit* (Simon 2021).

When one lives a long and fortunate life, one may receive honors and awards. I confess that I was pleased to receive honorary doctorates and to have a business school in China named in my honor. I was likewise happy and honored to receive various other awards both inside and outside Germany. The induction into the "Thinkers50 Hall of Fame" was a kind of climax in this regard. I cannot deny that as a scientist, consultant, author, and speaker, I enjoy such recognitions. After all, I am not indifferent to whether my research results are acknowledged, my advice accepted, my books and articles

---

[13] My personal record for interviews came on one Sunday in Beijing, when I was interviewed 14 times.

read, and my lectures appreciated. But I have at least been as happy for my family as for myself.

All in all, I have no complaints, neither about resigning as CEO, nor about the transition to the third phase of my life. In fact, I am very satisfied with how each of those processes unfolded and what they led to. The older I get, the less important success and recognition on the business side becomes. What is much more important now—and less dependable—is my health. I am lucky that I have control over my time at this stage of my life and can spend more and more time taking care of my health.

References

See Anja Müller, "Übernehmer statt Unternehmer," *Handelsblatt*, January 16, 2017, p. 22.

Hermann Simon, *Preisheiten—Alles, was Sie über Preise wissen müssen*, Frankfurt: Campus 2013/2015.

Hermann Simon, *Confessions of the Pricing Man*, Springer: New York 2015.

Hermann Simon, *Die Gärten der verlorenen Erinnerung—Eifel unvergessen, 2nd edition*, Südwest- und Eifel-Zeitung Verlags- und Vertriebs-GmbH: Daun 2017. Translated into English, the title is "The Gardens of Lost Recollections."

Hermann Simon, *True Profit! No Company Ever Went Broke from Turning a Profit*, New York: Springer Nature 2021.

Hermann Simon and Martin Fassnacht, Preismanagement, Wiesbaden: Springer-Gabler 2016.

Hermann Simon and Martin Fassnacht, *Price Management*, New York: Springer 2019.

Hermann Simon and Jörg Krütten, "Globalisierung und Führung—Kulturelle Integration und Personalmanagement in global agierenden Beratungsunternehmen" in Ingolf Bamberger (editor), *Strategische Unternehmensberatung, 5th edition*, Gabler Verlag 2008, pp. 175-195.

Lester G. Telser, "The Demand for Branded Goods as Estimated from Consumer Panel Data," *The Review of Economic Statistics*, 1962, No. 3, pp. 300-324.

12

Immersion in the Far East

In this chapter, I will focus on my adventures—and occasional misadventures—in two other Asian countries that endlessly fascinate me for different reasons: Korea and China.

Distant Cousins: Korea

The geographical distance between Germany and Korea is about 5000 miles. Despite this enormous distance, Korea and Germany are friends, if not cousins. Korea touched me in my early childhood for two reasons. The first was the Korean War. When it began in June 1950, I was still too young to understand. But at its end in July 1953, when I was six, my father told me about the tragedy that took place in the Far East.

War was an omnipresent topic for us anyway. My father, my family, my neighbors constantly told me about the horrors of World War II, which had ended only a few years earlier. Now there was widespread fear in Germany that the Korean conflict would trigger another World War. The second connection to Korea was the common destiny of Germany and Korea as divided countries. Today, it is difficult to imagine to what extent the issue of a divided Germany occupied us, both at home and at school. At Christmas, we put candles in the windows to greet the people in East Germany. Collections and parcels were sent to the East. From this situation arose compassion and understanding for the similar fate of the Korean people. In a way, these attitudes persist to this day.

© The Author(s), under exclusive license to Springer Nature Switzerland AG 2021
H. Simon, *Many Worlds, One Life*, https://doi.org/10.1007/978-3-030-60758-6_12

Pil Hwa Yoo

I owe my current deep relationship to Korea primarily to Professor Pil Hwa Yoo. Pil earned a BA degree at Seoul National University. At a young age, he went to the United States and got an MBA from Northwestern University. He then completed his doctorate at the Harvard Business School under the guidance of my friend Bob Dolan. Pil taught for many decades at the renowned SKK Graduate School of Business at Sungkyunkwan University in Seoul, where I also lectured several times.

Since Pil worked on pricing topics, he became aware of my publications and joined me as a visiting professor at Bielefeld and at Castle Gracht. These first efforts resulted in much more than just scientific cooperation. The encounter with Pil led to a fruitful relationship and decades of friendship. Pil and his wife Ki-hyang Lee, an extraordinary woman and a professor of design, became the go-betweens for Korea and me. Together with my wife Cecilia, we formed a group that was always inspired and never got tired of each other's company. The mutual visits to Korea and Germany have been highlights of our lives.

Pil Yoo and Ki-hyang Lee are fantastic hosts. They use the former home of Pil's parents in a historic quarter of Seoul as a guest house. Ki-hyang Lee furnished the ground floor in Greek style and decorated it tastefully with selected art. During our visits to Seoul, we have met extraordinary people and spent unforgettable hours in this house. On the first floor, there is a library with works by the world's famous philosophers. Professor Yoo reads these works in six original languages: Korean, Chinese, English, Japanese, French, and German. He is an unusual linguistic talent.

United in Destiny

The most emotionally moving moments in Korea were the visits to the Demilitarized Zone (DMZ) in Panmunjom. It is like a mirror of the Iron Curtain that divided Germany for decades and illustrates the common destiny of the two countries. It is possible to visit the narrow tunnels that North Koreans had dug to infiltrate the south. The descent into the tunnels is scary. Another strong symbol is the modern train station ending at the border (photo).

The station that ends at the border between North and South Korea

The topic of reunification is often discussed in my lectures and discussions in Korea. With respect to the unpredictability of such an event, I refer to the German reunification, whose form and timing was not foreseen by anyone. I believe the same will apply to reunification of Korea. It will come, but nobody knows when and in what way. It is impossible to say whether the recent rapprochements, and the meetings between US President Donald Trump and the North Korean ruler Kim Jong-Un, mark the beginning of a process that will ultimately lead to a united Korea. One can only hope that the reunification process will be as peaceful as it was in Germany. It would make me very happy to see a peaceful reunification of Korea in my lifetime.

Korean Personalities

I have met many important people in Korea: ministers, scientists, entrepreneurs, and CEOs. I have never encountered arrogance and snootiness. I briefly share four exemplary stories here, but reserve a very special Korean personality for Chap. 13, "Encounters."

In the early years of my career, I met Dr. Joong-hi Kang, the founder and first CEO of Dong-A Pharmaceuticals. Having studied in Germany, Dr. Kang had a strong affinity to my home country. When he was a student in Freiburg, he saw a statue of the Roman wine god Bacchus in a bar. He remembered this experience years later when he needed a brand name for the first product of Dong-A, and called the product Bacchus. Bacchus is a South Korean energy drink first launched in 1963. I have always perceived Dr. Joong-hi Kang as a very serious entrepreneur, and all our discussions have been very deep and substantive. He reminded me of typical German managers, a trait which may have its roots in his time as a student in Germany.

The next story is about Dr. Chang-Gyu Hwang, whom I first met in 2001 when he was the CEO of the Memory Division of Samsung Electronics. Later, he became the CEO of Samsung Electronics and then served as CEO of Korea Telecom. Back in 2001, Dr. Hwang gave me a small device to play digital music. The playback was high quality, but it was very difficult to store other songs on the device. That product flopped, but a successor device created by Dr. Hwang together with Steve Jobs had a much different fate. We know that product as the Apple iPod.

Another person whom I remember very fondly is Jun Chee Cho, who was the Chairman and CEO of the Industrial Bank of Korea (IBK) from 2010 to 2015. His mission was the promotion of a Korean *Mittelstand* and he was a big fan of the Hidden Champions concept. He proudly showed me a Hall of Fame of Korean Hidden Champions, which he had installed in the foyer of the IBK headquarters. During one of his visits to Germany, he surprised us with an unusual gift, the Korean national costume Hanbok for my wife Cecilia, our grandson, and me. He used photos to estimate the correct measurements. The beautiful dresses fit like gloves, and we wear them with enthusiasm when visiting Korea (photo).

With Cecilia and grandson in Korean national costume Hanbok

Another Korean entrepreneur whom I met repeatedly and whom I will not forget is Dr. Chang-Jae Shin, the chairman of Kyobo Life Insurance since 2000. The first major challenge he conquered was coping with the consequences of the Asian financial crisis of 1998. Kyobo Life Insurance is an enduring success today with more than five million customers. Dr. Shin always seems calm and confident. He is an avid listener and a truly "thinking" manager.

These four personalities—Dr. Kang, Dr. Hwang, Mr. Cho, and Dr. Shin— stand out to me thanks to our varied and extremely interesting encounters in Korea. They have enriched my life. For this I am grateful.

China

Though I had encountered China as child in many ways and in many aspects, it always seemed more abstract and distant than real. I could never have imagined that China would one day become a late love of mine. My uncle John Nilles, the missionary, told me about his travels to Hong Kong, Shanghai, and Qingdao, among other places. His stories made these faraway cities vivid, adventurous, and exciting for me. At the *Gymnasium,* we had a very modern teacher of religion who not only professed the teachings of Christianity, but also dealt extensively with Asian religions, historical and dialectical materialism, and Marxism. He was fascinated by Zhou Enlai, an intellectual and political force in the Communist Party of China and comrade-in-arms of Mao Zedong. He also introduced us to Lao Tzu and Taoism, Sun Tzu's *The Art of War*, and the teachings of Confucius. And of course, Mao Zedong played an important role in this context. In geography classes, we learned about the vastness of China. I found the Yangtse River and the city of Chongqing particularly fascinating. We learned that the city of Qingdao had been part of the German empire from 1898 to 1914. Although I do not usually drink beer, I always enjoy the famous Qingdao beer, a legacy of this German period, when I travel in China.

Later as a university student, I read the three volumes of *Das Kapital* by Karl Marx. I suspect that only a few Germans have read all three volumes. We also read the *The Little Red Book* by Mao, who had many followers among German students at that time. In the ensuing years we observed, with nervous interest, the Cultural Revolution and then in the late 1970s, the developments and reforms under Deng Xiaoping. We wondered where this new direction would take China. Setting these important political and economic trends aside, though, we also noticed another new development around that same time that enriched our lives directly: the first Chinese restaurants in Germany.

In the mid-1980s, the contacts to China intensified when I became the director of the German Management Institute (USW) at Castle Gracht. Among the highlights were the lectures by Professor Claus Kernig, a political scientist from the University of Trier, the hometown of Karl Marx. He had already traveled to China in the 70s and had taken photos. Ten years later, he visited the same cities again and took photos from exactly the same locations, thus documenting the radical changes and spectacular progress that had taken place in China in only one decade. I was flabbergasted by the contrasts.

It was a mystery to me how something like this could happen in a Communist system. The little we knew about East Germany, Poland, and Russia contradicted what we now saw from China. With fascination, we listened to the first reports of German managers who worked in China. One of the pioneers was the late Martin Posth, who started the Volkswagen operation in Shanghai in 1984 and built the largest assembly plant in China. This pioneering act is probably the main reason why Volkswagen remains the leader in the Chinese automotive market today. Posth came to Castle Gracht and gave us hands-on reports about what was happening in China.

The pace of change accelerated there. While I was the director at Castle Gracht, we received the first requests from Chinese state-owned enterprises for executive seminars. A contract to train Chinese managers in Shanghai was ready to be signed. But our German supervisory board ultimately refused to approve the project. Their argument was that our resources were limited and the China project would distract too much from our core mission to train German managers for top leadership roles. I still regret today that I could not realize this very early collaboration with the Chinese.

Nevertheless, I was able to establish a contact in China in an adjacent field. The Commission of the European Communities initiated an MBA program in Beijing at about the same time, and I joined their faculty council of professors from different countries. As a result, my signature—among several others—is on one of the first MBA certificates awarded in China (see photo).

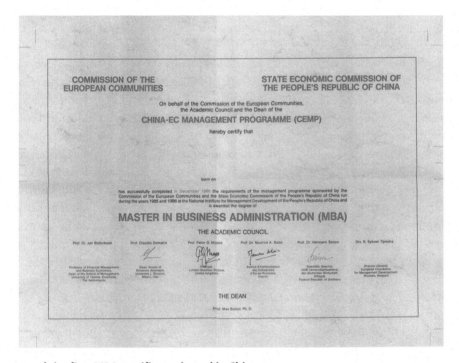

One of the first MBA certificates issued in China

From this early MBA program emerged the China Europe International Business School (CEIBS), based in Shanghai and now Asia's leading business school. Over the years, I have lectured several times at CEIBS. The school's success is an admirable achievement, and also reaffirms the old adage that "It's a small world." My good friend Professor Pedro Nueno from the IESE Business School in Barcelona played a very prominent role as the school's long-time president and now honorary president. The first headmaster was the Spaniard Alfredo Pastor. He was succeeded by Rolf D. Cremer, a German professor who had worked in Asia and Oceania for many years. He was followed for two years by Professor John Quelch from Harvard Business School. After him came Professor Hellmut Schütte, with whom I had held management seminars in Asia as early as 1982.

In the 1990s, the development in China accelerated yet again. A large conference in Guangzhou, where I gave a lecture, brought another "a-ha" experience. A professor from the Communist Party University in Beijing said that value is created mainly by private companies. I was amazed. With each new visit, I saw that China was serious about long-term growth and progress. This seriousness became particularly impressive during our first consulting project in China: win over German investors for a new high-tech industrial park in Wujin, part of the city of Changzhou. When I traveled to Wujin for the first time, I only saw fields and small farmhouses in the area intended for the high-tech park. When I returned 18 months later, those formerly empty fields now held a university with six colleges. The managers of Wujin knew what they were doing. Their goal was not to win over investors who were seeking low-cost labor, but rather to attract high-tech manufacturing facilities that needed suitably qualified employees. Thus, their first step was to build a university. That really impressed me.

In those early years, I visited numerous Chinese factories where thousands of workers were doing simple jobs. I remember a factory that produced 160 million microphones and loudspeakers for mobile phones. Thousands of female workers were sitting on long benches and manually assembling the miniature components. At that time, China was competing on the world market almost exclusively with low costs and low prices. The products were simple and of poor quality. A typical example was a company from Guangdong Province that manufactured scissors and nail clippers and became the global market leader in this field. The entrepreneur ran six factories that made these simple products. He sold his products primarily through a sales office in Hong Kong and at trade fairs in Europe and the United States. His competitive advantage lay in the low price. His strategy at the time was representative of Chinese companies: low costs and high quantities. This phase of low costs was necessary to achieve the phenomenal growth.

But the nail scissors entrepreneur also symbolizes the decline of this strategy. When I saw him again a few years later, he reported that the strategy was unsustainable. His costs had risen massively, but he was unable to increase his prices because he lacked a strong brand. His customers had turned to cheaper countries like Vietnam or Bangladesh. He also experienced major problems with staff turnover. Other companies offered higher wages, and his workers migrated in droves. He ultimately shut down production, and later founded a company in the training sector. In 2018, I met up with him and his daughter, who studied in the United States and is now running that training company. His pivot to an entirely new sector illustrates how flexible Chinese entrepreneurs are.

Despite the decline of the low-cost industry, Chinese exports rose very strongly. In 2009, China overtook Germany and became the export world champion for the first time. Since then I have been on numerous lecture tours to speak about the strategies of the German Hidden Champions as well as about pricing strategies. I visited companies from all kinds of industries. It struck me that the maturity of these companies varied greatly. I saw an increasing number of very modern plants, but still quite a few that look antiquated. On these trips, I was often accompanied by Professor Deng Di from Jinan University in Guangzhou, formerly Canton. Self-taught in English, he acted as my very dependable translator and guide. He also visited me in Germany and got to know quite a few Hidden Champions personally. Our friendship has endured and deepened over the years, and today Prof. Deng Di is a Chinese specialist for Hidden Champions. Another expert on this topic is Dr. Jan Yang of Simon-Kucher. I invited Dr. Yang to be the co-author of the fifth edition of the Chinese Hidden Champions book.

In Changsha, where Professor Deng came from, I visited the Sany concrete pump factory. In just a few years, Sany had become the world market leader in this field and had ousted the German Hidden Champion Putzmeister from first place. I was amazed by the state-of-the-art factory. Sany used the best components—such as hydraulics from Bosch Rexroth, control units from Siemens, and truck chassis from Volvo—and instituted modern workflows and production process. I had seen practically the same setup just a few months earlier in a showcase Scania truck factory in Sweden. Remember that was in 2008! In 2012, Sany acquired Putzmeister. The cooperation has developed very well. Even Karl Schlecht, the founder of Putzmeister who had a hard time separating from his "baby," confirmed to me this positive outcome a few years later.

How has the Chinese economy changed in recent years? Every time I return to China, I am amazed by the progress, the new buildings, the ultra-modern factories. I ride everywhere on high-speed trains, see huge airports, and luxurious hotels. Over the years, I have been particularly interested in the development of exports. Here, too, China has shone in every respect. If you take exports not just for one year, but for the ten years from 2010 to 2019, China is by far the number one, followed by the United States and Germany. One can say that China and Germany are the big winners of globalization although they have followed fundamentally different paths. In the late 1980s and early 1990s, German companies began to enter the Chinese market and to build factories there. In the city of Taicang alone, there are more than 300 German companies, around 200 of which operate factories. Kern-Liebers, Hidden Champion and global market leader for safety belt springs, was the first German company to settle there in 1993. In the same year, Phoenix Contact, a Hidden Champion in electronic interface technology, opened its first factory in Nanjing. These pioneers were followed by thousands of German companies. Today, there are around 8500 companies active in China today, and more than 2000 of them operate their own factories there.

On the other hand, there are only four Chinese greenfield factories operating in Germany as of 2019. Several are under construction, including ones for car batteries and automotive components. Chinese companies mostly export and trail far behind the Germans in their international presence. Their approach is to take over German companies instead. Between 2014 and 2018, there were 204 takeovers of German companies by Chinese firms. In the opposite direction, the number in the same period is only 50. This internationalization strategy of Chinese companies makes sense. Through the takeovers, Chinese companies gain production capacity, know-how, and strong brands in one fell swoop. In a way, they leapfrog a development stage. All in all, there are about 4000 Chinese companies active in Germany today.

The Beauty of China

I had seen beautiful images of Chinese landscapes in Chinese restaurants, illustrated books, and films. I suspected that many of these paintings and illustrations were exaggerated, romanticized, and unrealistic. But much of the scenic beauty we saw in China was truly breathtaking, exceeding our expectations and proving that the pictures in the Chinese restaurants were no fantasies.

The first time we came to Guilin with its karst mountains, we could not believe our eyes at first. This landscape did indeed resemble the paintings I had seen. Only in New Zealand, where films like "The Lord of the Rings" were shot, I have seen similar scenery. The photo shows Cecilia and me in front of the picturesque Karst Hills of Guilin.

Hermann and Cecilia in Guilin in 2002

When I think of our voyage down the mighty Yangtze River from Chongqing to Wuhan, pictures of the Three Gorges pop up in my mind, with their rocks that used to rise hundreds of yards high on both sides of the river. A few years later, these rocks disappeared under the dammed-up waters of the gigantic Three Gorges Dam. We saw the hanging monasteries of Datong and the 50,000 Buddha statues in the province of Shanxi. One unforgettable trip, together with our friend Yang Shuren and his family, brought us the endless grasslands of Inner Mongolia. We got to know a China that is strikingly different from the megacities I visit so often. In Inner Mongolia, we were guests of the couple Guo Xiuling and Cao Xiaoxu. Both grew up there and today sell the finest cashmere products all over the world through their Shanghai-based company Sandriver. There is even a Harvard-type case study called "Sandriver—The Preacher of Cashmere." They immersed us in their homeland and showed us the huge herds of goats that supply the precious cashmere wool. Their hospitality cannot be described in words.

Tasting China

I do not know if the reincarnation I mentioned in the first chapter really exists. But why should it be more improbable than the eternal life in which Christians believe? If there is indeed reincarnation, I must have lived in China in one of my former lives. That would be a convincing explanation for my great preference for Chinese cuisine. My friend Professor Savas Tumis, who has lived in Shanghai for 15 years, says that he still discovers a new, unknown dish at least once a week. The diversity of Chinese cuisine eclipses everything else. I think I have eaten almost everything except dog meat and monkey hands. Even when trying exotic foods such as sea cucumbers (actually a swimming crab), goose feet, and sheep eyes, I have never had a bad experience, never an upset stomach, and never failed to enjoy a meal. On the contrary, it has always been a pleasure for me to dine at a round table with a rotating "Lazy Susan" in friendly company. Over the years, I have learned to be reasonably skillful with chopsticks. Chopsticks have the advantage that you eat slowly and do not get prematurely full. The eating process and the feeling of fullness are in harmony, so to speak. That is undoubtedly better than the German way of overloading your fork and eating meals in a hurry. The diversity and richness of Chinese food strengthens my assumption that China must have been a prosperous and well-fed country in its history. Such a cuisine could only have developed amidst sufficiently high prosperity and productive agriculture. I am already looking forward to my next meal in China.

Chinese Hospitality

The vast majority of people I meet anywhere in the world is friendly. Nevertheless, there are differences. Germans are rather serious and often seem reserved or even disapproving. It can take time to develop a closer relationship. In contrast, it is easy to connect with Americans, but relationships may remain superficial. The greatest hospitality I have experienced in China. I felt at home everywhere. My journeys have taken me to many Chinese cities and provinces, and the hosts always do their best to spoil their guest from Germany.

I have noticed that Chinese hosts devote a lot of time to their guests. The same cannot be said of Western people, and unfortunately that also applies to me. We in the West are always under time pressure, rushing to stick to our rigid schedules. The Chinese, on the other hand, are far more flexible, masters of improvization, and trust that things will work out—which is usually the case. I recall one evening in Guangzhou. We sat at dinner and were supposed to fly to Shanghai the next morning. Shortly after 8 p.m. I asked our host for the departure time. He told me that he still had to figure out the flight, and that I should not worry. Later that evening, I learned that our plane would depart at 11 a.m., and the next day everything went like clockwork. That evening was no exception. The improvization always seems to work.

I find it a great personal weakness that I do not speak Chinese. I am a hopeless case. My unmistakable German accent comes through, even in European languages, and of course, correct pronunciation is an absolute must in Chinese. So I have to live with the fact that I cannot fully exploit the potential of communication with Chinese friends and acquaintances. Nevertheless, I have the impression that we often understand each other, even if there is a problem with the language. I find it difficult to remember Chinese names. One reason is that some surnames like Wang, Yang, Xu, etc. occur frequently. On the other hand, I have no associations with many of the first names due to my lack of language skills. Because of this weakness, I occasionally find myself in embarrassing situations when I cannot remember the name of a Chinese conversation partner.

Academic and Publication Activities

Over the years, contacts with Chinese academics have increasingly developed. Professor Deng Di became a constant, valuable advisor and contact person for my Chinese activities. The University of International Business and Economics (UIBE) in Beijing granted me an honorary professorship. Tsinghua University organized a lecture series on the Hidden Champions. The Hermann Simon Business was founded in Shouguang, Shandong Province, at the initiative of entrepreneur Yang Shuren, owner of Moris Technologies. The school devotes itself to research and teaching on the Hidden Champions concept. Yang Shuren has been practicing the Hidden Champions strategy since 2002. Today, his company is the global market leader in three specialty chemicals. Dieter Boening, managing director of the German subsidiary of Moris Technologies, played a key role in this initiative. The renowned Professor Liu Hongsong from Beijing acts as dean of the new school.

Hermann Simon Business School in Shouguang/China

More than a dozen of my books have been published in Chinese and several have achieved higher sales figures than in Germany. I remember a dinner with publishers in Beijing. Among them was the publisher of the books by Karl Marx. He reported that his sales figures were in the hundreds of millions, an order of magnitude unimaginable for European and American publishers. But that is China. Whatever the figure, it makes the numbers from other countries seem tiny.

I have been able to publish dozens of articles and more than 100 interviews in Chinese newspapers and magazines. Several times, I have been on the front pages of Chinese magazines, an unusual honor for a foreigner. Here are two examples.

On the front pages of Chinese magazines

I was also invited to numerous appearances and interviews on Chinese television and radio stations. The photo shows an interview with the CCTV Business Channel. On the right is the moderator, and on the left Professor Deng Di who acted as translator.

Interview with CCTV Business Channel in 2005

I have given more than 100 speeches, many of them at large conferences with up to 3000 people. On my speaking tours, I often come to a city whose name I did not know three months earlier, only to find out that this city has a population of ten million and is the capital of a province that is larger than Germany. Someone advised me not to see China as a single country, but to think of the provinces as countries. This is a novel view that helped me to better comprehend the vast dimensions of China.

Little Adventures in China

In one of China's giant cities, an acquaintance picked me up with his car to take me to the conference center where I was supposed to give a lecture. We drove three quarters of an hour through this megacity. Suddenly I asked: "Isn't this my hotel? Where are we?" The city was so big that even a local could not find his way around. We asked a taxi driver to drive ahead of us, and after another quarter of an hour we finally reached the conference site.

The situation was different in Beijing. The distance between my hotel and the conference place was only 8 km. To be on the safe side, we left two hours before the beginning of my lecture. But we got into a terrible traffic jam.

Nothing moved and I arrived one hour late, an embarrassment because more than 500 people had to wait. But the attendees took my delay in stride. They were familiar with the traffic in Beijing.

On journeys lasting several days, especially long ones, one constantly lives in the uncertainty of having forgotten something. This starts at home with packing and continues at every place you visit. Even a thorough inspection of the hotel room is no guarantee that everything has been packed. I was particularly shocked when, after a lecture and already on the way to the airport, I realized that I had forgotten my passport in the hotel safe. There was no alternative. We had to drive back. Thank God the passport was still there, and I reached my plane on time. Generally speaking, it is also risky to place objects on one's own or the free neighboring seat in an airplane. There is a good chance that you will forget it when you leave. That is how I have left my dictation machine behind several times. Through pure luck, though, I always got it back. I sometimes find objects like mobile phones on my seat that my predecessor had forgotten. I am obviously not the only forgetful person.

During one of my first official trips to China, I was accompanied by a police escort. Whenever necessary, the police car used blue lights and a siren to clear the road and get us through quickly. It also accompanied me on the way to the airport, which was in a different province. I asked the policemen if they would go with me to this airport. "Absolutely not," they replied. "We would not venture into the territory of the other province."

Once I took advantage of a stay in China to consult a Traditional Chinese Medicine (TCM) doctor about a knee problem. My escort team took me to the appropriate clinic and the doctor asked me to go to the examination room. As a matter of course, the team accompanied me to this room. This was quite unusual for me, but it seemed completely normal for everyone present. Under the eyes of half a dozen spectators, the doctor examined me and then prescribed me a black, foul-smelling ointment. I applied it for a few days and my knee got a little better. But in the long run, even a TCM remedy cannot heal arthritis.

Once my Chinese publisher invited me to dinner together with a professor from Karlsruhe Institute of Technology (KIT). The trip to the restaurant, which was beautifully situated on a hill, should take about 20 minutes. At first everything went well, but then there was a steep road, and the car could not make it uphill with the three passengers. The KIT professor explained that the clutch was slipping. It smelled burnt.

"Let's get out before the car starts to burn," I said to my companions. Said and done. We got out and went up the hill. The car followed, and at the top of the hill we got in again and drove at walking speed to the restaurant.

I experienced exemplary service at the Ritz Carlton Hotel in Shenzhen. One evening I suddenly started seeing flashes of light. I called my German eye doctor and he said I needed to go to an eye clinic immediately. Without hesitation a hotel employee agreed to go with me, and she helped me find an emergency service for eye problems. The matter turned out to be harmless but without the help of the lady from the hotel I would not have known what to do. My friend Horst Schulze, the founder of Ritz Carlton, should be proud of this example of excellent service.

Bathing in the Crowd

When you live in a geographically small country like Germany, it is hard to imagine the size of China. Its area is 27 times that of Germany, and its population of 1.4 billion is 17 times larger than that of Germany. The gigantic distances, the huge cities, the railway lines, the roads, the airports, the endless plains of Inner Mongolia—all of this far exceeds what I am used to. When I come to China, I always need a few days to adapt to these dimensions. America has always seemed bigger to me than Europe, but China is bigger than America by the same factor.

What does a population of 1.4 billion really mean? It is hard to imagine. On a trip with Professor Deng, I had an "a-ha" experience. We took a train from Jinan, the capital of Shandong Province, to Beijing. When we got off the train in the huge Beijing South station, we literally sank into a sea of people. I lost sight of Professor Deng. Luckily, he noticed me, because I was tall enough to stand out above the crowd. Cecilia and I had a similar experience with huge crowds in 2010 at the World Expo in Shanghai. We suddenly found ourselves in a vast mass of people, a situation totally unfamiliar to us. Cecilia got claustrophobic, but nothing happened.

I highly value my experiences in the West, but my times in the East have been at least as valuable. When I was young, I could never have dreamt that I would undertake these explorations. Now I cannot imagine my life without them. I have been blessed to get to know so many countries of the world, so many different peoples and cultures. I am grateful for that.

13

Encounters

In my life, I have met countless people who stood out from the masses. Many of them held or still hold important positions. But the number of them who left an indelible impression on me—who "blew me away," to use the colloquial expression—is rather small. In this chapter, I will describe some of those amazing people.

Peter Drucker

The first time I met Prof. Peter F. Drucker was around 35 years ago in Düsseldorf. We were participating in a day-long seminar held by Econ, which had published Drucker's books in German and where I was also an author. In the ensuing two decades we corresponded regularly, and I visited him several times at his home in Claremont, California, outside Los Angeles. But my last planned visit never happened. We had agreed to meet on Saturday, November 12, 2005. I called his home on Friday evening to confirm our get-together, as I would be flying in from Mexico City. His wife Doris answered.

"Peter died this morning," she said.

I was shocked and took the next available flight back to Germany. The picture below shows us together at our last face-to-face meeting in Claremont on August 11, 2002.

© The Author(s), under exclusive license to Springer Nature Switzerland AG 2021
H. Simon, *Many Worlds, One Life*, https://doi.org/10.1007/978-3-030-60758-6_13

Last meeting with Prof. Peter F. Drucker on August 11, 2002 at his home in Claremont, California

I once asked Prof. Drucker whether he considered himself more a historical writer or a management thinker. With little hesitation, he answered, "more a historical writer." Shortly before that, I had read his memoirs, *Adventures of a Bystander* (Drucker 1978), in which he immersed his readers in a fascinating bygone world. Another famous native of Vienna, the author Stefan Zweig, called that era "The World of Yesterday" (Zweig 1944)

Peter Drucker was born and raised in the upper middle class of the Austro-Hungarian monarchy. That unique environment prized education, culture, art, music, historical consciousness, urbanity, and international openness. But those words do not fully capture life at that time in Vienna. For a richer description, one should read Drucker's *Adventures of a Bystander* and Zweig's *The World of Yesterday*. In their era, it was taken for granted that upper-class children would grow up multilingual, in part because they were usually raised by an English or French nanny.

One unique aspect of this era is the great minds that it produced. The courses of their lives have an uncanny resemblance to Drucker's. The end of the Austro-Hungarian Empire in 1918, the rise of Bolshevism in Russia, and the Nazi era in Germany—the "almost unceasing volcanic eruptions of our European earth" as Zweig called them—uprooted an entire generation but also unleashed their incredible creativity. Often far from their original homes, they made immense and enduring contributions to the cultural heritage of mankind.

In addition to Drucker and Zweig, this generation and its cultural circle included philosopher Karl Popper, the mathematician John von Neumann (whom we can thank for game theory and the computer), author and philosopher Elias Canetti, journalist Arthur Koestler, art historian Ernst Gombrich, and sociologist Norbert Elias. Last but not least, that cohort also includes Karol Woytila (1920–2005) from Krakow, Poland, whom the world would come to know as Pope John Paul II. Peter Drucker's own path through life—from Vienna to Hamburg and Frankfurt, to England and then ultimately to the United States—fits seamlessly into that group.

The children of this long-lost monarchy were well prepared to make their lasting achievements because they were raised as exemplary citizens of the world. Long before anyone thought about globalization in the current sense of the term, these children were highly educated, culturally flexible, multilingual, and aware of both their own history and the history of others. "The World of Yesterday" had prepared them for the "World of the Future." The echoes of their achievements, rooted in this unique culture, continue to reverberate in our lives today.

But that is only what lies on the surface, the general impression. What makes some of these individuals special runs much deeper. Because Peter Drucker understood history as few others do, he could peer into the future in his own unique way. He repeatedly impressed me with his detailed and extensive knowledge, and how he cleverly made unusual associations. Several moments illustrate this.

Many years ago, I was impressed when I read that the famous German philosopher Arthur Schopenhauer learned Spanish just to enable himself to read *The Oracle Manual and the Art of Worldly Wisdom* (Gracian 1998) by the Spanish Jesuit Baltasar Gracian (1601–1658) in its original language. Later, I corresponded with Drucker about the book and learned that he was well versed in Gracian's work. He wrote me:

"My father gave it to me as a present 72 years ago when I left Vienna to become a business apprentice in Hamburg.... A few months later I discovered [Danish philosopher Soren] Kierkegaard. And these two have become the poles of my life. Because of Gracian, I taught myself enough Spanish to read his work in its original language—and along with that I learned enough Danish to also read Kierkegaard's work in its original language."[1]

---

[1] Personal letter from Peter F. Drucker, July 26, 1999.

To learn Spanish in order to read Gracian and to learn Danish to read Soren Kierkegaard (1813–1855) in their original languages shows how ambitiously but also how naturally Drucker absorbed and integrated philosophical discourse into his thinking even though he probably was not a virtuoso in the foreign languages.[2]

Let us look at another special case. Drucker frequently cited Deutsche Bank in his articles and books as the first corporation to be organized according to modern business principles. Aware of his interest in that topic, I once sent him an article about one of the bank's founders, Ludwig Bamberger (1826–1899).[3] I did not expect that Drucker would be familiar with this name, which I myself had never heard. Wrong again! He was very familiar with Bamberger's life and deeds through the diaries of his own grandfather, Ferdinand von Bond. Drucker wrote back to me that his stories about Ludwig Bamberger and Georg Siemens (another founder of the Deutsche Bank) "fascinated me and I still remember some of them."[4] This attests once again to Drucker's rare power to retain details.

Remarkable as well was how close he was with notable personalities from all walks of life. In *Adventures of a Bystander,* he recounts his acquaintances with Buckminster Fuller, the physicist, and Marshall McLuhan, the communication scientist. I noticed that whenever I mentioned a famous name to Drucker, he seemed to know him or her personally. Three examples: He knew Ernst Jünger (1895–1998), the famous, but controversial German writer from the 1930s. Drucker considered him to be an opportunist. Drucker first met Reinhard Mohn, the man who built Bertelsmann into a global media empire, in the 1950s. I asked him if he knew art historian Ernst Gombrich, who was also from Vienna. He was the same age as Drucker and his voluminous *The Story of Art* sold more than six million copies. Drucker said he had not known him from Vienna, but that he spent a very long and pleasant evening with him in London a few years ago. The two continued the relationship by regularly exchanging books, letters, and articles with each other.[5] The

---

[2] In an e-mail from October 17, 2016, his daughter Cecily Drucker questioned this: "Dear Hermann: A friend of mine sent me the article of yours which recently appeared in the Harvard Business Review. Enjoyable, but I would like to make one comment. Just as he used history (and sometimes bent the facts to get the desired result) to explain a situation, he also gilded the lily about some of his own work—I cannot say this, for a fact, but I find it highly unlikely that he learned either Spanish or Danish well enough to read (and deeply comprehend) either Gracian or Kierkegaard. I may be wrong but this was never revealed around the dining room table when I was growing up! With warmest regards to you and your wife. Cecily Drucker".

[3] "Ein bärtiger Revolutionär und erfolgreicher Bankier," *Frankfurter Allgemeine Zeitung*, February, 1999; see also Koehler and Bamberger (1999).

[4] Personal letter from Peter F. Drucker from March 4, 1999.

[5] Personal letter from Peter F. Drucker from November 28, 2001.

world is small. Outstanding personalities seem to attract each other across vast distances, and their paths do cross. Drucker often found himself at those intersections at the right moment.

Drucker also possessed the skill of bi-sociation, the ability to make connections between seemingly disparate things. He transcended time and space and recognized relationships and analogies that escape the average person. He drew parallels and recognized commonalities between historical, current, and future developments, stretching broad intellectual arcs between them. That requires not only encyclopedic knowledge, but the ability to make bi-sociative connections. The journalist and author Arthur Koestler, also a child of the Austrian-Hungarian monarchy, considered this competence to be true source of creativity (Koestler 1968).

Drucker's book *Management Challenges for the 21st Century* is elegant proof of this ability. Viewing digitalization through the lens of the art of printing led him to surprising insights. He concluded that the long-term winners of the digital revolution would not be among the hardware or software companies, but rather the companies that have access to data, knowledge, and content.

Drucker had the gift of drawing valuable insights by interpreting current developments and potential future events in light of historical analogies. This was one of his greatest strengths. But in my opinion, it is also one of the biggest weaknesses of most management authors, whose knowledge of history is spotty and superficial, if not totally lacking. Drucker possessed a broader and deeper foundation of historical knowledge that set him apart from those who have dubbed themselves specialists on business history, but cover only a small portion of that field. Lacking Drucker's kind of historical understanding and consciousness, business managers risk falling prey to prevailing buzzwords and trends.

History was one of Drucker's most effective teaching tools. By holding a mirror in front of us, he opened up new perspectives and helped us to understand the future better. As Kierkegaard said: "Life can only be understood by looking back, but can only be lived by looking forward." Precisely because he was a man of the past, Peter Drucker shined as a thinker of the future. I always profited from our exchanges and owe him a lot.

Herman the German

I have met only a few true adventurers in my life. "Herman the German" was one of them. Born Gerhard Neumann in the eastern German city Frankfurt an der Oder on October 8, 1917, he passed his engineering exams at age 20 at the Mittweida College. Germany was too risky for him in the 1930s because of his mother's Jewish heritage. So in 1937, he took a job with a company in Hong Kong. But when he arrived there—on a flight that had to make 16 stopovers en route—the company he had joined was bankrupt.

By chance, though, he was able to get a job instead with the legendary US airline Pan Am. Later on, he joined the Flying Tigers, a group of former American soldiers. First known as the "American Volunteer Group," they were fighting against the Japanese in China, with the tacit approval of the US government. While with the Flying Tigers, Neumann received the nickname "Göring," after the notorious supreme commander of Germany's *Luftwaffe*. But after the commander general of the Flying Tigers, General Claire Lee Chennault, heard that nickname, he issued an order: "Don't call him Göring. Call him Herman the German."[6]

Since then Neumann never shook off the "Herman the German" moniker, and even used the name as the title for his autobiography (Neumann 1984). He was responsible for the maintenance and repair of the Flying Tigers' aircraft. But he was not satisfied with the performance of the mechanics. There were too many accidents occurring after maintenance work. That is when he instituted one of his famous management principles. Each and every mechanic needed to take the plane's first flight following their maintenance work. From that moment on, there was a radical improvement in the quality of maintenance. There were hardly any accidents again.

Japan's most important fighter plane was the "Zero." At the request of the forerunner organization of the US Central Intelligence Agency (CIA), Neumann salvaged the wreckage of four crashed Zero Fighters and assembled an airworthy machine. The plane was flown to Karachi, Pakistan for inspection. Four American planes accompanied the rebuilt Zero on its flight over the Himalayas, but the only plane that arrived undamaged in Karachi was the Zero.

Sometime later, Neumann himself flew to Karachi for interrogation. He wondered whether any of the Americans played chess, a game he sorely missed. Someone gave him the name of a young woman at the Pentagon. That is where Neumann met Clarice, and they married three weeks later. Clarice was Neumann's intellectual equal, and the two would experience many adventures together.

After World War II, Neumann returned to China with Clarice with the goal of starting an airline together with General Chennault. The plan

---

[6] Chennault is famous in the United States. There was a stamp with his portrait, and Chennault International Airport in Louisiana is named after him.

collapsed, though, when Chiang Kai-Shek was forced from the mainland by Mao Zedong and retreated to the island of Formosa (now Taiwan.) Neumann commandeered a Jeep and fled with Clarice on a daring 10,000-mile drive clear across Asia. They eventually reached Israel, from which they made their way to the United States. Herman the German was so valuable to American interests that they passed a special law to grant him American citizenship. At his house in Swampscott, Massachusetts I saw the original document—"An Act—To provide for the naturalization of Master Sergeant Gerhard Neumann"—with my own eyes.

As the jet age began, Neumann joined the aircraft engines division of General Electric. It took only a few years before he rose to become CEO of the global market leader in jet engines. One can truly say that Herman the German wrote the history of the jet age. Under his leadership, GE developed both the best-selling military engine (GE J79) and the best-selling civilian jet engine (CFM 56). The latter was co-developed with the French company Snecma, now known as Safran Aircraft Engines. In the mid-1950s, Neumann negotiated with the German defense minister at the time, Franz Josef Strauss, to equip the Starfighter with the GE J79 turbine. The Starfighter whose crash I witnessed at Bomber Fighter Wing 33 had that engine.

Neumann was infamous for his sayings. Behind his desk hung a sign that read "Feel insecure." Another saying, borrowed from the Prussian General von Steuben was "a danger which one recognizes is no danger." Under the conference table in his office, he had a button installed at each seat. If someone pressed the button with one's knee, a bell would ring to signal that the current speaker must stop talking immediately, regardless of the topic. He hired a kind of "court jester" who was outside the hierarchy and whose job was to grill Neumann before he made any important decisions. He was also famous for his Items of Importance (IoI) System. Managers were required every day to write a note with the most important items (maximum one page) and distribute it to their supervisors and colleagues.

Neumann cultivated his own myth. He would show up at factories in the middle of the night, always accompanied by his dog, a German shepherd. He refused to be bossed around by Jack Welch, who took over as CEO of General Electric in 1982 and thus became his direct superior. Neumann claimed that Jack Welch tolerated his individualism and self-will, but I have not been able to confirm that that is true. Neumann was once sent to a seminar for division heads at GEs renowned management training center in Crouton-on-Hudson. The seminar began on Monday morning. That afternoon, he left the seminar, claiming he was not learning anything relevant to the real world. He also forbade his own top managers from attending such seminars.

Neumann and Clarice once survived a plane crash. They were lucky that the plane landed in the water in Mexico instead of crashing on land. "Just lucky I guess" was his motto, and not just after surviving that brush with death. At age 72, he and Clarice went skydiving for the first time. Similar to Erhard Gödert, Neumann also broke the sound barrier while flying below sea level. But he was not the pilot. He was a "back seater" in the two-seat training version of the F-104 Starfighter.

I met Neumann in the 1980s through my contacts at MTU Aero Engines in Munich. We would visit each other. He was excited to show me his yacht in Swampscott, which he captained himself and which was outfitted with the most modern navigation instruments. On the occasion of his receiving the Otto Lilienthal Medal on June 15, 1995, we held a reception at our house in Bonn with representatives from the aerospace industry. At the University of Mainz, he gave a speech in which he explained his simple but effective management principles. The auditorium was too small to hold the crowd, and the 1,200 people who ultimately attended gave him a standing ovation. His speech was the best I had ever witnessed in my university career.

In the foreword to his autobiography, Anna Chennault, the widow of General Chennault, wrote: "The first time I met Gerhard Neumann was in Kunming, China, during World War II. Ever since, I have been fascinated by the kaleidoscopic adventures crowding his life. An astonishing career as a maverick-type manager added more adventure to his amazing life" (Neumann 1984, p. 5). Herman the German was indeed a true adventurer.

Even in his old age, Herman the German retained a youthful vigor. He was witty and fun-loving, and he was always thinking about jet engines, a topic which interested me as well. I will always have found memories of every encounter we had. He passed away in 1997.

Ted Levitt

Ted Levitt was an unbelievably stimulating discussion partner. Ideas literally poured out of him. He challenged everything and was careful not to offer quick answers or make a rush to judgment. He seemed able to make a meaningful contribution to any topic.

Levitt did not publish much, but what he did publish was sensational. The first and most famous of his works is "Marketing Myopia," published in the Harvard Business Review in 1960 (Levitt 1960). In that article, he asked the question—"What business are you in?"—and his question has preoccupied generations of marketing academics and practitioners ever since. The question sounds simple. But as is often the case, asking a simple question can lead to important insights. He illustrated the problem by using the US railroads as an example. In the 1930s, the railroads failed to recognize that they were in the personal transportation business, not the railroad business. Ironically, the US government apparently did recognize the transport commonality, when in 1934 it subsumed the laws for air travel companies under the railroad laws. The railroad companies were financially very strong at that time. If they had realized that their customers were paying for personal mobility and not for train trips, they would have entered the market for air travel and could have taken control of that sector. Instead, they left that market to newcomers, and from those start-ups emerged the large US airlines.

We can also thank Levitt for popularizing the word "globalization." The term was first coined in 1917, but it did not gain traction. Then in 1983, Levitt published "The Globalization of Markets" in the *Harvard Business Review* (Levitt 1983). Today, Google turns up 70 million hits for the search term "globalization." But when one filters for hits through 1982, there are only 137 entries.

Ted Levitt was born into a Jewish family in 1925 in the small town of Vollmerz (population 800) in the German state of Hesse. The family migrated to the United States ten years later. During my time at Harvard, he and I never discussed his childhood. In all of our interactions, I only caught one brief glimpse of his German origins. At my farewell party at Harvard's Faculty Club, Levitt appeared and asked in Hessian dialect whether we were serving blood sausage. I said "nein" ("no" in German). We then continued talking as usual in English.

When I returned to Germany, an amateur historian from Vollmerz, whom I had contacted, provided me with information about the history of the Jewish community there. In the files, the original family Levy appeared. But I was hesitant to send the documents directly to Levitt. How would he react? After careful consideration, I sent the material to Bob Dolan, who was both my friend and Levitt's colleague. He passed the documents to Levitt.

The next time I visited Levitt, he was an emeritus professor and had an office in the Emeriti Faculty Center at the Harvard Business School. On this occasion, he spoke openly about his childhood in Vollmerz. The family name was Levy. His father was a poor, struggling cobbler, and it was that relative poverty that may have ultimately saved his family. They escaped the attention that wealthier Jewish families attracted. He and his family made it to the United States with the help of a refugee organization that Levitt continued to support for his entire life. He passed away in 2006.

Joseph Cardinal Höffner

On Sunday, December 4, 1983 we anxiously entered the hall of the German-speaking Catholic community in Tokyo. The Stüber family had invited us to attend the confirmation of their two sons, who attended the German school in Tokyo along with our daughter Jeannine. For several years, Alfred Stüber had been the CEO of the Japanese subsidiary of a German corporation. He and his wife Emma came from the same village as Cecilia and were friends with her parents.

The atmosphere in the hall was festive. Everyone's attention was focused on one person who stood in the middle of the room and greeted every guest individually with a handshake. This person was Joseph Cardinal Höffner (1906–1987), the Archbishop of Cologne. The archdiocese of Cologne had a sort of patronage over the diocese of Tokyo and particularly over its German-speaking community. Under these auspices, Cardinal Höffner performed the confirmations. That was my first encounter with him. We shook hands and exchanged a few words which I do not recall. But I was deeply impressed, even though our exchange was limited to just a brief conversation.

Three years later, I met with Cardinal Höffner one-on-one in his episcopal see in Cologne. The reason for my visit was a conference on the topic "Business and the Church" that we planned to hold at Castle Gracht. I came to extend a personal invitation to Cardinal Höffner. He seemed to be the perfect key-note speaker for this event, not only because of his high-ranking status in the Catholic Church, but also because of his extraordinary academic qualifications. He held four doctorates, including one in economics, and had earned his undergraduate degree in economics. I told him what we had in mind with the conference and that a C-level audience would be present. He listened very intently and welcomed the conference topic as important and current from the perspective of the church. Then he fell into a pensive silence which seemed to me to last for an eternity.

"I will not do it," he said with complete calm and without emotion.

It was intuitively clear to me that that statement was final. There was no point in trying to persuade him to change his mind. To this day, I have rarely heard an answer so clear and definitive from anyone. My disappointment was evident. But then he added: "I will find you an appropriate speaker."

I had the impression that he had not said that out of mere courtesy. On the contrary, I felt his word was binding. And he did indeed keep his word. He arranged for Paul Josef Cordes, a bishop from the Vatican who would later become a curia cardinal, to speak at the conference. Cordes was highly qualified for the topic, and at the conference he delivered a first-rate keynote speech.

I have often asked myself who among the people I have met has left the most profound impression on me. Cardinal Höffner is one of the few candidates for the top of that list. In an interview with the magazine *w&v* in 1990, I was asked to name the person—past or present—who had impressed me the most. My spontaneous answer was "Cardinal Höffner."[7] But it is difficult for me to explain precisely why. What was it about him that left such an indelible impression? Was it my perception that he was totally at peace with himself? Or was it the certitude that emanated from him? It could also have been the way he gave his answers, which seemed calmly indifferent but also left no room for doubt or discussion. My hunch is that the deep roots of this calm and certitude rest in his steadfast and unwavering faith. I have never met a person who was later canonized, but a former colleague described to me a meeting with Mother Teresa in Calcutta. His story reminded me of what I experienced in the presence of Cardinal Höffner.

Philip Kotler

If Philip Kotler is not *the* reason why I turned my attention to marketing, he certainly played an important role in my decision to follow that path. In 1967, he published his groundbreaking book *Marketing Management. Analysis, Planning and Control.* As a student, I read this textbook enthusiastically. Marketing—understood as customer-oriented management—was a totally new concept for me. In my own research, I came across Kotler's articles, and many of them were directly relevant to the topic of my dissertation. That was especially true for his 1965 article in *Management Science* about the influence of marketing on the life cycle of new products (Kotler 1965). As I mentioned in a previous chapter, I was able to use mathematical analyses to show that his model could lead to some nonsensical results. My article criticizing these results appeared in *Management Science* in 1978 (Simon 1978). The criticism of the great master by a "nobody" from Germany struck a nerve with many people in academic circles.

In January 1979, I visited Northwestern University in Evanston, where Kotler taught, and requested a meeting. To my amazement, he agreed immediately and greeted me very cordially. I sensed right away that there was a good chemistry between us. He gave me several pieces of advice, one of which was to contact the Chicago "price consultant" Dan Nimer. What would have happened to me without Kotler's suggestion to meet with a price consultant?

---

[7] *w&v*, November 2, 1990, p. 180.

Out of that first meeting with Kotler grew a lifelong friendship. There are few marketing academics I have met as often as him. Even in his later years, he is in high demand around the world as a speaker at conferences, many of which I participated in as well. Over the years, our paths have crossed in places such as Shanghai, Mexico City, Sao Paulo, Bangladesh, Vienna, Milan, Castle Gracht, Tokyo (see photo), and many other locations.

With Philip Kotler in Tokyo, October 2016

I have met few people who are as friendly, balanced, and indefatigable as Philip Kotler. He has handled a workload that would have crushed others. He wrote more than 60 marketing books and has received 22 honorary doctorates. His Hirsch Index is 198, and his i10-index is 1216.[8] I do not personally know any other author with higher values of this citation index.

I am impressed by Kotler's ability to immerse himself in new topics. He touches on digitalization in all of his current speeches. Despite his advanced age, he is well versed in the most modern methodologies and contemporary case studies. His curiosity is unquenchable. Although I know his work very well, he surprised me in many ways with his 2015 book *Confronting Capitalism*

---

[8] The Hirsch index is the number n of publications that have been quoted at least n times. The i10-index is the number of publications that have been quoted at least ten times. https://scholar.google.com/citations?user=g9WIbh0AAAAJ&hl=en, called up on February 17, 2021.

(Kotler 2015). First, it is highly unusual that a marketing expert—someone who is the very embodiment of marketing science—would write such a fundamental critique of capitalism. His treatment of the topic shows that his view extends beyond the horizons of the typical marketing academic. The book was also an impressive example of his broad base of knowledge and his deep understanding of the interactions between economics, politics, and the society at large. His doctorate from MIT's economics department shines through.

Kotler still writes one or two books per year across an increasingly wider spectrum of topics. Together with his brother Milton, two years his junior, he wrote a book in 2014 on the future role of megacities (Kotler and Kotler 2014). Milton Kotler, whom I have also had the pleasure of meeting, is a Washington-based consultant who specializes in China. Though he is over 80 years old, he still travels once per month to China. I hope for many more meetings with Philip Kotler and am indebted to him.

Marvin Bower

I was a Marvin Bower Fellow during my time at the Harvard Business School. Marvin Bower (1903–2003) became the spiritual father of McKinsey & Company after founder James McKinsey passed away in 1937 and his partner A. T. Kearney split off to run his own independent firm. The firm McKinsey's Code of Conduct and corporate culture trace their roots back to Bower. One single dinner with him left a deep impression on me. For that occasion, he had made a special trip from New York to Boston, and at age 85, he was still as sharp as ever.

That same impression comes across in the book *The Will to Lead,* which he published in 1997 at the age of 94 (Bower 1997). A previous book with a similar title *The Will to Manage* came out in 1966 (Bower 1966). The titles recall Friedrich Nietzsche's controversial concept "will to power."[9] The term "will" appears rarely in the management literature, even though "will" is an indispensable trait of leadership and management. Interestingly, the concept of "will" is reminiscent of a saying from Seneca: "Willing cannot be learned."

What impressed me so much about Marvin Bower? I believe it was his combination of "soft" and "hard." The soft side comprised his composure, the

---

[9] "Will to Power" is not one of Friedrich Nietzsche's independent publications, but a concept he introduced in *The Gay Science* and *Thus Spoke Zarathustra.* He refers at least briefly to this concept in all of his following books.

wisdom of his age, and his modest appearance. But behind that was a decisiveness and an unbreakable will that came across with strength but without a hint of aggression. Meeting Marvin Bower was a highlight of my life. He passed away a few months before his 100th birthday on January 22, 2003.

Hans Riegel

Hans Riegel (1923–2013) was one of the most extraordinary entrepreneurs that I have ever met, comparable in some ways with Johann Rupert on the luxury goods group Richemont. Riegel was born in Bonn in 1923 as the oldest son of Hans Riegel, the founder of Haribo. The name Haribo stands for "Hans Riegel Bonn." After serving in World War II and time afterwards as a prisoner of war, the younger Hans returned to Bonn, where he needed to take over leadership of the family firm at a young age after the unexpected death of his father. He led Haribo for 67 years, from 1946 to 2013, with unstoppable and undiminished creativity. He read teen magazines, understood the language of young people, and succeeded time and again in the creation of new products that appealed to children and teenagers.

Riegel was a man full of contradictions. He was completely focused on his company. If someone had woken him up at 2 a.m. and asked what he was thinking about, he would probably have said "Haribo" or "gummi bears." But at the same time, he was passionate about his hobbies, especially hunting. High in the Austrian mountains he owned 11,000 acres of land that he had purchased from a nobleman. Not far from Bonn, he operated the Hotel Kloster Jakobsberg and its adjacent hunting grounds. In his younger years, he introduced badminton to Germany and in 1953 he became the first German badminton champion in men's doubles. He also participated in speedboat racing together with his brothers.

He was efficient and effective at the same time. Discussions with him always centered on the essentials, and then he would make his decision. His quest for efficiency penetrated all parts of his business. Early in his career, he purchased a helicopter in order to save time on traveling. He even got his own pilot's license.

He and I had a somewhat strange relationship. I felt that I was one of the very few people that he trusted. At the same time, like most others, I was unable to discover what truly made him tick. The basis of his trust in me lay probably in the fact that I would occasionally contradict him or at least disagree with him. Employees or others who depended on him could hardly risk doing that. In his will, he assigned me a custodial role over the foundation that would control his assets. After careful consideration and talks with people involved, I ultimately declined the offer. I was deeply saddened when Dr. Hans Riegel passed away in 2013. Unfortunately, I could not attend his funeral because I was in New Zealand at the time.

Tomohiro Nakada

My relationship to Tomohiro Nakada came about through Takaho Ueda, a professor at Gakushuin University in Tokyo and a long-time friend. Gakushuin University plays an important role in Japanese society. The children of the imperial family traditionally study there. The photo shows Nakada (left) and Ueda (right) with Cecilia and me.

Tomohiro Nakada, Hermann Simon, Takaho Ueda, and Cecilia Simon in Nakatsugawa, Japan, 2015 (l. to r.)

In many respects, Tomohiro Nakada is an unusual entrepreneur. His firm Salad Cosmo is the Japanese market leader for fresh vegetables such as chicory and sprouts. He led his company successfully for a long time. In the Salad Cosmo facilities, I saw large-scale, industrial biological production for the first time. Computer-guided palettes move the plants through the factory. The plants are continually exposed to optimal amounts of water, nutrients, light, and humidity. The company uses neither artificial fertilizer nor pesticides, so that its products meet standards for organic production.

But it was not just his competencies as a businessman that impressed me. The headquarters of Salad Cosmo is located in the central Japanese city of Nakatsugawa, a small city by Japanese standards. What I experienced there—the hotels, the food, and the people—was so much different than what I encountered in the major metropolitan centers such as Tokyo and Osaka. Hardly anyone speaks English. One feels totally foreign as a European in that environment.

But the friendliness of the people is extraordinary. I can barely find the words to describe what Nakada organized for us in his hometown. The highlight was a drama piece performed by 150 students from the Yukikomakei Dancing School, where Nakada is a benefactor. Although we could not understand the dialog and songs in Japanese, Cecilia and I were moved to tears, as was Nakada himself. The photo captures the mood after the performance.

Drama performers in Nakatsugawa, Japan

The professionalism of that evening was first-class in every way: the performance, the choreography, the singing, the set design, and the motivation of the students. I cannot imagine that a German school could match that kind of show, which demanded meticulous preparation and endless hours of practice.

Another unforgettable experience came during my second visit to the city, when I held a speech at Nakada's school with 600 students in attendance. Before entering the auditorium, all attendees removed their shoes and put on slippers. Mine were a couple of sizes too small, so I waddled awkwardly into the hall to the sounds of the German national anthem. Once on stage, I removed the slippers and delivered my speech—on career prospects in a globalized world—while standing in my stocking feet. As I departed, a band of 60 students played the Radetzky March, a famous melody from Vienna. Cecilia and I were on the verge of tears again.

Nakada treated us to other unique experiences such as receptions, visits to traditional craftsmen, and trips to historical villages. He invests his ideas and his energies into leading his hometown into the future. One highlight will be the inauguration of the new magnetically levitated train—the so-called Linear Shinkansen—planned for 2027. That line, which will cut a straight line deep under the mountains, will effectively transform the rather remote town of Nakatsugawa into a suburb of Tokyo and Nagoya. I have accepted Nakada's invitation and hope that both of us can attend the inauguration of the service in 2027.

Nakada is down-to-earth, but at the same time he is a true global player. He has visited me many times in Germany. He and 40 other Japanese once stood on the terrace of my house and passionately sang the Japanese national anthem. In Argentina, he has been growing seeds for his plants on 3000 acres of his own land. And in 2019 he bought another 17,300 acres. He procures the seedlings for his chicory production in Holland and buys other materials in Italy. He personally inspects all of these activities several times a year, even though he is only a few years younger than I am. I have always found him to be friendly, full of energy, and constantly coming up with ideas. He chartered two big planes to take the students in his performing troupe to South America where they performed for the Japanese who had settled there decades earlier. Despite our geographical and cultural distance, Nakada and I have a deep friendship.

Yang Shuren

In 2002, the Chinese entrepreneur Yang Shuren read the first Chinese-language edition of my Hidden Champions book and became an enthusiastic fan of the strategic concept. His company, Moris Technologies, is located in

Shouguang (Shandong Province), not far from the city of Qingdao, a former German colony famous for its beer. Thanks to the nearby Yellow Sea, Shouguang possesses a unique source of brine that is the basis for a specialty chemical industry. Moris Technologies operates nine production plants in Shouguang.

Inspired by the Hidden Champions concept, Yang Shuren decided to focus only on products that gave his company a chance to achieve international market leadership. Today, his company is the global market leader for three kinds of flame-retardant materials.

When I walk next to him, I need to work hard to keep up despite my height advantage. His small stature belies the amount and intensity of his energy and ideas. But he does not only come up with ideas. He implements them relentlessly and with breathtaking speed. He sees every problem as a business opportunity.

When the roughly 50 chemical plants in Shouguang had problems with their water supply, he built a treatment plant to provide water customized to each plant's needs. One of the most serious problems in China's chemical industry is worker safety. Deadly accidents are common. Thus, safety became an important topic for Yang. So what did he do? Professor Deng Di, a Chinese expert on Hidden Champions, describes his actions:

> "Mr. Yang had an amazing idea that I refer to as 'turn your problem into a business!' Safety is the biggest problem for chemical companies in Shouguang. He was the first one to make meaningful investments to educate his employees and a special team on the topic of safety in the chemical industry. Second, he set up facilities—such as a 'safety museum'—where his own staff and employees from other companies could receive safety training. Then he founded a consulting firm to advise the other chemical companies in the region on safety."[10]

Systematic vocational training is another underdeveloped area in China. To address that, Yang founded a trade school based on the German model. Beyond that, he has recognized the need for sound management training. His response was to establish a business school, and I am truly honored that that school bears my name.

One might get the impression that Yang suffers, as many Chinese entrepreneurs do, from an acute case of "diversification syndrome." But that is not the case. Everything he does is focused on the chemical industry and the

---

[10] E-mail by Deng Di from November 20, 2017.

Mittelstand in his home region. His clear goal has always been to advance Moris Technologies as well as the whole chemical industry in Shouguang.

The business relationship with Yang has led to a personal friendship that also includes our families. It is difficult to top his hospitality. We have taken many trips together. The picture shows us on our way to the Great Wall of China. We stopped to buy some freshly picked apples from a passing trader. One highlight was a trip through Inner Mongolia that we took in the summer of 2018 with our families. He showed us a side of China that offers a sharp contrast to what I encounter in the huge cities I usually travel to. Yang Shuren opened up China to me. I have much to thank him for.

With Yang Shuren and Cecilia on an outing to the Great Wall of China

Miky Lee

In Asia, it is a rare honor to be invited into someone's private home. My friend Professor Pil Hwa Yoo from South Korea is an exceptional host in that regard. He uses his parents' old house in Seoul's historic district as a guesthouse. His wife Ki-hyang Lee, a professor of design, has decorated the ground floor in Greek style. On the second floor, there is a library with the works of all famous philosophers, which Professor Yoo reads in five original languages. Cecilia and I are regular guests at this house when we visit Seoul. At one dinner occasion, the guest list included Dr. Chang-Gyu Hwang, the CEO of Korea Telecom and his wife, and the CFO of a large company. Another woman was expected to join us later on.

We felt at home in our small group and had a wide-ranging conversation. I asked Dr. Hwang's wife, who used to be responsible for economic development for the city of Incheon (population three million), why Bonn lost out to Incheon in the competition to host a United Nations department.[11] She said that the Korean president invited the heads of state of various developing countries to visit Incheon and let the city win them over. When the vote came, that tipped the scales in Incheon's favor.

Then the last guest of the evening finally entered the room and drew everyone's attention. Wearing an eye-catching dress and gym shoes, she looked more like a young girl than a businesswoman. She was Miky Lee, whose name in Korean is Mie Kyung Lee. She is the oldest granddaughter of the founder of Samsung, Byung Chull Lee. She studied at the elite Seoul National University as well as in Taiwan, Japan, and China. She also earned an MA from Harvard, where she taught for several years.

But Miky Lee was not resting on her family legacy. Together with her brother, she founded and leads the company CJ E&M, which is active in media, entertainment, and retail. It is part of the CJ Group, which has an annual revenue of almost $25 billion. She was also one of the early investors in the film studio DreamWorks SKG, founded in 1994 by Steven Spielberg, Jeffrey Katzenberg, and David Geffen. For her outstanding business and cultural achievements, she has received numerous national and international honors and awards. But in 2014 Bloomberg Markets had written "little is known about her" (Lee 2014). Only after her brother was convicted of tax evasion in 2013 did she come increasingly into the limelight.

Miky Lee's entrance immediately changed the mood in our dinner group. Her charisma pervaded the room. She was unpretentious, relaxed, and had a great sense of humor. She has implemented her vision—"to create new industries, jobs and heroes" (Lee 2014, p. 54)—to an incredible degree. Katzenberg, one of the biggest names in the film industry said: "I hold her in extraordinarily high esteem as a businesswoman, a manager and a leader" (Lee 2014, p.57). Others may have a similar level of accomplishments, but that is not what makes her so special. Few people if any have overcome health issues as

---

[11] The international airport of Seoul is located in Incheon, about 40 miles from the capital.

chronic and severe as Miky Lee's to reach those heights.[12] The true measure of her person is that she has overcome these obstacles while maintaining an exemplary positive outlook and attitude.

When people ask me who has left the deepest and most enduring impression on me, there are only two candidates for first place. Miky Lee is one of them.

References

Marvin Bower, *The Will to Manage: Corporate Success Through Programmed Management*, New York: McGraw-Hill, 1966.

Marvin Bower, *The Will to Lead: Running a Business with a Network of Leaders*, Cambridge, MA: Harvard Business School Press, Cambridge, 1997.

Peter F. Drucker, *Adventures of a Bystander*, New York: Harper & Row, 1978.

Balthasar Gracian, *The Oracle Manual and the Art of Worldly Wisdom* (Spanish original title: "Oraculo manual, y arte de prudencia"), translated into German by Arthur Schopenhauer, 11th edition, Frankfurt am Main: Insel, 1998.

Benedikt Koehler, Ludwig Bamberger, *Revolutionär und Bankier*, Stuttgart: Deutsche Verlag-Anstalt, 1999.

Arthur Koestler, *Der göttliche Funke*, Munich: Scherz, 1968.

Philip Kotler, "Competitive Strategies for New Product Marketing over the Life Cycle," *Management Science* 12 (1965), p. B-104.

Philip Kotler, *Confronting Capitalism: Real Solutions for a Troubled Economic System*, New York: AMACOM, 2015.

Philip Kotler and Milton Kotler, *Winning Global Markets: How Businesses Invest and Prosper in the World's High-Growth Cities*: Hoboken: Wiley, 2014.

Yoolim Lee, "Selling Korean Cool," *Bloomberg Markets*, March 2014, p. 57.

Theodore Levitt, "Marketing Myopia," *Harvard Business Review*, July/August 1960, pp. 45–56.

Theodore Levitt, "The Globalization of Markets," *Harvard Business Review*, May/June 1983, pp. 92–102.

Gerhard Neumann, *Herman the German: Enemy Alien U.S. Army Master Sergeant #10500000*, New York: William Morrow, 1984.

Hermann Simon, "An Analytical Investigation of Kotler's Competitive Simulation Model," *Management Science* 24 (October 1978), pp. 1462-1473.

Stefan Zweig, *Die Welt von gestern—Erinnerungen eines Europäers*, Stockholm: Bermann-Fischer, 1944.

---

[12] It is the so-called Charcot–Marie–Tooth disease, one of the hereditary motor and sensory neuropathies of the peripheral nervous system characterized by progressive loss of muscle tissue and touch sensation across various parts of the body. Currently incurable, this disease is the most commonly inherited neurological disorder.

14

Magic Moments

This chapter includes stories about personal experiences that remain etched in my memory. Some of those memories are tied to significant moments in history—such as German reunification and the terrorist attacks on 9/11—while others arose from events with no relevance to the wider world. This chapter is partially inspired by Stefan Zweig's book *Decisive Moments in History (Sternstunden der Menschheit* in German,) but that in no way implies that the personal events I describe have the weight and impact of the decisive moments Zweig described.

Nonetheless, there are some commonalities. Zweig writes that in history "a vast number of insignificant and mundane things occur" while "sublime, unforgettable moments are rare" (Zweig 2014). The same holds true for most people's private lives. But science has still not definitively explained why some experiences stay present and vivid in our memories forever, while the memories of other events—perhaps even more important ones—fade away completely.

A Forecast Far Off the Mark

At the invitation of *Manager Magazin,* the CEOs of 12 German corporations gather in Munich on October 25, 1989 to discuss the topic "What will become of Germany?" Because I had written a column for the magazine since my days at Harvard, I am invited to attend the meeting. The developments between East Germany and West Germany have intensified in the weeks prior to that meeting. The citizens of East Germany have received permission to

H. Simon, *Many Worlds, One Life*, https://doi.org/10.1007/978-3-030-60758-6_14

travel outside the country, and the dramatic scenes of Germany's foreign minister, Hans Dietrich Genscher, at the German embassy in Prague are still very fresh in everyone's mind. René Jäggi, at the time CEO of Adidas AG, arrives to the meeting somewhat late because he has just signed a contract with the East German Olympic organization. The contract is for sports equipment for the forthcoming Summer Olympics in Barcelona in 1992. Jäggi notes he is "assuming that this is the last contract that Adidas will ever sign with an East German Olympic team."

"Are you trying to say that in 1996, when the Olympic Games take place in Atlanta, there will no longer be an East German team?" one CEO asks.

"Exactly!" Jäggi answers abruptly. The rest of the participants look at him incredulously. Most think his vision is pure fantasy.

Two weeks later, on Thursday, November 9, 1989, I teach in Paris at an executive seminar for the accounting firm Price Waterhouse.[1] The discussion turns inevitably to the ongoing events in the two Germanys. Regarding the topic of potential German reunification, I state that I would no longer rule it out before the end of the twentieth century, meaning it could happen within the next ten years. Little do I know that the Berlin Wall would fall within the next ten *hours*! When I return home to Bonn late that evening, I hear the official news. For all practical purposes, the state of East Germany no longer exists. The official German reunification takes place within a year.

***

I tell this story often when I visit Korea, and end it with the following sentiment: Korean reunification will eventually happen, but no one can say when. Perhaps the flow of events will make it impossible to foresee the timing with any certainty, just as it happened with Germany. One can only hope that the process transpires peacefully. It still amazes me today that the German reunification happened so peacefully and smoothly. As I described in the chapter "Years of Thunder," the parties on both sides of the Iron Curtain were heavily armed. But no shots were fired and no bombs fell. "The future lies in darkness," according to a German song. That has always been true and always will be.

Two days after the fall of the Berlin Wall, on November 11, 1989, I flew with our two children to Berlin. Jeannine was 14 at the time and Patrick was nine. I wanted to show them the Wall and East Germany, because both would soon no longer exist in their present forms. We rented a car and drove through gaps in the Wall—now open in many places—into East Berlin. Little had

---

[1] In 1998, Price Waterhouse merged with Coopers & Lybrand forming PricewaterhouseCoopers, PwC. Today PwC is the second largest auditing firm worldwide.

changed since my class trip there 25 years earlier. Everything seems cloaked in a somber shade of gray. On the side streets of East Berlin, one could still see bullet holes from the battles at the end of World War II.

Prior to that trip, I had only visited East Berlin a handful of times. For a West German citizen, the rest of the country of East Germany was off limits. Now we could drive out to Potsdam, outside Berlin, without a problem. But the same somber gray scenes filled that city as well. I was very surprised how quickly we were in the open countryside once we left Berlin. As we drove down a country road lined with poplars, we encountered a Russian military convoy of heavy trucks. The trucks seemed threatening, and the whole scene made me very uneasy.

I had a similar feeling again when I visited the Eastern German city of Jena in February 1990. We arrived in the evening and were going to visit a professor there. The city was pitch dark. We asked a passerby where we could make a phone call. He said "at the post office" and offered to show us the way. He climbed into my BMW. Apparently, the short trip in such a car was quite an experience for him.

There was no hotel in Jena where we could stay for the night. We finally found some acquaintances of West German friends and they put us up for the night. Several months later, I was in Jena again for a lunch meeting with the CEO of Carl Zeiss, the famous optical systems firm. The local residents who had made us feel at home on our first visit now viewed me with suspicion and acted very cautiously around me. They didn't know what to make of my meeting with an important figure such as the CEO of Zeiss. A few months later, East Germany formally ceased to exist, and that CEO was also replaced by a manager from the West. However, the vestiges of the Communist system show their effects to this day. One example is the voting tendencies in the Eastern German states.

Return from Nowhere

My home city of Wittlich once had a large Jewish minority. More than five percent of the residents were Jewish, supposedly the second largest share in Germany behind Frankfurt. The last Jewish resident disappeared from the city in 1942, but the synagogue remained intact. Built in 1910, it had survived the nationwide destruction during the Night of Broken Glass (*Kristallnacht*) on November 9, 1938.

After World War II and during my entire time in school, there was a cloak of silence over the fate of Wittlich's Jews. The first attempts to discover their history and their fate came in the 1980s at the initiative of the younger generation that was not tainted by the Nazi past. In 1991, the city invited the surviving Jews to return to Wittlich. About 70 people accepted, most of them elderly. They came all the way from Israel, the United States, Argentina, and other countries.

Meeting these people touched me profoundly. Before my time they had lived among us. The ones who had not escaped the Nazis in time were transported to the ghetto in the city of Lodz in Poland and from there to Auschwitz or other extermination camps. The ones who returned to Wittlich from "nowhere" belonged to the fortunate ones who got away ahead of the Nazi onslaught.

Because of the pervasive and stifling silence during my youth, I had not been aware of their existence. We knew nothing about them. They had just disappeared into nowhere. Now a considerable number of them stood in front of us. Many still spoke our Moselle-Franconian dialect. They did not appear to be vindictive, but rather happy to return to their hometown—perhaps one final time. For almost all of them, it was indeed the final time, but that one time seemed to be enough. None returned for good.

Some were accompanied by their children. They included 90-year-old Erna Baumann, nee Mayer, from Buenos Aires. Coming back to her hometown was an extremely touching experience not only for her, but also for her son Réné Baumann. Cecilia and I met up with him years later in Buenos Aires, and he told us in perfect German how unique and special that event was for him.

Wittlich has done a lot in the meantime to account for its Jewish past. In 1997, the Emil Frank Institute, named after the last leader of the Jewish community, was established. It carries out research on Jewish history in the region as well as interfaith dialog among Christians, Jews, and Muslims. The city's synagogue, hidden undisturbed for years behind fences and barbed wire, was renovated true to its original style. It now serves as a culture and community center. Several academic research projects have explored the history of Wittlich's Jews. The book *Juden in Wittlich 1908–1942* by Maria Wein-Mehs covers 681 pages and offers the most comprehensive view (Wein-Mehs 1996). I do not know if any of Wittlich's Jews are still alive. But my encounter with them was a magic moment I will never forget.

At this point, I would like to mention another moment that fits in this context, even though it is not related to Wittlich. On March 25, 2016, I received an email from someone in Israel, Zvi Harry Likwornik, whom I did not know. He referred me to the second edition of his book *Als Siebenjähriger im Holocaust* (*Into the Holocaust as a seven-year-old*) (Likwornik 2012/2014). Zvi Harry Likwornik grew up speaking German in the city of Czernowitz (now Chernivtsi in Ukraine) and was sent to different ghettos starting in

1941. The tortures inflicted on him as a child are beyond comprehension. He and his mother finally made it to Israel. Deeply shaken after reading his book, I sent him an email spontaneously, and he called me overjoyed about my response. Think about that: one receives a phone call from someone who survived the Holocaust as a seven-year-old. The past can be so close.

An Ancestor Re-Appears

On January 19, 2001, I have a mysterious dream. In the dream, my uncle Jakob Simon—who reportedly drowned in the Black Sea in 1944 and was the last person in my family to pass away before my birth—is either living in Switzerland or had lived there. Then he shows up again in my hometown in 1959. We are in an auditorium. I'm sitting in the balcony, while Jakob is sitting upfront and is summoned to the podium. He speaks about Germans that fled Germany during the Nazi regime. He speaks eloquently and seems perfectly calm and in control of the situation. He is fit and well-groomed in a dark, pinstriped suit. But his face looks thin. I get a long and very precise look at it, and notice a certain resemblance to my father.

After his interview, I try to get close to him, but that proves difficult because he is surrounded by people. Finally, I reach him and ask him if he will be returning to our hometown again. He says no. I ask him for his address, so that I may visit him, but he refuses to give it to me. He shows me identification issued by a mysterious German agency. On his papers, a box labeled "Endangered Person" is checked off. I give him my business card in order to nudge him to give me his, but to no avail. He leaves, and I do not know how to find him again.

Then I wake up, very anxious and soaked in sweat. I have forgotten almost all the dreams I have ever had, but not this one. Why is that? Could it be the interconnection of souls that I hinted at in Chap. 1?

Crossing to Africa

When we were young, how often each of us dreamt about the big wide world! Some of my friends did go to sea, and that only intensified my wanderlust. Our forefathers had traveled to faraway lands during the wars. Two of my uncles fought under Field Marshall Erwin Rommel in Africa. A young man from our neighborhood joined the French Foreign Legion and served in Sidi bel Abbes in Algeria. Africa beckoned, but we seemed to be trapped in our village.

The trip I described in Chap. 2—to Spain, Morocco, and Portugal—was our break-away moment. The emotional high point was the sea crossing to Africa on the "Virgen de Africa," which brought us from Algeciras in Spain to the Spanish enclave Ceuta on the Moroccan side of the Straits of Gibraltar. The pose in the photo below captures my emotions during that journey.

Crossing the Straits of Gibraltar to Africa, July 1965

I felt like Vasco da Gama as I left Europe for the first time and set foot on another continent. By definition, you experience such a first departure from your home continent only once in your life. Was this crossing the first step toward the global player I would one day become? That is still the way I view that trip to this day.

In Morocco, we entered a fascinating world. Only a few years earlier, Morocco had gained its independence from France and Spain. At that time, the country had a population of 14 million, but in 2019 the population is 37 million and the cities have modernized accordingly. When we visited in 1965, however, it was still the old, almost medieval Morocco. The pungent odor that permeated the tanning district in Fez remains in my nose today. The market square Jemaa el-Fnaa in Marrakesh—with its jugglers, snake charmers, traders, and storytellers—seemed like a fairy tale straight out of *Arabian Nights*. We spent three days and three nights in Marrakesh. Without any air condition, we suffered in the unbearable heat and hardly slept. Making matters worse, a sandstorm erupted and blew sand between our teeth.

I bet a schoolmate a case of beer that I would nonetheless return to Marrakesh someday. I won the bet, but lost the city. Upon my return 30 years later, the Marrakesh that enchanted me in my youth no longer existed. Jemaa el-Fnaa had lost its magic. Perhaps that was due to my rational view of things. Time travel into one's own past is not possible. But the crossing on the "Virgen de Africa" and my first immersion in the wonders of Marrakesh will always rank among my magic moments.

9/11

At Frankfurt's *Alte Oper* concert hall, I am preparing to moderate a conference with two prominent keynote speakers: Ernst Welteke, the president of Germany's Bundesbank (Federal Reserve Bank), and Henry Kissinger, the former US secretary of state. The picture below shows us at lunch. It is September 11, 2001, about 2 p.m. Frankfurt time.

Lunch with Henry Kissinger, Frankfurt, September 11, 2001. In the photo from left to right: Henry Kissinger, Ernst Welteke (president of The German Bundesbank, seen from the back), Franz Alt (TV journalist), Kajo Neukirchen (CEO of Metallgesellschaft AG), representatives of the conference organizer Ernst & Young, Hermann Simon

Our conference starts at 3 p.m., which is 9 a.m. in New York City. As the moderator, I briefly introduce Kissinger, who launches into a talk with the title "Years of Renewal." In hindsight, both the timing and content of his opening remarks are eerily ominous.

"Mainland America has never been attacked by an external enemy," he says. No one in the room has any idea that a mere eight minutes later, his statement would no longer be true.

Kissinger concludes his talk at 3:30 p.m. and opens the floor for discussion. A journalist asks a provocative question about Kissinger's involvement in the US intervention in Chile and the 1973 coup d'état against Salvador Allende. As the tension rises in the room, a man approaches me on the podium and whispers in my ear that New York City and the Pentagon have just been bombed. I approach Kissinger to pass along the news, but he does not appear to grasp what I have said. He gives me a dismissive wave and suggests that we continue with the discussion.

I disagree and decide to interrupt the discussion. The journalist who asked the provocative question calls out loudly that my interruption is only a trick to silence him (an action for which he later apologizes). I ask the audience if they know anything more precise about what is happening. A Bloomberg journalist who has just arrived speaks up and gives us a quick update. In the meantime, the technical team has projected a live German television broadcast on the big screen. In total disbelief, we all witness the scenes in New York and the collapse of the World Trade Center buildings. In such moments, one feels the touch of history.

Eckhard Kucher, co-founder of Simon-Kucher, is in Washington at the time. I attempt to contact him via our Boston office, but that is no longer possible. All lines are blocked. The internet emerges as the savior. About two hours later, we receive an email that all of our colleagues in Washington as well as in Boston—where two of the hijacked flights originated—are safe. Kucher remains stuck in the United States for a week before catching a flight back to Germany.

The events of 9/11 demonstrate another consequence of globalization. International interconnections bring tragic events close to home, regardless of where they happen or where one is. The shock is immediate. A few days later in Tokyo, I met a consultant from the Nomura Research Institute. He said that two of his colleagues died at the World Trade Center that day. Danger is near, no matter how far away it seems to be.

Moscow Nights

It is autumn 1971, still in the midst of the Cold War. The Soviet Union does not trust any foreigners. But at the same time, Russia's black market is flourishing Young Russians find typical western products irresistible.

It is in that environment that a motley mix of students from Bonn decides to undertake a trip to Moscow. Each of us packs suitcases with products that would sell well on the black market: jeans, button-down shirts, but also seemingly trivial items such as ballpoint pens. We know that taxi drivers in Moscow accept the pens as payment. The ruble-to-dollar exchange rate in the black market is four to five times the official rate. Ten dollars, converted into rubles, give us enough purchasing power for a wild night on the town. We indulge in Crimean champagne, caviar, and other Russian delicacies that we could have never afforded at home as students.

The large bookstores in Moscow offer German-language books from East German publishers, and at the black-market exchange rate we can buy bound classical books for around 1 DM (0.50 euros) apiece. Shipping costs with the postal service are also very low, so we literally buy books by the meter and send them back home. We are students, and none of these transactions gives us any guilty conscience at all.

On a trip back to his native Afghanistan, my friend Sami Noor also plans to make a stopover in Moscow. We live in the same dorm in Bonn, and we had agreed to meet up at the office of the Afghani airline Ariana, which is located in the famous Hotel Metropol. I go to our agreed meeting point and ask if Sami Noor has arrived. The staffer from Ariana tells me that he indeed arrived, but then departed again right away. That strikes me as highly unusual. I do not find out what happened until we are both back in Germany. Sami had taken a Russian taxi from the airport to the hotel. His suitcase was in the trunk. When he exited the taxi at the hotel, the driver sped off. Sami did not go to the police, though. He wanted nothing to do with them. Instead, he bought a new ticket and flew back to Germany.

In Moscow, our group also has a few unpleasant surprises. On the street, I look to exchange a $20 bill. The dealer gives me a piece of paper that looks like a 100-ruble note, and then suddenly and excitedly yells "Police! Police!" I turn around and the money trader runs off quickly in the other direction. When I first have a calm moment to look at the piece of paper, I notice that it looks like a 100-ruble lottery ticket. I have been ripped off. The $20 bill is gone, and that bothers me for quite a while.

I sent that anecdote to my Russian publisher Dmitry Pasechnik. On March 25, 2018, he answered by email: "I think there's a mistake in your story. That isn't a lottery ticket. It's a 100-ruble bearer bond issued by the Russian government. One could bring the bond to Sberbank [at the time the only bank in the Soviet Union] and exchange it for 100 rubles. Don't throw it away! Maybe you can still get the money."

I am holding onto it. Who knows?

It looks like a lottery ticket (which I had received from a black-market money trader for $20), but in reality, it is a government bearer bond

***

After this trip, I was happy to leave Russia. Let us just say that the mixture of youthful exuberance, late nights, and lots of alcohol did not always induce our best behavior. We even had a few run-ins with the police. There was an American student in our group, and one night we sang "God Bless America" and similar songs while riding the Moscow subway. That did not exactly endear us to our audience. We were even less disciplined after another night of drinking in Leningrad, which is now St. Petersburg. Somehow a vase flew from the fourth floor of the hotel and shattered on the floor of the lobby. The police ultimately let us off. But the lessons from those events did not stick with everyone in our group. One student traveled a short time later to Prague, where the black market was similar and the alcohol flowed just as freely. His late-night antics landed him in jail for a month. Those were wild times!

Immobilization

At the age of seven, I was immobilized—in the literal sense of the word—for eight weeks. It is hard to measure the impact such a state has on a farm kid used to all the freedoms that growing up in the countryside offered. I faced two problems. First, I had grown very quickly. Second, I probably suffered to some extent from malnutrition. Except for the absolutely disgusting cod liver oil my mother gave me regularly, we lived almost entirely from what we produced ourselves. I stopped drinking milk when I was three and was very picky about the vegetables I ate. By the time I was six, I had hip problems that left me with a limp and with chronic pain. Our doctor diagnosed "growth pains" and an infection of the hip joint. He had me admitted to the Hospital of the Brothers of Charity (known as the *Brüderkrankenhaus*) in Trier, a leading regional hospital with more than 600 beds and 2400 employees.

I had never been away from home alone, and being admitted to the hospital was a shock. But that was only the beginning. They placed the lower half of my body in a cast which had ran from my bellybutton to the knee on the left side and the full length of my leg (including the foot) on the right side. I was immobilized and doomed to remain that way for eight long weeks. The first few days were horrible, but somehow I made it through. Sundays were both the best and the saddest days. That is when my parents came to visit. Once they brought my sister with them, and another time they brought my friend from next door. I felt so alone every time they left. After the cast came off, I needed to learn how to walk again and spent another four weeks in the hospital.

The day I returned home was one of the happiest days of my life. My schoolmates showed up to welcome me back, along with half the village. There was no rehab after that, even though it was probably urgently needed because of the extent of the muscular atrophy. I was weak in sports and did not win a competition until I was 15, when I had grown strong enough to win an honorary certificate at the German Youth Games.

To what extent did this hard experience in my childhood leave its mark on me? I do not have a sense of trauma when I think back to my time at the hospital. Instead, I feel that it taught me firsthand that you just have to endure and fight through the hard times in life. That helped me overcome a complicated shoulder operation in 2014, which effectively immobilized me again for several months. Patience has never been my strong suit, but in such situations it helps me to think back to the hospital in the fall of 1954. Perhaps my strong, lifelong attachment to my hometown has its roots in that childhood experience as well. I was never sadder in my life, nor have I experienced greater homesickness than during that episode. And I learned to work hard to improve my athletic ability even though that took years. I lacked the systematic training to become a top performer, but I still managed to become a local champion in the javelin toss and took part in the championships of the second division of the German air force.

When the Earth Shakes …

Earthquakes are an experience I could have easily lived without.

Shortly before midnight, on a night in 2005, I am in my hotel room on the 21st floor of the ANA Hotel in Tokyo.[2] I am drifting off into sleep when I feel a strange trembling. In my half-awake, half-asleep state, I cannot figure out what is happening. Am I dreaming? Or is this a real earthquake? One is not quite sure what is going on the first time one is caught in an earthquake. I stand up and have no clue what I should do. Should I stay in the room or take the stairs down 21 flights to the lobby? I start to get uncomfortable when I realize that the hotel has 37 stories total, which means that I have the weight of 16 floors looming over my head.

Eventually, there is an announcement over a loudspeaker: "This is an earthquake. Do not leave your room. This building is earthquake-proof. Wait for further instructions." In such a precarious situation, one can only hope that the building is indeed earthquake-proof, but doubts always creep in. The most unpleasant part, though, is the total lack of control. The only thing to do is wait. A half-hour later, the announcement comes that the earthquake is over. But it is still a restless night.

The next morning, I am due to fly back to Germany and take the bus to the Narita Airport about 40 miles north of downtown Tokyo. A huge bank of dark, threatening clouds is coming in behind us as we drive north. It is a typhoon. Shortly after take-off, the pilot announces that we have left the airport just in time. A few minutes later and we would have been grounded.

About a dozen years later, Mother Nature strikes again. On September 19, 2017 I am scheduled to speak at a conference in Mexico City. The conference program includes an earthquake drill at 11 a.m. That is an annual event throughout Mexico meant to commemorate the catastrophic earthquake that struck that same day in 1985 and killed 10,000 people. The well-disciplined drill lasts around 30 minutes. Afterwards the attendees file into the

---

[2] ANA (All Nippon Airways) is the second largest Japanese airline. At the time, I used the ANA hotel as it was right next to our Tokyo office.

auditorium at the Centro University. My talk begins promptly at noon and is scheduled to run until 1:30 p.m. I cruise through my program until 1:14 p.m. That is when a jolt goes through the building and the stage begins to shake. Two hours after the drill, the real thing is here!

The crowd of several hundred jumps up and rushes for the exits, but without panic. I leave everything behind and head for the exit as well. The auditorium is on the first floor, so we make it outside the building quickly. But the modern building has about 20 floors, and we can see people using the external emergency staircases. They need much more time to reach the ground outside than we did, and I would not want to trade places with them. The building emits sounds I have never heard in my life. The sound of steel girders bending but not breaking under the immense pressure penetrates deep into my bones.

Traffic in Mexico City comes to a standstill, but my hosts find a clever solution. They get their hands on a bicycle which allows me to reach my hotel over three miles away. Because it would have been impossible to find my way through the chaos that afternoon, one of my hosts runs alongside me. He is an amateur marathon runner, and I am very thankful for his help and guidance.
***

The Tokyo earthquake measured 5.8 on the Richter scale, and the typhoon also caused extensive damage. The Mexico City earthquake measured 7.1 on the Richter scale, more than an order of magnitude stronger than in Tokyo.[3] Fortunately, no one in the Centro University building was injured. But throughout the rest of Mexico City, numerous buildings did collapse. A total of 370 people died and more than 6000 were injured.

Such events help me appreciate that Germany is relatively safe from such major natural disasters. Then again, my homeland in the Eifel is a volcanic region, and who knows when the now dormant volcanoes will erupt again. Scientists say that it could happen anytime.

In the Year 40,000

On April 5, 2000, the entrepreneur Reinhard Mohn receives the Jakob Fugger Medal. That is a prestigious media award presented by the Bavarian Magazine Publishers Association for "outstanding and extraordinary service to promote the freedom, independence, and integrity of the magazine press and raise the public consciousness." Mohn took control of a small publishing house in

---

[3] The Richter scale is not linear but logarithmic, meaning that the energy of earthquakes increases exponentially.

Germany's eastern Westphalia region and built it into the global Bertelsmann Group, which has a revenue of more than $19 billion and owns a majority stake in Penguin Random House, the largest book publisher in the world.

In the run-up to the year 2000, the newspaper *Die Zeit* has asked me to name the "Businessperson of the Century" and write a tribute. Among others, I am considering Henry Ford and Bill Gates. But my choice is Reinhard Mohn (Simon 1998). Then I am invited to give a speech on "Leadership Challenges in the 21st Century" at the award ceremony. My speech, however, is not the reason why that evening stays in my mind.

The award ceremony takes place in the Residence Theater in Munich. The speaker before me is Edmund Stoiber, the prime minister of Bavaria. While I am rehearsing my own speech in my mind, I close my eyes. That is a technique, I often use ahead of such talks. But on this occasion, my attention wanders and I fall into a "lucid dream." That is a state of mind in which the dreamer is aware that he or she is dreaming (Green and McCreery 1996). In my dream, I am flying like a cloud from Bonn southward to the city of Koblenz, following the Rhine River below me. At Koblenz, I make a westward turn toward the Eifel. Somehow I am aware that I am 40,000 years in the future. The land below me sparkles wonderfully, with green fields alternating with dark forests. The landscape looks well maintained, but I notice that something is missing. I do not see any people, nor houses, nor villages. Humans have disappeared and the ensuing millennia have removed all traces of them. The Eifel has returned to the idealized state that the German Emperor Wilhelm II wished for in 1889 when he said "the Eifel is a beautiful hunting ground. It's a shame that people live there." One could imagine that I am saddened by the disappearance of mankind, but the opposite is true.

I wake up from my daydream in an easy-going good mood. Relaxed and loose, I follow Stoiber to the podium and deliver my speech.

***

Was it my soul that had flown over my homeland in the far distant future? When I think of this daydream, the last verse from Joseph von Eichendorff's poem "Moon Night" wells up inside me:

"And my soul
spread out its wings,
and flew over the quiet land,
as if it were flying home."[4]

---

[4] It is the third verse of the poem "Mondnacht," which Joseph von Eichendorff (1788–1857) wrote in 1835. The poem was first published in 1837. The German original:

"Und meine Seele spannte

Weit ihre Flügel aus,

References

Celia Green and Charles McCreery, *Träume bewusst steuern. Über das Paradox vom Wachsein im Schlaf.* Frankfurt am Main: Krüger, 1996

Zvi Harry Likwornik, *Als Siebenjähriger im Holocaust,* Konstanz: Hartung Gorre Verlag, 2012/2014.

Hermann Simon, "Fit für die Zukunft – Hermann Simon kürt den Unternehmer des Jahrhunderts," *Die Zeit,* December 30, 1998.

Maria Wein-Mehs, *Juden in Wittlich* 1908-1942, Wittlich 1996.

Stefan Zweig, *Decisive Moments in History,* Riverside: Ariadne Press 2014.

Flog durch die stillen Lande,
Als flöge sie nach Haus."

15

The School of Life

Life is a never-ending school. In this final chapter, I will present some simple lessons that life has taught me. Such a collection of lessons is always subjective, incomplete, and certainly selective to avoid putting the author in a negative light. Mine is no different.

Appreciate the Support You Receive

There is no way I could have chartered the course described in this book without the support and backing of my wife Cecilia and my family. Cecilia Sossong comes from a family of craftsmen and grew up in a small village on the southern and climatically rougher side of the Moselle. Her mother's family were millers in the Saarland. There were also millers among my ancestors, and my mother also came from the Saarland. Cecilia and I met in Bonn, where we were both studying. We were married in 1973 and raised two children: Jeannine (born 1975) and Patrick (born 1980). Cecilia worked as a teacher at a special needs school from 1972 to 1988.

After our time at Harvard, she gave up her teaching job and founded Lingua-Video Medien GmbH, a firm that publishes audio-visual media for use in educational institutions such as schools, libraries, and media centers. She led the firm for 27 years until 2016, when our daughter Jeannine took over as CEO.

Cecilia and I once discussed why both of us gave up our tenured positions as teacher and professor and struck out on our own as entrepreneurs. One reason is that both her and my parents were self-employed. But ultimately, we agreed that we both sought out an independent, self-employed lifestyle because neither of us wanted to have a boss.

My parents were independent and self-sufficient. What effect did that have on me? There was no one who could tell them what to do, nor when and how to work. They were certainly constrained by external forces such as weather, nature, and annual cycles. Nonetheless, they could decide freely how to deal with those forces. They did not have a boss. They were free people.

Perhaps those circumstances have shaped me more than I am aware. In any event, I find it very pleasant to think that for most of my adult life, no one could tell me what to do or not do. As a professor, I was technically an employee of the state government, but I had essentially free rein in my research and teaching. As an entrepreneur, I was totally self-responsible and free. To this day, I am surprised that more people do not follow the path of freedom and self-responsibility instead of placing themselves under the command and control of other people. I do not mean to say that such independence is for everyone. Many, if not most people probably feel more comfortable when they do not have to bear the burdens of self-responsibility and constant self-motivation.

Cecilia also comes from an independent family and felt the same influences. She has an unusual gift for organization. She takes care of everything and frees me up as a result. She supervised the construction of two houses. She renovated my parents' old farmhouse in the Eifel from the ground up and transformed it into an absolute gem. She managed the family, took care of the household, and organized parties—all while building her own small business. During the many intense years of my time-consuming work and travel, she was my constant pillar of support. On top of that she was my trusted advisor, the only one whose word and advice I really follow. She often shows more courage than I do because with every new challenge, she tells me "of course you can do it."

There is no doubt that I could have never realized the full extent of my potential without her organizational and moral support. Our children, who are successful on their own, also made big contributions. They tolerated the nearly constant physical and spiritual absence of their father. They missed out on a lot because of my incessant travel and business priorities. The family paid a large price for my professional success, without receiving their due recognition from me. That is because someone in my situation tends to take the comforts of family and home for granted and underestimates the effort that goes into creating and preserving them. But one thing that I can say for certain is that the most wonderful part of my projects and trips has always been returning home.

And what do single people do when they pursue a life full of intense work and travel? If they want to have a halfway stress-free existence, they must delegate many of the tedious day-to-day tasks of life. In other words, they need to pay money for those services. Otherwise, it is not possible to maintain that intensity over a long period.

In the worst case, however, it is primarily—and often only—the family that pays the price. Friendships that can withstand extremely long, enduring "worst case" periods are rare. That is another lesson life teaches. Most so-called friendships reveal themselves as fair-weather phenomena when things get rough.

Cecilia was also active in many other fields. She served for several years on the city council of Königswinter, but over time she found the political process tiresome and decided to organize her own cultural events. When Germany faced a choice in 1991 on where to locate its capital city—Bonn or Berlin—she became involved. She printed up "Bonn remains the capital"[1] stickers and distributed thousands of them via businesses, hotels, and other multipliers.

BONN BLEIBT HAUPTSTADT

Sticker created by Cecilia Simon for Germany's capital city decision (Bonn vs. Berlin) in 1991

There was a second similar action called "Yes to Bonn." The mastermind behind that movement was my friend from back home, Friedel Drautzburg, an "Eifeler" and Rhinelander through and through.[2] On June 20, 1991, the parliamentary decision went in favor of Berlin, 338 votes to 320. Drautzburg relocated to Berlin and opened the bar "Ständige Vertretung" (STAEV) in the former representative office of West Germany in East Berlin. Their goal was to bring some flair from the cheerful Rhineland to stern and Prussian Berlin.

Cecilia was also involved in various clubs and charitable causes, such as conservation. In my hometown, she established a children's choir, cultivated fields of wildflowers, and planted more than 50 nut trees. She simply needs to stay active.

---

[1] A kind of early "Remain" campaign, 30 years before Brexit.
[2] See the portrait of Friedel Drautzburg in Simon (2008).

Do Not Worry About Tomorrow

When someone is having a bad day or faces an acute problem, it is natural to feel worried and burdened. Often, if not in most cases, the worries are about the future. Will I make it to my meeting on time tomorrow? Will I get the project? What will the results of my check-up be? Will my child pass the exam?

One of the mottos my mother lived by was: "Don't worry about something that might not happen tomorrow." The inventor of the Reiki meditation technique, Dr. Mikao Usui (1865–1925), had a similar saying: "Just for today, do not worry." From him comes the simple insight that we all should work on the things that we can improve and accept the things we cannot change.

Human beings have the ability to imagine themselves in the future, to think about it, to plan it, and to mentally anticipate events. This ability creates the problem mentioned above because it generates both hopes and fears. The latter is the wellspring of worry. But one should not be weighed down by these worries because many of the things we fear will never occur. The time to worry is when the fears actually manifest themselves in real events. The advice of my mother may come from a simple farmer's wife, but it has helped me tremendously. The more one succeeds in heeding that advice in day-to-day life, the more easygoing and carefree life becomes. Personally, there is hardly a day when her saying does not cross my mind. And when I occasionally forget it, Cecilia brings it up.

Live Healthy

Writing about the topic of health under the heading "The School of Life" creates some obvious risks. One risk is that the discussion degenerates quickly into clichés and platitudes such "exercise, eat right, and reduce stress." Another is that the writer assumes the role of a missionary trying to win over the rest of mankind with his or her personal recipes for promoting and maintaining good health. Without getting too deep into personal details, I would like to describe some experiences in a way that tries to avoid those risks.

One cliché is that good health is less of a given the older one gets, and therefore becomes more important. This is basically a universal truth. But what I have observed—and what draws far less attention—is that many of the ailments that my contemporaries suffer from at an advanced age are self-inflicted. Their root causes often lie in behaviors practiced far in the past for an extended time. Professor Rudi Balling, a world-class scientist and former head of the German Institute for Infection Research, a 600-person organization, told me: "Old-age illnesses are mostly childhood illnesses." Included are risky behavior in the youth, smoking, excess weight, alcohol consumption, and high stress levels. In most cases, aging will not reverse the effects of these behaviors although it can lessen them. This leads to the recommendation for parents and young people to think about the long-term consequences of such behaviors and eliminate them early in life rather than stopping only when the permanent negative effects have begun to show.

A second personal experience: changes to nutrition can have miraculous effects. In 2014, I was diagnosed with a mild case of diabetes. I did some research and was shocked to read about the serious damage that this increasingly common disease can wreak. The doctor wanted to prescribe me medication. I objected and promised that I would solve the problem through nutrition. I made radical changes to my diet. Six months later, all of my blood test values were not only at safe levels, but at optimal ones.

But I also realized that many people fail to make such adjustments. The bottleneck is not always a lack of knowledge. Instead, it is the person's social environment, which plays a detrimental role when people express intolerance toward an unusual or markedly different dietary habit. For example, I do not drink alcohol. Nowadays, it is easy for me to resist the pleas of "Come on, just one drink." That applies even in Russia and China, where refusing to drink alcohol is often considered abnormal. In that regard, I received a very clever and useful tip from Dr. Peter Zinkann, co-owner at Miele. I knew that he does not drink alcohol either and asked him how he gets around that in Russia. His answer: "You must not drink the first glass." His wise advice works. Ironically, he gave me that tip while we were at the famous Russian Tea Room near Carnegie Hall in New York.[3]

Although I have read and researched a considerable amount, I am reluctant to give specific recommendations on nutrition because that lies outside my expertise. What amazes me, though, is the extent of the discrepancies and outright contradictions in the recommendations from experts in the field. Over the course of time, prevailing assessments can change in spectacular ways. Cholesterol is one example. Some doctors consider high cholesterol levels to be very dangerous, others do not share this assessment at all. And over time, opinions have changed substantially several times.

I have personally settled on a particular dietary approach and do not worry about whether there is a better one although I cannot rule that out. What helps me—and what I can recommend—is strict discipline with a diet. I have

---

[3] http://www.russiantearoomnyc.com/

seen friends and acquaintances who remain strictly disciplined all week, but cannot resist having cake with their coffee on a Sunday afternoon. That is not only a question of will power, but also a question of biology. Some diets create such intense cravings for certain kinds of foods that people eventually cannot restrain themselves. That is why a diet should be balanced to prevent cravings.

My second recommendation is to avoid episodes of short-term starvation. As a consultant who was constantly traveling, I would often come home with a voracious appetite, and as a result would consume a massive amount of calories in one sitting, often late in the evening. Nowadays, I snack much more frequently to quell my appetite instead of letting it build up for too long.

Stay Grounded

When someone's life is shaped by a childhood on a farm seemingly straight out of the Middle Ages, and then travels across centuries (metaphorically speaking), it is inevitable that that person's own frames of reference will change. I have confronted the Latin phrase *"tempora mutantur et nos mutamur in illis"* ("The times change, and we change with them") head on since I turned 20 years old. Success is seductive. Pride is human weakness that can turn into arrogance. No one is immune to its charms. Have I forgotten where I come from? Have I lost my bearings due to the radical changes in my life? These are important questions.

Otto von Bismarck, who unified Germany in 1871, once said "character is talent minus vanity." I first heard that phrase used to characterize a speech at the WHU in Koblenz by physicist Peter Grünberg, who won the Nobel Prize in 2007. Professor Grünberg impressed me not only with the content of his speech, but also with his modesty, the opposite of vanity. During the dinner that evening, he patiently explained to me how magnetism works although I cannot truly claim I understood his explanation. I witnessed similar modesty in my encounters with Peter Drucker, Marvin Bower, Joseph Cardinal Höffner, and many other major personalities.

Bismarck was clever. Why did he give vanity (with a minus sign) equal weight in his equation, alongside talent? One likely explanation is that leaders who have fallen victim to vanity expend considerable mental effort, time, and energy into cultivating their self-image. They are playing a zero-sum game, which means those leaders are diverting their mental effort, time, and energy away from actual problem solving. If this hypothesis is true, it implies that modest leaders are more effective. Vanity and long-term success are negatively correlated. Unfortunately, academic management science has little to say about such questions, despite their relevance in the real world. Ted Levitt once said that the importance of particular phenomena in the real world is inversely proportional to how much academics investigate those phenomena. Vanity could certainly fall into the category of "very important in real life" but "neglected by academic research." But at the same time, some findings indicate that that inverse relationship between vanity and success exists.

The US management researcher Jim Collins has found empirically that the less the CEO of a company appears in public or is widely known, the more successful that company is over the long term (Collins and Porras 1994; Collins 2001). Collins draws a stark contrast between "show horses" and "plow horses." The latter spend less time and energy on external appearances and therefore more on taking care of their business. I think Bismarck would have appreciated this distinction.

My own experiences tend to validate Collins' hypothesis. As a young man, I was impressed when I saw charismatic entrepreneurs and managers. But over the decades, I have learned that those who perform their jobs quietly and outside the limelight—most CEOs of the Hidden Champions, for example— are in general better managers than "show horses." The negative correlation between effective leadership and vanity holds true, even though I cannot prove this with simple statistical criteria. One could supplement Bismarck's equation with one attributed to Albert Einstein. According to Einstein's formula, success = a + b + c, where a stands for intelligence, b for industriousness or diligence, and c is "keeping one's mouth shut." That is not bad and is directionally similar to what Bismarck said.

Now, how do I connect vanity with being down-to-earth? For that I refer back to a commemorative speech I gave on November 24, 2011, at the ceremony to award the "Best Human Brand Lifework Award" to Germany's most famous and beloved actor, Mario Adorf. He has appeared in more than 200 roles in film and television, and has left his personal stamp on every role he played, not vice versa. In other words, he was always Mario Adorf.

In the movie, *Blechtrommel* ("The Tin Drum") by Nobel laureate Günter Grass, he played his most important early role, Alfred Matzerath, the cook from the Rhineland who expressed his feelings by cooking soup. The film's famous director, Volker Schlöndorff, wrote to me about that role: "Mario Adorf was at the top of the list of actors to cast. From the first rehearsals on, we had a great degree of trust in each other, almost as if we were partners in crime."

Adorf came from the town of Mayen in the Eifel, not far away from where I grew up. We conversed with each other in our Moselle-Franconian dialect. In our preparation interview ahead of my speech, he described himself as "down to earth and grounded." One of his mottos is, loosely translated, "never spit further than you actually can." That is how people from the Eifel are, I can vouch for that!

The German word for vanity is *Eitelkeit*. To underscore Adorf's modesty and link it to his upbringing in the Eifel, I coined the word *Eifelkeit* as a play on words to use in my speech. It fits him perfectly. Modesty and being down-to-earth—the opposites of vanity—are two characteristics of good leaders.

The simple formula from Bismarck has proven to be a very valuable way to evaluate employees and colleagues as well as business leaders and politicians. I have applied it often, and it has frequently led me to eye-opening insights. What I have also noticed is that this "vanity syndrome" is not very widespread, but in those who do have it, it is usually so pronounced that it plays a significant role in the evaluation.

Keep It Simple, Stupid: The KISS Principle

People should not make the world more complicated than it already is. Unfortunately, simplification, or at least avoidance of additional complication, is a skill many people lack nowadays. It drives me crazy when anything—from a process to a business issue to a general topic—gets made more complicated than it ought to be. In the same vein, I am impressed when someone simplifies something without harming or diminishing the overall outcome. Simplification saves time and energy and avoids superfluous discussions. Here, I can cite a striking example from Denmark.

In previous times, merchants that wanted to ship their goods from Denmark to Sweden needed to pay a customs duty based on the value of their goods. Putting a value on all these different goods is inherently difficult for a variety of reasons. Complicating matters further was the fact that there were no uniform documents to record the appropriate information.

So the Danish king thought out a new process. The merchants were allowed to determine the value of their goods themselves, but under one condition: the king would have the right to purchase the goods at their given price. The system was ingenious! Additional controls, complex evaluation guidelines or strategies, etc. were no longer necessary. Actual purchases by the king were rare.

Nowadays, would it be possible to set customs duties or taxes, such as property taxes, using that process? An interesting thought! That would at least eliminate the problem of making valuations and assessments.

Another example is the required deposit of one euro for the use of a shopping cart in German supermarkets. This extremely simple method preserves order without any supervision or interference from anyone. Prior to the introduction of this deposit system, the large supermarkets each employed several people who rounded up the carts in the parking lot and stored them in an orderly fashion. Now the shoppers need to bring their shopping carts back themselves and store them properly in order to get their deposit back. The German flat-rate withholding tax is another example of simplification. Instead of collecting individually assessed capital income taxes from millions of individuals, the government receives its tax revenues directly from a relatively small number of banks.

All kinds of trivial decisions make day-to-day life needlessly complicated. What should I buy? What tie should I wear? What do I choose from the menu? The physicist Richard P. Feynman, who won the Nobel Prize in 1965, knew how to radically simplify such problems. He said: "When you're young, you have all these things to worry about ... And you worry, and try to decide, but then something else comes up. It's much easier to just plain decide. Never mind—nothing is going to change your mind. I did that once when I was a student at MIT. I got sick and tired of having to decide what kind of dessert I was going to have at the restaurant, so I decided it would always be chocolate ice cream, and never worried about it again—I had the solution to that problem" (Feynman 1985).

I have made Feynman's advice my own and have always tried to organize my activities as simply as possible. I maintain three offices: one at Simon-Kucher in Bonn, one at my home in Bonn, and one at my farmhouse in the Eifel. All three offices have the same setup. I do not need to make any adjustments when I switch from one office to the other. For 40 years, long before the internet, I ordered the same supplies from the same vendors. All that process requires is one phone call with the message "the same as last time." It is that simple.

This method only works, however, when one opts not to follow the latest fashion trends, for example, in shoes or shirts. I buy in the same stores and thus avoid spending my time searching around. I prefer the same hotels and the same airlines. This eliminates unnecessary decisions and means I have to make few adjustments when I travel. That may sound boring and obsessive, but it saves time and stress.

Simplicity is one of the most effective means of cost reduction. It has helped to massively reduce the number of parts in products such as printers or antilock braking systems. Toyota is the poster child for the global automobile industry in terms of both the simplification of production processes and the resulting quality improvements (Jones et al. 1990). Simple processes require less time. The popular concept of "business process reengineering" is in essence about time savings through simplification (Hammer and Champy 2006). In this regard, the internet has yielded enormous progress. A shining example is the one-click ordering process on Amazon. Buyers do not need to identify themselves. One click triggers both the order and the payment.

Another person who impressed me with his clear commitment to simplicity is Andreas König, the former CEO of Teamviewer. Teamviewer is a Hidden Champion based in Germany and is the world market leader for the global networking of personal computers and similar devices. The Teamviewer software is installed on more than two billion devices worldwide and as simple to use as can be. Yet there are still quite a few e-commerce processes that are unnecessarily complicated and tedious. Many internet companies totally underestimate the importance of simplicity and convenience.

A company's employees play a key role in simplification. As I learned from Professor Albach, I always insisted that my associates decide matters for themselves. That makes a lot of things simpler because it eliminates follow-up or "permission" questions, keeps processes flowing smoothly, and avoids delays. But it also demands that the individual employees have the necessary competencies and—more importantly in my view—are willing and prepared to assume responsibility. I always wonder how often leaders get called by their employees with unnecessary questions, and vice versa.

Simplicity requires that tasks be completed as quickly as possible. As I return from a business trip, I am already preparing my travel expense report on the way back. If one lets that task sit for a long period, there are inevitably gaps in one's memory. Reconstructing the trip after several weeks or months can be a painstaking and time-consuming exercise, especially if the receipts are not all in one place. Fast means simple and simple means fast.

To sum up, you might conclude that I am addicted to simplicity. That may be true. But it has served me well throughout my career, and that is why I strongly recommend the KISS principle.

Polarized Leadership

Leadership is always an oscillating balance between two poles: the authority of the leader and the self-responsibility of those being led. If the pendulum swings too much toward the former, the result is authoritarian leadership, a command economy, or similar structures. If the leader gives employees too much free rein without clear objectives, then the situation collapses into an uncoordinated state or in the worst case, chaos. Overly authoritative leadership—when that style does not suit the team—leads to demotivation,

performance strictly by the book, and resignation, either internally or explicitly. Top team performance comes only under a leadership style that sets clear
objectives and strict performance standards while sustaining a high level of
motivation. How does one achieve that inherently contradictory
combination?

The answer is to strike a balance by doing both at the same time, namely to
have an authoritarian and a participatory style. The late Berthold Leibinger of
Hidden Champion Trumpf referred to that leadership style as "enlightened
patriarchy." Dietmar Hopp, one of the founders of business software champion SAP, addressed his employees as a "strict but caring patriarch." One CEO
of a Hidden Champion told me that his leadership style is both group-oriented
and authoritarian. The authoritarian style applies to the principles, the values,
and the goals of the business. There is no discussion, and the chain of command runs clearly from top to bottom. But a much different style applies to
how the actual work gets done. The employees enjoy a considerable amount
of leeway and influence over how they accomplish their tasks.

This form of two-sided or balanced leadership found an unexpected confirmation in the findings of the Israeli military historian Martin van Creveld. In
his book *Fighting Power,* he compares the German and American armies in
World War II (van Creveld 2011). As a Jew who lost members of his family in
the Nazi concentration camps, sugarcoating the crimes of the Nazis would be
the furthest thing from Creveld's mind. Yet he came to the conclusion that the
fighting power of the Germans was 52% greater than that of the Americans.
The key factor for this enormous gap was the differences in the leadership
systems.

The German system, which traces its roots back to Prussian Field Marshall
Helmuth von Moltke (1800–1891), is called mission-oriented, while the
Americans use a process-oriented system. Under the mission-oriented system,
the commander assigns his troops a mission or task, but leaves them a large
amount of freedom regarding how they complete it. The Americans, in contrast, analyze a particular situation thoroughly and then define specific process
steps to resolve it. This is the system that most American businesses still practice today. One example is the meticulously detailed list of individual steps
and actions in the kitchens of the McDonald's fast-food chain. Personally, I
am a staunch advocate and devotee of the mission-oriented system, which
grants employees considerable latitude. But one must be honest about the
prerequisites for such a system to work. It requires a team with the appropriate qualifications as well as the ability to think on its feet.

Another aspect is: who controls the system? As Lenin once famously said:
"Trust is good; control is better." The control can come from above or from

the group or team. Within the Hidden Champions, the social control through the group—combined with self-control based on the firm's values—plays a much greater role than within the staffs of large companies. Manfred Bogdahn, the founder of Flexi, the world market leader for retractable dog leashes, counts on the teams themselves to exercise quality control in the manufacturing process. This control is part of the normal production process, and according to Bogdahn it is much more effective than any downstream checks or controls. Mistakes are caught and remedied during the production process rather than after the finished product has left the line. Heinz Hankammer (1931–2016), the founder of Hidden Champion Brita, the world market leader in point-of-use water filters, explained to me that it is not his job to track and select the right people during a probationary employment period. His team does that on its own. Similar to a sports team, the colleagues know that the team is as strong as its weakest link. They will not tolerate colleagues who are unwilling or unable to do their jobs properly. Control through the group is an indispensable part of effective leadership.

The two sides of the leadership style also manifest themselves in the attitudes of the employees. It is not unusual for employees to see their bosses through two often contradictory lenses. There are complaints about the leader's authoritarian style, or perhaps his or her harshness or unpredictability. Yet those same employees will express their admiration for their boss and stress that there is no other company they would consider working for. This split mindset recalls the stories that students often tell about strict or demanding teachers. The students do not like those teachers all that much, but at the same time, they know that they learn more from those teachers than they do from the ones who do not push them. Ron Chernow, who has written a number of best-selling biographies, notes that: "A leader should be neither too remote nor too familiar. They don't need to like you—much less love you—but they need to respect you."[4] Effective leadership means uniting precisely these two aspects. That reflects the polarity that one finds in good leaders.

Ration Your Time

The only resource that we cannot increase or reproduce is time. One can earn back lost money. The human body, in some cases, is capable of healing itself and restoring lost health. But lost or wasted time is gone forever. No one has a cleverer statement on this point than the Roman philosopher Seneca, who

---

[4] "George Washington's Leadership Secrets," *The Wall Street Journal*, February 13, 2012, p. 15.

wrote in *De brevitate vitae* ("On the Shortness of Life") that: "We are not given a short life but we make it short, and we are not ill-supplied but wasteful of it. Life is long if you know how to use it."[5]

Managing one's own time is indeed a major challenge. When I look back at my own life, I realize that time had no meaning during my childhood and youth. Our life on the farm was determined by the course of the days and years. Granted, there was some time pressure during the harvest, but in general we had a surfeit of time. I myself wasted staggering amounts of it on unproductive activities. Perhaps that is the reason why I have made much more effective and more conscious use of my time in subsequent phases of my life. My attitude toward time changed abruptly when I began my university studies. Time became a driving force in my life. My classmates tell me to this day that I was very deliberate and sometimes even stingy with my time.

During my tenure as a professor, and especially in my years as CEO of Simon-Kucher & Partners, I placed a high priority on the conscious management of time. Whenever possible, I hired a driver for long car trips. I never traveled enough to warrant hiring a full-time driver, so I employed part-timers. I am amazed by the amount of time that top executives and others waste because they drive themselves. There is no easier and more inexpensive way to save time than to let someone else do the driving. One can use the free time to work, or to relax on the way back home. Both are better ways to spend one's time than driving.

Should autonomous driving ever become mainstream, this form of time savings will not only be available to top managers and the wealthy, but to everyone. Saving time would the true revolution sparked by autonomous driving. This is tantamount to an increase in one's life span. Having said that, I have my doubts about the acceptance of autonomous driving. The barriers in my view are ethical rather than technological, as I outlined in an article on "The Ethics of Autonomous Driving."[6]

When students and colleagues wanted to have a longer talk with me, I often invite them to accompany me on a car or train trip. They are usually very thankful because under normal circumstances they would have not had a chance to talk with me one-on-one in a relaxed environment for two hours. Sometimes I have even invited myself on such trips. In one case, I needed to discuss some urgent business with a government minister. We were scheduled to appear at the same conference. I called his office and asked if he planned to

---

[5] Seneca, *Von der Kürze des Lebens*, Kindle-Version 2017, Position 4238.

[6] https://www.2025ad.com/in-the-news/blog/ethics-of-autonomous-driving/

drive back. His office confirmed he did, so I took him with me on the way back. We had two hours to discuss the topic.

When I was CEO of Simon-Kucher, the partners' demand for my time exceeded the available supply. One possibility to address the excess demand is a rationing or allocation system. But how should I decide how important a particular matter is, and how much time I should budget for it? In such cases, I always prefer a market-based answer, which is no surprise seeing that I am a pricing consultant. I introduced an internal price for my time. This price only applied when the demand for my time came from a partner. When I myself requested time from a partner, the price of course did not apply. This simple mechanism allowed me to bring my available time into a reasonable balance with the demands on it. Only once have I heard of an entrepreneur that uses a similar system. This entrepreneur also comes from my home region, but wants to remain anonymous. He has made a fortune of several billion euros.

Time management remains a constant struggle. Ever since I stepped back from an active management role, I am exposed to greater external demands on my time. People seem to think that I must now have enough time on my hands, so they request some of it. That means I risk experiencing firsthand what Seneca described as follows:

"I am often filled with wonder when I see some men demanding the time of others and those from whom they ask it most indulgent. Both of them fix their eyes on the object of the request for time, neither of them on the time itself; just as if what is asked were nothing, what is given, nothing. Men trifle with the most precious thing in the world; but they are blind to it because it is an incorporeal thing, because it does not come beneath the sight of the eyes, and for this reason it is counted a very cheap thing—nay, of almost no value at all. No one sets a value on time; all use it lavishly as if it cost nothing."[7]

I have nothing to add to that. I cannot express the dilemma better than Seneca did.

One final thought: While writing these lines I ran across seven pages of notes from 1990. In those pages, I had written down—in great detail and very specifically—how I could manage my time better. How well have I implemented those ideas? I was only partially successful, and in some cases only years later. There is an ocean between having an idea and implementing it. And according to an Italian saying, that ocean is vast.

---

[7] Seneca, Position 4401.

Avoid the Legal System

The local courts once sent my parents a letter that caused a small panic in our home. Like most people, they did not want to get unsolicited letters from the courts. This particular one threatened them with foreclosure. It turned out that an agricultural machinery company, from whom we had purchased equipment, had made a mistake. Another local farmer with a similar name had failed to pay his bill.

Feelings ran high again when I was arrested by the local police for riding my father's moped without a driver's license and with a friend of mine as a passenger. I was 15 years old at the time. Then I compounded by my stupidity. When the police officer asked me who allowed me to ride the moped, I said "my father."

The result was that both my father and I received citations. My father needed to appear in court, the same court where he had served several times over the years as a juror. He was fined 42 DM (about 21 euros) and the citation remained part of his permanent record. As a minor, I got away with a warning.

During my time in Japan, I learned something which stunned me. In North America, there are ten times as many lawyers per capita as there are in Japan. Apparently, the interactions between people are handled in very different ways in these two societies. I clearly prefer the Japanese way.

The relatively harmless events I just described were enough to permanently spoil my appetite for anything to do with courts and lawyers. Both privately and professionally, I have tried whenever possible to avoid using lawyers or settling matters via the courts. But there have been a few instances where their involvement was unavoidable. One was the case of plagiarism of my German book *Preismanagement* (Price Management), a story I told in Chap. 9. But there was another case of plagiarism that required considerably more time and effort to clear up in our favor.

In 2007, we learned by coincidence during a project with BMW in Germany that "our Chinese office was also working for BMW in China." Why was that a surprise? At that time, we did not actually have an office in China. Instead, there was a Chinese consultant using our name and logo. The imitator had brazenly copied our homepage and other documents. At first, I sought a political solution, in part through high-level channels, to stop the unauthorized imitator, but to no avail. So we hired a private detective to investigate the matter. He provided us pictures of the sign on the office door, which not only included our name and logo, but also the names of the other cities where we really did have offices. In November 2010, we brought our case to court in Beijing. Our efforts eventually paid off, and the imitator was shut down. That decision freed us up to use our name and logo in China for the first time.

During my tenure as CEO, I kept the use of lawyers to an absolute minimum. At one time, we felt the need to make our contracts more legally robust and engaged an independent attorney. For a flat-rate of 5000 DM (around 2500 euros) per month, he would take care of all of our legal issues. From that point on, life became complicated. After one year, I cancelled the contract and we went back to our time-tested approach of resolving our issues "by hand."

Today, Simon-Kucher has reached a size and level of complexity that makes it impossible to get by completely without lawyers. There is still no internal house counsel among our more than 1500 employees, but we require the outside services of notaries, lawyers, and tax advisers to support us with transactions, partnership contracts, and similar matters. The negotiation I described in Chap. 11 is another example of when having a lawyer was both necessary and worthwhile.

A few preventative measures can help stave off legal battles. First, one should avoid doing business with people whom one either does not trust or whose cooperation requires a level of legal finesse to ensure. In one case, we decided not to purchase a certain property—even though we really liked it—because the neighbor had the reputation of being a difficult lawyer to deal with. The same thinking applies to employees and colleagues. If at all possible, one should avoid dealing with squabblers, people who enjoy exploiting their legal leeway, and other generally litigious people.

In the rural community I grew up in, one's word and handshake were a bond. Written contracts were rare. Nonetheless, I do not recall any lawsuits, nor anyone having contact with lawyers. Admittedly, that world was less complex than the one we currently live in. But at the same time, I am convinced that my desire to avoid legal battles has served me well, even in this occasionally incomprehensible world. There are probably not many people with a comparable range of activities who spend less time and money on legal matters than I do. This principle will continue to guide me, and I gladly recommend it to my children and other young people.

Do Not Be Overly Sensitive

I know many people who are easily irritated by what others say. They react in a very sensitive way to criticism, accusations, or perceived insults. I learned something about this from our strict German teacher. She often gave us unsolicited criticism. Once she said to me: "Simon, you can sure dish it out, but you can't take it." Probably, she was right. Out of that experience came a resolution, namely that I would not make a big deal out of criticism. That does not always work. But I believe that this advice early in life has enabled me to cope well with criticism, which I encounter all too often. Later, I formulated a personal motto based on this idea: "I will decide for myself who will upset or insult me." That motto likewise does not work 100% of the time, but overall it has proven to be useful. It keeps potentially distracting external influences in check. I know so many people whose moods are highly dependent on what others say or think. All it takes is one remark to put them in a bad mood for hours. One should definitely strive to avoid falling into that trap. This is not a recommendation to blunt or reject the criticism, but rather to view it objectively rather than personally. Of course, I am aware that this topic is closely tied to a person's self-confidence. If this is weak, self-protection becomes even more important.

Do Not Burn Bridges

Life brings encounters with pleasant and unpleasant people. You cannot always choose schoolmates, colleagues, or neighbors. You stay in constant contact with some, while you lose sight of others you and have some you would rather not meet again. In the worst case, a person becomes an enemy and the bridge is burned. Regrettably, I have even observed this between siblings. Often the cause lay in inheritance disputes. Burning a bridge should be avoided at all costs.

There are only a few people with whom a reunion would be unpleasant for me. One example is someone who cheated me. I took him to court and he was ultimately given a heavy prison sentence. What would I do if I ran into him and we made eye contact? I am not sure how I would react. But I do not rule out that I would talk to him.

"Many enemies, much honor" is a German proverb.[8] I do not think much of this wisdom. I avoid having enemies and burning bridges. You never know when and how you will meet again. It could even be in the afterlife. Who knows?

---

[8] German Original „Viel Feind, viel Ehr".

Little Pearls of Wisdom

In the course of our lives, we encounter so many pieces of good advice. Much of that advice goes unheeded or disappears from our memories, while others become ingrained habits. I offer several examples of the latter type.

When I started attending the *Gymnasium* in Wittlich, my mother considered it important that I always carried some money with me. One never knew what could happen. I have maintained that habit throughout my life. I never leave the house without some cash. If I accidentally do leave without money, I get very nervous.

Sometimes having cash on hand has helped me out of a tight spot. I once had a flight delay of seven hours in Bangladesh. That meant that I would miss my connecting flight from Kathmandu to Seoul, a flight which departs only every three days. I managed to reserve a seat on a flight to Hong Kong and wanted to purchase the ticket. But the Bangladeshis did not accept credit cards. Figuratively speaking, my habitual cash reserve was worth its weight in gold at that moment. On trips to countries where transactions might be problematic, one should always have sufficient cash in one's pocket. A leading expert, Princeton Professor Markus Brunnermeier, has said "for the foreseeable future, it will be predominantly be cash that safeguards the private sphere" (Brunnermeier 2018). I have nothing to add to that.

Another pearl of wisdom that I still take to heart came from our biology teacher, Ms. Monkenbusch. She advised us to change our brand of toothpaste on a regular basis. Her rationale was that the individual brands contain different active ingredients. Switching brands allows one to fight or prevent a more diverse range of dental problems. That has become a habit. I never buy the same brand of toothpaste twice in a row.

In our basic training, a sergeant in the medical corps told us that he frequently treated soldiers with head injuries. He knew exactly what had happened: the soldiers had stood up and hit their heads on the open locker door. Every time I see an open cabinet door above eye level in the kitchen, I think of that sergeant's implicit advice. And I have never banged my head on a door when standing up. An interesting question, though, is why the army does not install these doors differently. That sergeant was certainly not the only person who saw the effects of that problem on a regular basis.

From Professor Albach I learned a very important habit beyond all of the valuable academic content he taught me. He was the one who helped me recognize and appreciate the tremendous efficiency of dictation. The voice recorder has become one of my most important tools. Getting that high level of efficiency, however, does require discipline and concentration. My favorite time and place to dictate is during walks along the Rhine. That is how I formulated large portions of this book. My abilities with the recorder are not so developed that I could dictate academic books or sophisticated articles. In such cases, I still prefer to express my thoughts by putting pen to paper.

As I get older, I have started to notice the gems of truth and useful wisdom in popular sayings. Over the years, I have collected many such sayings, especially ones about management or leadership. Few of my books were more fun to compose than a compilation of those sayings which I published in German under the title *Geistreiches für Manager ("Wit and Wisdom for Managers")* (Simon 2000/2009). Unfortunately, the theoretical power and insight behind those sayings does not always lead to implementation. One often remembers a piece of advice only after ignoring or neglecting it has led to something going wrong. Or as the philosopher George Santayana (1863–1952) once said: Those who do not remember the past are condemned to repeat it.

Epilogue

To conclude, I come back again to the two distinct worlds of my life, which are my hometown in the Eifel and the globalized world I call Globalia. The most important formative experiences in one's life occur in two phases: during the first six years of life and during puberty (Huber 2017; Yalom 2017). The personality traits embedded in us during those two phases are permanent and determine the rest of our lives. The personality of a "child of the Eifel" came about in that first phase. My childhood was blessed with positive memories. But during puberty, the world of the Eifel became too confining for me. My trips to Italy and Morocco kindled a wanderlust for the global world. This striving intensified over the decades and transformed me into a global player. But along the way there was some occasional alienation from that first world that shaped me. I noted in 1996 that "between 'then' and 'now' there is an awkward chasm that is getting harder and harder for me to bridge. A temporary return to 'then' tends to leave me frustrated rather than satisfied." I looked for my childhood, but did not find it again. I could return to the physical place, but not to the old times. The past exists only in our memory.

As I entered the eighth decade of my life, however, that first world has started to draw me back in without severing my connection to the global world. For as long as possible, I want to feel at home in both worlds, because both are integral parts of my life. I am thankful for that.

References

Markus Brunnermeier, "Kryptowährungen und der Schutz der Privatsphäre," *Frankfurter Allgemeine Zeitung*, March 23, 2018, p. 22

Jim Collins, *Good to Great: Why Some Companies Make the Leap … And Others Don't*, New York: Random House 2001.

Jim Collins, Jerry Porras, *Built to Last: Successful Habits of Visionary Companies*, New York: Harper Business 1994.

Martin van Creveld, Mili*tärische Organisation und Leistung der deutschen und der amerikanischen Armee 1939-1945*, Graz: Ares-Verlag 2011

Richard P. Feynman, "Surely You're joking, Mr. Feynman!"*: Adventures of a Curious Character* New York: W. W. Norton & Company. Kindle Edition, 1985, p. 235

Michael Hammer and James Champy, *Reengineering the Corporation: A Manifesto for Business Revolution*, New York: Collins Business Essentials 2006.

Johannes Huber, *Der holistische Mensch – Wir sind mehr als die Summe unserer Organe*, Vienna: edition a 2017; and Irvin D. Yalom, *Wir man wird, was man ist*, Munich: btb Verlag 2017.

Daniel T. Jones, Daniel Roos and James P. Womack, *The Machine That Changed the World: The Story of Lean Production*, New York: Free Press 1990

Hermann Simon, Geistreiches für Manager, Frankfurt: Campus 2000/2009

Hermann Simon, Kinder der Eifel—Erfolgreich in der Welt, Daun: Südwest und Eifel-Zeitungsverlag 2008, pp. 53–54.

Index